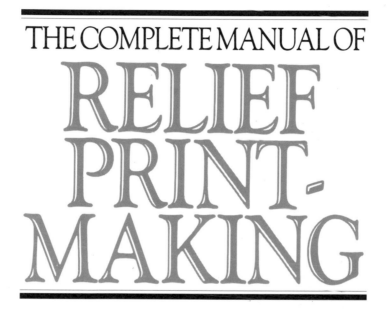

# THE COMPLETE MANUAL OF
# RELIEF PRINT-MAKING

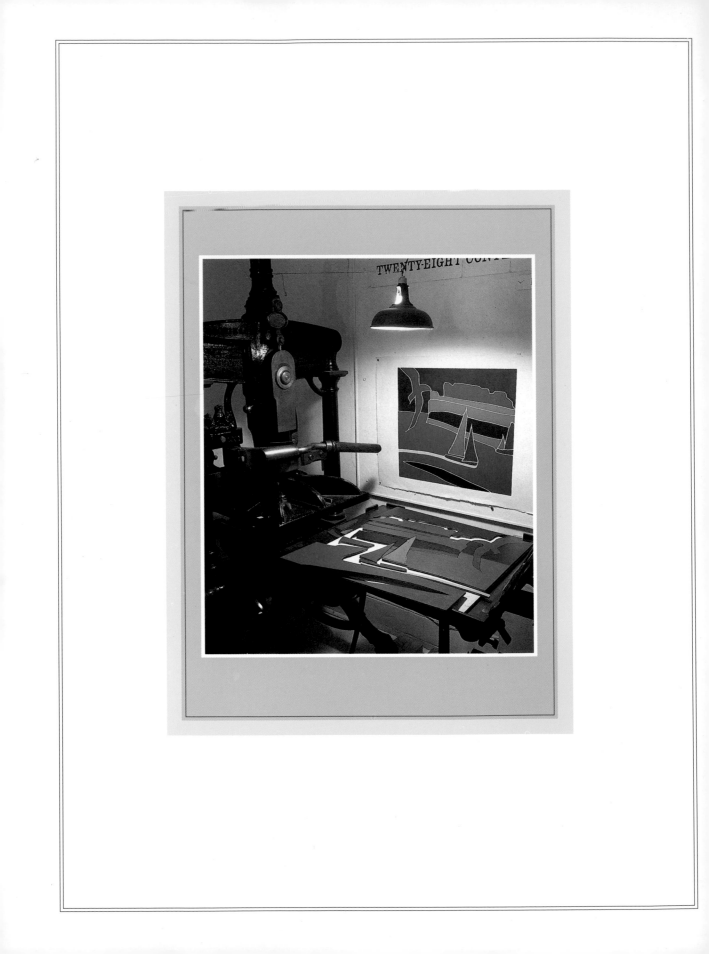

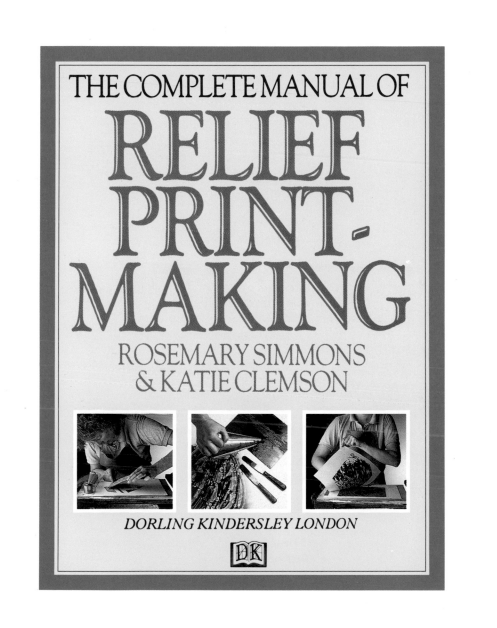

# THE COMPLETE MANUAL OF
# RELIEF PRINT-MAKING

## ROSEMARY SIMMONS
## & KATIE CLEMSON

*DORLING KINDERSLEY LONDON*

First published in Great Britain in 1988
by Dorling Kindersley Limited
9 Henrietta Street, London WC2

British Library Cataloguing in
Publication Data

Clemson, Katie
The complete book of relief print making:
a practical guide to the tools and
techniques of linocutting, woodcutting
and engraving.
1. Relief printing
I. Title   II. Simmons, Rosemary
761 NE850
ISBN 0–86318–280–1

Manufactured in Hong Kong

**Relief Printmaking**
was produced by Nigel Osborne
115J Cleveland Street
London W1

**Art Director** Nigel Osborne
**Editor** Linda Sonntag
**Photographer** Mark French
**Artwork** David Ashby

*This book is dedicated to all the printmakers
who told us about their techniques so generously
and have allowed us to reproduce their prints and
to our husbands who have been models
of patience throughout.*

# Contents

**THE COMPLETE MANUAL OF RELIEF PRINTMAKING**

**FRRATA**

*Page 94:* "White Water Rafting" is by Fiona Hamley;
*Page 101:* The cross-reference under "Card" should read "Introduction";
*Page 114:* The text on this page should read as follows: ". . . less obvious with water-based colours. When very intense colours are required it may be necessary to print the same colour more than once – Japanese woodblock printers frequently do this because their water-based inks are somewhat diluted. When you mix opaque colours with transparent ones the resulting colour will be opaque. You can keep a colour opaque and make it lighter by adding white, although some mixtures containing white dry a slightly different shade from wet ink. Another curiosity is that semi-opaque colours look cold and dull when printed on a dark background, but warm and clear on a white background. Simple experiments with basic colours will demonstrate all these points.
**Additives** Additives are mixed with ink to reduce the strength of a colour, to thicken or thin the consistency, or to make it dry more quickly or more slowly. Inks, paints and dyes are not always the right consistency for printing. Water-colours, gouache and some fabric dyes are diluted with water and will then need thickening with gum arabic or glue. Oil-based inks that you have had for some time will thicken as their oils evaporate, but they can still be used if thinned with a very little linseed oil. Colours applied with a brush need to be slightly thinner than roller-applied inks.
**Reducing mediums, extenders or tinting mediums** Strong colours can be used straight from the tin or tube, but most colours will need to be reduced from full strength ink. Note that full . . ."
*Page 126:* The pictures for steps 4, 5, 6 belong with captions 1, 2, 3, and vice versa;
*Page 144:* Under "Temporarily fixed studs and holes", the diagram annotation should read "Tabs taped to paper";
*Page 161:* The heading should read "Printing Wallpaper on a Converted Proofing Press".

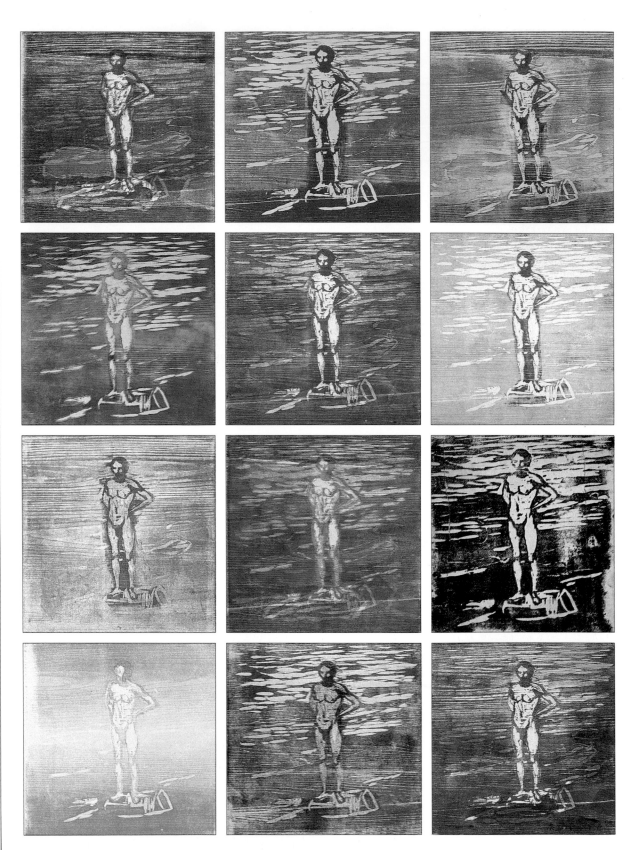

# RELIEF PRINTING

This book is about the most ancient method of taking an impression from one object and putting it on to another – relief printing. It is also about the most up-to-date and exciting methods used by print-makers today.

Handprints made in soot or earth colours can be seen in many caves once occupied by prehistoric peoples. The northern Chinese first took rubbings from carved stones, and then developed true printing some thousand years before any other civilization. They first pressed a carved seal on to some colour and then on to a document written on silk. The seal is a prototype of a relief printing block, in which the non-printing parts are carved away leaving only the design to take colour and be impressed. From a small seal it was a short jump to the carving of a larger area in wood.

The simple idea of a carved block of wood with the design covered in ink and pressed on to a sheet of paper is at the very heart of civilization: the replication of text and illustration spread know-ledge, power and religion quickly. From northern China printing spread along the Silk Road to the Mediterranean and on to the New World.

Relief printing has been used by famous artists as well as anonymous illustrators; it can be delicate and subtle, or bold and colourful. It was the method of printing used for all books and newspapers until this century. Now, while its commercial use is rare, the basic idea thrives in the hands of printmakers who have developed and refined the techniques leading to a revival that is noticeable everywhere.

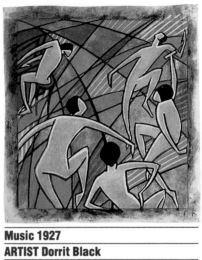

**Music 1927**
**ARTIST Dorrit Black**
**SIZE 24 × 21.5cm (9½ × 8⅓in)**

This colour linocut expresses the subject in its rhythmic composition. The artist, an Austra-lian, studied linocutting with Claude Flight at the Grosvenor School of Modern Art in Lon-don. Note the texture from the brush applica-tion of the ink. The print was intended to be shown behind a window mount so the im-mediate border would be hidden.

**Bogenschutze (Archer) 1908-9**
**ARTIST Wassily Kandinsky**
**SIZE 16.5 × 15.2cm (6½ × 6in)**

A four-colour woodcut executed during the transitional period when the artist was moving from figurative to purely abstract imagery.

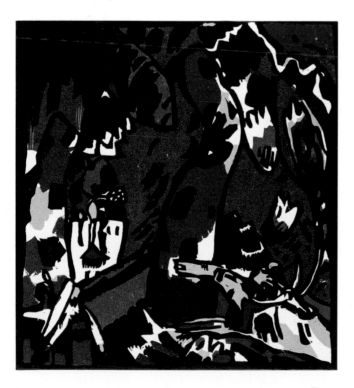

**Male Bather**
**ARTIST Edvard Munch**
**SIZE Unknown**

A single-block woodcut. Munch experi-mented with inking by hand on the block and also on the print itself. He was more interested in the variations that he produced from one block than in printing an edition of identical prints. He used printmaking to explore the possibilities within an image and not for its ability to be replicated. These 12 variations show how different the image becomes with different inking patterns.

# A CHRONOLOGY OF RELIEF PRINTING

The invention of paper, as well as of printing, took place in China. The inks used were water-based. Contrary to popular belief, movable type with ceramic, wooden or metal letters was also an Asian invention. Generally, however, the use of relief woodblocks remained the preferred method, with hand-burnishing the means of printing. The mechanical press was, however, a western invention, based upon the screw-operated oil or wine press. This, in combination with metal type, led to the use of oil-based inks since water-based ones adhere poorly to metal. The increased pressure exerted by the screw led to modifications in the structure of the paper and to the widespread use of size, which is not a feature of Asian papers. Until the introduction of the power-operated press in the 19th century, hand-burnishing, with teams of two men, had a higher output per hour than printers using western screw presses. It is of interest that all the developments listed below, including power (hydraulic) presses, are still being used by artists, although many of them are no longer to be found in commerce.

Entries in **bold type** relating to world history are intended to set these developments in a wider context.

**336-23 Alexander the Great**
**218 Hannibal crosses the Alps**
c.167 Block-printed gauzes in Tomb 1, Mawang-tui, China
**140-87 Han Wu-ti, emperor of China**
Earliest examples of paper, mostly hemp-based
**44 Assassination of Julius Caesar**
**0 Birth of Jesus Christ (traditional)**
105 The eunuch Tsai Lun formally reports to the Emperor the invention of paper. It was probably silk-rag based. Other developments employed old fishing nets, mulberry bark and various fibres
c.110 Trajan's column, Rome. The inscription was the model for capital letters
Mid 2nd c. Lampblack ink made by Wei-t'an. Use of ink for seal impressions on paper increased rapidly, as did the size of seals
175-83 Cai Yung's brush-written text of the Chinese Classics cut on stone slabs at the Great University, Chang-an: paper rubbings were made of these
**407 Romans leave Britain**
**460 Alaric sacks Rome**
6th c. Chinese Buddhist monks duplicate charms and protective images using woodblocks and ink on paper
**618-907 T'ang dynasty in China**
Enormous increase in paper production of all grades in China
**622 Hijra: Mohammed's flight from Mecca; beginning of Muslim era**
Before 751 Pulguk-sa, Kyongju, Korea: 12-sheet woodblock print of a Buddhist sutra
c.770 Nara, Japan: Empress Shotoku organizes printing of Buddhist charms in ten editions of 100,000 each. Many still exist
**800 Charlemagne crowned emperor in Rome**
Paper was manufactured in Baghdad, probably by Chinese prisoners-of-war
868 Tun-huang, China: first dated, printed scroll with frontispiece of the Buddha preaching the Diamond Sutra (488×30.5cm, 184×12 in). From seven woodblocks
877 Tun-huang: calendar with zodiacal animals and other illustrations
**899 Death of Alfred the Great**
951 & 952 Two rival and complete editions of the Chinese Classics, based on stone-cut originals, were presented to the government. The printing of these fundamental political documents was made a state monopoly
947-9 Tun-huang: earliest surviving book, on accordion-pleated pages, rather than scrolls as hitherto
972-83 Buddhist Tripitaka in Chinese printed on scrolls from 130,000 woodblocks

c.1040 Pi Sheng said to have invented movable ceramic type set in resin and wax on an iron base

**1066 Battle of Hastings**
c.1150 First papermills in Europe at Xátiva and Toledo, Spain
1186-91 83,198 block edition of the Taoist scriptures printed in north China

**1215 Magna Carta**

**1271-95 Marco Polo in China**
His widely read account of printed paper money appeared in 1298
1280 Animal-glue size developed at Fabriano papermill, Italy, to strengthen short-fibre European paper
c.1300 Etching used to decorate armour
1313 Wang Chen gives account of tin type (unsuccessful) and of wooden movable type. His fount to print a regional history had 60,000 units. The type was held on two huge revolving tables with compartments
1392 Korean government establishes state printing-works and type foundry. Bronze type was sand cast from wooden originals
c.1400 Block books common in Europe

**1415 Battle of Agincourt**
c.1430 Earliest engraving on metal
c.1450 Johann Gutenberg, Mainz, Germany, developed movable type. His special contributions were the invention of the mould or matrix and certain improvements to the press

**1453 Fall of Constantinople**
1465-7 *Virgin and Child with bird*. Relief-printed engraving by Master E.S.
c.1460-80 Anonymous German coloured metal-cuts (in the dotted manner)
1476 Westminster, London: Caxton's printing press established
1480 Earliest known drypoint by the Master of the Housebook
1482 Earliest colour woodcut by Erhard Ratdolt

**1492-3 Christopher Columbus' first voyage.** His account for the Spanish Treasurer is immediately printed and available throughout Europe
1493 Nuremberg World Chronicle published. Dürer served his apprenticeship as a form-cutter for this immense book
1499 *La Grant danse Macabre des Hommes* published at Lyons, France, showing earliest known picture of a wooden printing press
1510 Earliest chiaroscuro woodcuts by Lucas Cranach
1511 Dürer publishes first major independent prints, *Life of the Virgin*
1513 Earliest etching by Urs Graf
1514 Luther's Bible

**1519-22 Magellan's circumnavigation**
Early 16th c. multi-coloured woodcuts: Albrecht Altdorfer and Georg Lemberger
1539 Mexico City: first print shop opened by the Italian Giovanni Paoli
1548 Antwerp: commercial distribution of prints begins
1572 First catalogue of prints by Laferg available on demand

**1577-80 Francis Drake's circumnavigation**
1588 Amakusa, Japan: missionaries set up a press to print translations of texts into colloquial Japanese using Latin characters. Although the Japanese already knew of movable type through Korea, they generally remained faithful to woodblocks
1619 First European book about printing ink; the first Chinese books on ink were four centuries earlier
1620 Holland: lever principle for press invented by Willem Jansz Blaeu. This meant that only one pull instead of two was required
1620 Mayflower reaches Cape Cod
c.1625. Beginning of Ukiyo-e: colour added to black and white prints by hand
1625?-1694 Hishikawa Moronobu, who did much to popularize Ukiyo-e woodcuts and to refine their style

**1666 Great Fire of London**
1698-1777 Michel Papillon inventor of end-grain wood engraving
1701-1754 J.B. Jackson developer of large scale, multi-colour, chiaroscuro woodcuts which could be used as wallpaper
1725?-1770 Suzuki Harunobu, developer of the nishiki-e 'brocade', i.e. full colour print. His books were among the first Ukiyo-e ones in full colour printing
1753-1806 Kitagawa Utamaro. Creator of the *Insect Book* 1788, but mainly renowned for his portaits of women of the Yoshiwara
1753-1828 Thomas Bewick raised white-line wood engraving to great heights in numerous closely observed book illustrations from nature
1760-1849 Katsushika Hokusai, woodblock cutter turned artist, who produced almost the whole range of Ukiyo-e prints, but principally famed for his later landscape series

**1776 American Declaration of Independence**

**1788 First convict convoy reaches Australia**

**1789 Paris: storming of the Bastille**
1797-1858 Ando Hiroshige, originally book-illustrator, who turned increasingly to magnificent series of landscape and scenic prints

1798 Essones, France: N-L Robert invents first paper-making machine
1798 Alois Senefelder invents lithography
1801 Gamble obtains first British patent for a paper-making machine
1803 Robert's patent developed in England by Fourdrinier brothers who obtained a new patent of their own in 1806
1804 Earl Stanhope invents the Iron Press, the first all metal one
1807 Philadelphia: Columbia Press invented and brought to Britain
1810 Friedrich König invents steam-powered press

**1815 Battle of Waterloo**
1822 Acorn Press, forerunner of the Washington Press, made in USA
1827 London: R.W. Cope starts to make Albion Press: 4,300 made by 1862
1848 Rotary press invented
1863 Watson obtains patent for a proposed 'Floorcloth…called…linoleum'

**1869 Official opening of Suez Canal: Verdi's *Aida***
1893 Paul Gauguin makes woodcuts on his return to Paris
1896 Having seen Gauguin's work, Edvard Munch makes woodcuts
1890s Vienna: Franz Čisek first uses lino

**1897 Diamond Jubilee of Queen Victoria**
1905-12 Dresden: Die Brücke group
1909 Munich: Der Blaue Reiter group founded
1910 Vojtec Preissig introduces lino to artists in USA
1911 Horace Brodsky brings lino from USA to Britain as an artist's material

**1914-18 First World War**

**1917 Russian Revolution**
1917-21 Russian artists produce many works on lino: Liubov Popova (multicoloured), Aleksander Rodchenko (monochrome), the ROSTA 'windows' in Moscow and Leningrad
1927 Claude Flight's book *Linocuts*
1930s Silkscreen printing developed in USA
1937-44 Henri Matisse makes lino illustrations for de Montherlant's *Pasiphaé*

**1939-45 Second World War**
1958-62 Pablo Picasso makes 107 linocuts, his only relief prints
c.1960 Screenprinting taken up by Pop artists in Britain and USA
1975 Revival of all aspects of relief print-making.

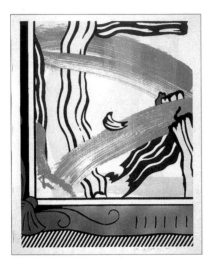

**Painting in a Gold Frame**
**ARTIST Roy Lichtenstein**
**SIZE 184.7 × 293.2cm (78¼ × 115½in)**

This very large mixed media print combines relief printing from lino, screenprinting and collage. This artist likes to emphasize the different qualities of various materials and techniques available to the printmaker today.

**Tigers Drinking**
**ARTIST Norbertine Bresslern-Roth**
**SIZE 21 × 21cm (8¼ × 8¼in)**

Four-colour linocut. This Austrian artist travelled extensively making studies of animals. Her linocuts were shown widely in Europe and Australia during the 1920s and 1930s.

The reason for the survival of relief printing over two thousand years is its versatility. You can use a beautifully prepared block of a rare wood, but you can also rescue a piece of driftwood to cut into a block. You can use the finest handmade paper to print on, but you can also print on quite ordinary paper. You do not need much equipment – a table to work on, a knife, a simple roller and a wooden spoon to burnish the impression – it involves no great outlay to start a series of experiments in relief printmaking. Later you may well be intrigued with the possibilities and want to acquire a printing press, but remember that the Oriental woodblock prints were printed without a press by hand-burnishing.

Many materials other than wood are now used, giving a wide choice in both price and availability. People who are unable to use the solvents and chemicals essential in other printmaking methods will find that relief prints can be made with non-toxic substances and the solvent can be water. Although we urge a professional attitude on the reader, we also encourage simple techniques and free experimentation.

## THE DEVELOPMENT OF PRINTING

Printing developed over the centuries in response to new inventions, improvements in materials and demands from the user. There are four basic methods of printing: in historical order they are, relief, intaglio, lithography and screenprinting. All are used by printmakers, and all give different results.

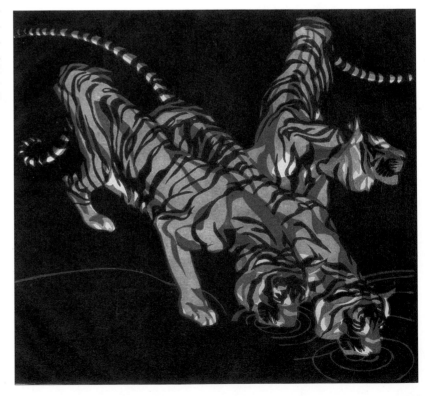

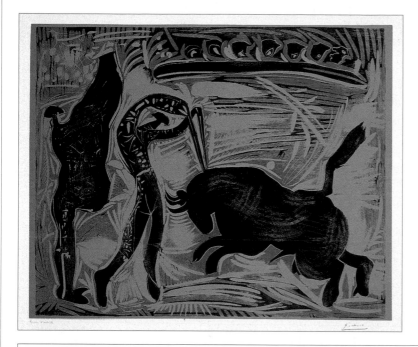

### Les Bandereilles 1959
### ARTIST Pablo Picasso
### SIZE 62 × 75cm (24½ × 29½in)

This three-colour reduction linocut is typical of the 107 linocuts he produced between 1952 and 1963. Note the scratched textures, which enliven the flat areas.

### Puddle
### ARTIST Maurits Cornelis Escher
### SIZE 24 × 32cm (9½ × 12½in)

Woodcut printed from three blocks. Escher is famous for his metaphysical visual inventions but in this print he records nature as it is. He made some linocuts in his youth and occasionally one or two later but he is best known for his woodcuts, wood engravings and lithographs.

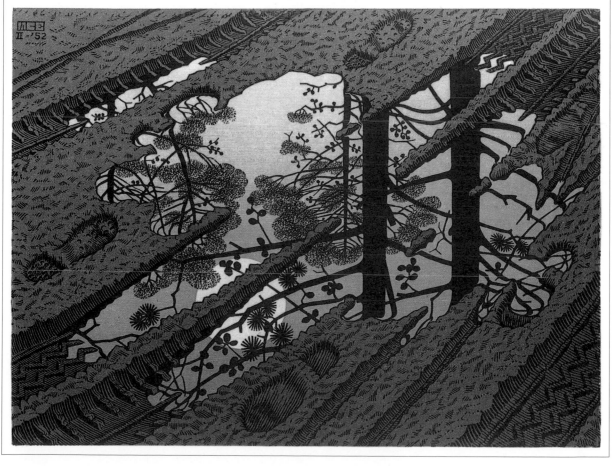

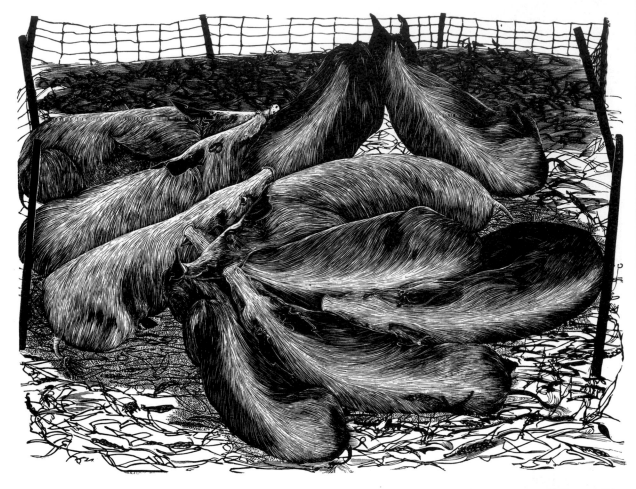

## Mr Henson's Young Tamworths
### ARTIST Sarah van Niekerk
### SIZE 15.2 × 20.4cm (6 × 8in)

This wood engraving shows the contrast between white line on the animals' backs and black line in the fence and foreground litter.

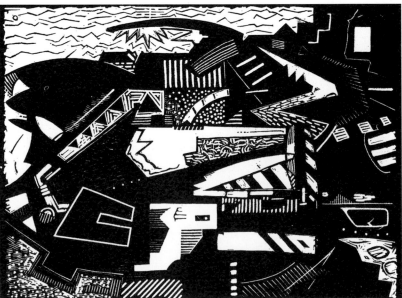

## Folkestone
### ARTIST Roy Willingham
### SIZE 10 × 7.5cm (4 × 3in)

This wood engraving is unusual in that the artist does not follow the traditional figurative manner of most wood engravers. He responds to the abstract patterns seen in urban landscapes when viewed from above.

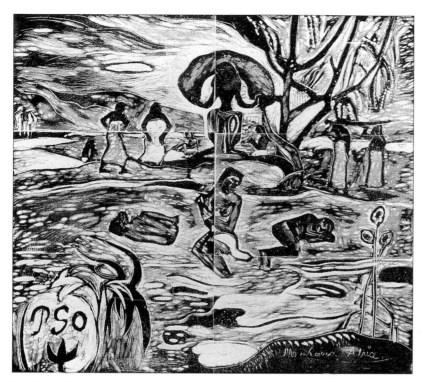

**Mahana Atua 1894**
**ARTIST Paul Gauguin**
**SIZE 18.5 × 20.3cm (7¼ × 8in)**

Gauguin began making woodcuts during his self-imposed exile in Tahiti. Using tropical wood, he hacked and scraped expressive images of life and the women of his ideal land. The rounded ends to the cuts suggest he used mostly u-gouges. Also note that six sections of wood have been joined to make the block.

## Relief printing

In simple forms it has been used since earliest times. Examples are seals, rubber stamps, woodcuts, wood engravings, linocuts, relief etchings, prints from card, stone, plastic and collaged blocks.

The raised surface of the block is inked, put in contact with paper and burnished or put through a press to transfer the image.

## Intaglio printing

Developed during the 14th century. Examples are etching, engraving, aquatint, mezzotint; made from metal and plastic plates.

The incised design on the plate has ink rubbed into its depths, the surface is cleaned and it is put in contact with paper. A press is required to transfer the image on to the paper.

## Lithographic printing

Invented in 1798, based on the antipathy of grease and water. Examples are stone, transfer, zinc, aluminium and continuous–tone lithographs.

The design is drawn in greasy ink on stone or grained metal plate. It is alternately dampened and rolled with greasy ink. A press is required to transfer the image to paper.

## Screenprinting

Developed in the 1930s from stencilling. Examples are silkscreen (hand–drawn) or screenprint if photographic techniques are used.

A fine textile mesh is stretched over a frame and parts are sealed. Ink is pushed through unsealed areas on to paper beneath.

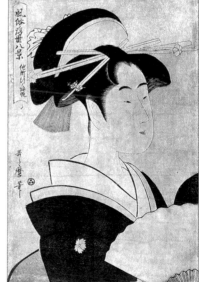

**The Courtesan with a fan**
**ARTIST Kitagawa Utamaro**
**SIZE 38 × 25cm (15 × 9⅞in)**

Colour woodblock print utilizing a key block printed in black with other colour blocks cut to fit. The inks are water-based, the paper handmade and printing is done by burnishing. Utamaro's prints are considered to be the finest in the whole of the Ukiyo-ē or Floating World school of Japanese printmaking.

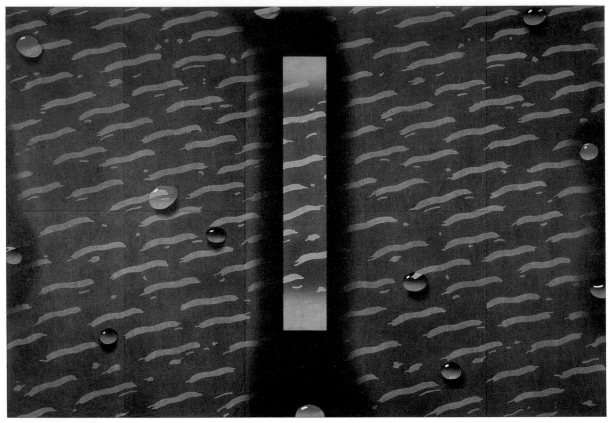

**Between Moments (1984)**
**ARTIST Akira Kurasaki**
**SIZE 56 × 82cm (22 × 32½in)**

This contemporary Japanese woodblock print features blended colours and is printed in the traditional way by hand using a baren and water-based inks.

## THE METHOD OF MAKING A RELIEF PRINT

The sequence starts with the visual idea that you want to transform into a print. If you already have an idea worked out in a drawing or perhaps a painting, it needs to be analyzed in terms of blocks to be cut and colours to be printed. The materials must then be collected together and each block planned in detail. Next, the blocks are cut and proofed. Further cutting and proofing may follow until the proofs are satisfactory. The edition is printed, using the proofs as a guide. Finally, each print is checked, signed and numbered and is ready to be exhibited.

### Relief printing as an experimental method

Not every printmaker wants to make an edition of identical prints. The trend recently has been to use printmaking as a creative method in its own right. The effect of a printed image is quite different from one that is drawn in pencil or pastel, or one painted in water-colour or oil paint. Printed passages can be used in combination with drawn or painted areas, either one on top of the other or perhaps as part of a collage. Works that are entirely printed may be classed as unique prints, or called monotypes or monoprints and still be accepted for most international and national print competitions. There will always be printmakers who prefer to work within a discipline that has been established over the years, and who frown on experimentation for its own sake. Relief printing offers both.

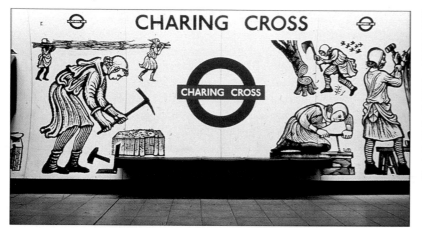

### Charing Cross Mural
### ARTIST David Gentleman
### SIZE 183cm × 82m (72in × 284ft)

The Charing Cross was built at the last resting place of Queen Eleanor's funeral cortege in the 13th century. The artist illustrated the story of the building of the cross in a series of wood engravings. Proofs of these were greatly enlarged and screenprinted on to plastic laminate panels. These panels were installed in 1979 on two platforms of the Underground station.

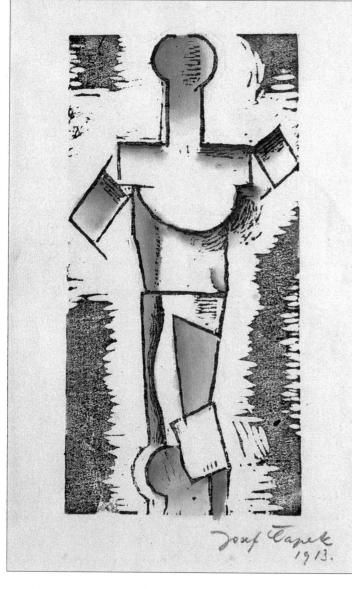

### Cubist Figure 1913
### ARTIST Josef Capek
### SIZE 20.7 × 10.2cm (8½ × 4in)

This three-colour linocut is one of the few examples of relief printmaking by Cubist artists. Note how the colour is rubbed to produce a shaded effect.

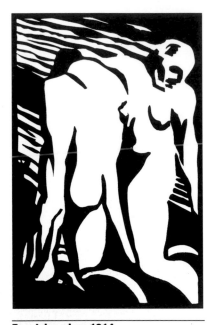

**Expulsion circa 1914**
**ARTIST Horace Brodsky**
**SIZE 46 × 35.5cm (18 × 14in)**

This Australian artist learnt about linocutting in New York and brought the medium to Britain when he settled there in 1908. He was noted for using pieces of lino as a sketchbook and cutting it freely without previous drawing. His linocuts have a characteristic vigour that comes from the ease with which the material can be cut.

# LINOCUTTING PAST AND PRESENT

Linoleum might seem to be too prosaic a material to inspire artists, yet the variety of images that can be printed from it is impressive. From its development as a flooring material in the 1860s until about 1900 it was known only for the warmth and hygiene it brought to cottages, mansions and battleships (hence the name for the thickest variety). Then a remarkable Viennese art educator, Franz Čisek, introduced lino into his classes for children for cutting and printing. Čisek was against the formal methods of teaching art through copying old masters; instead he encouraged children to use all sorts of materials freely. The results were as lively as we would now expect from children, but in the Vienna of 1896 they were shocking– and exciting. Čisek's friends, artists and architects of the Sezession Movement, immediately recognized the imaginative vitality inherent in this work, and they also adopted lino as an art material for themselves.

Linocuts first started appearing in artists' magazines in about 1900, and then as illustrations for books and posters throughout Europe. For some years linocuts developed in two directions: educational and illustrative. Čisek exhibited the work of his pupils very widely – an exhibition in London in 1908 caused a sensation. His principles were soon adopted world-wide, which accounts, in part, for the still common association of lino with schools. At the same time Viennese artists took lino to the United States, where it was used as a popular material for illustration because it could be printed directly alongside type. From New York it was brought to Britain by Horace Brodsky, where it was eventually lifted out of its illustrative role to be used in printmaking at the influential Grosvenor School of Modern Art. This private art school attracted many students from what were then the British Dominions and Colonies, who eventually returned home with new ideas and skills. That heritage remains, and is strong in Southern Africa, Canada, New Zealand, and pre-eminently in Australia. Australian linocutters of the '20s and '30s are almost all deeply influenced by the Futurist inspiration of Claude Flight, teacher at the Grosvenor School, yet they endowed it with their own special character. In contrast the European tradition of that time was of Abstraction and Expressionism – in the early days of the Russian Revolution some of the best linocuts were splendidly abstract.

Today we associate linocutting primarily with figurative and expressionist work. Why this should be so is an interesting question. The answer lies in the nature of the material itself. To begin with lino was used as a cheap substitute for wood; later its special qualities made it ideal for a certain type of work. It was not, however, just that it was cheap and readily available; it was more important that it was not saddled with an impressive history, such as wood has, and which has had such an inhibiting effect.

So, mentally lino was liberating, and physically it was quite different to work from wood. It was much easier and therefore quicker. It was also ideal for dramatic responses to political events: it was used by Soviet artists to create overnight posters as part of the Agitprop movement; it was used by Jews in hiding to satirize Nazi thugs: when all other printing equipment has been seized you can still cut out a piece of the floor, make ink from soot and oil, and burnish a print on the coarsest of paper.

These down-to-earth realities have made lino a first choice as an introduction to printmaking. It was used in the American Works Relief programme during the Depression of the '30s. It is used today to teach printmaking to aborigines in distant parts of Australia. It is also used in the most sophisticated ways by artists of recognized world stature. Its versatility makes it ever more popular.

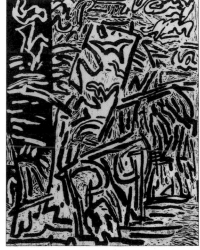

**Untitled**

**ARTIST John Walker**

**SIZE 117.5 × 91.4cm (46 × 36in)**

This very large monochromatic linocut belongs to the revival of Abstract Expressionism and the renewed interest in relief printmaking.

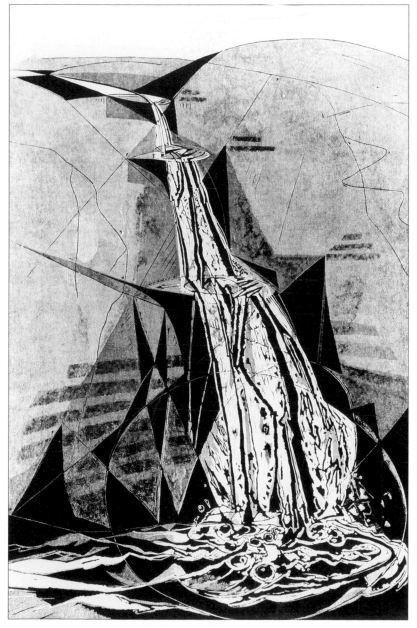

**The Waterfall**

**ARTIST Gertrude Hermes**

**SIZE 94 × 66cm (37 × 26in)**

Two-colour relief print from one block of plywood and one of lino. This British artist was unusual in that she made both very detailed small wood engravings and large wood- and linocuts. Most printmakers tend to work either small or large, but not both.

### Cockerel Turning Round
**ARTIST Michael Rothenstein**
**SIZE 47.5 × 72.5cm (18¾ × 28½in)**

Colour linocut that won first prize in the 1956 Giles Bequest Competition for colour relief prints. Note the blended inking on the tail and the overprinting of a dark colour with a light one on the breast.

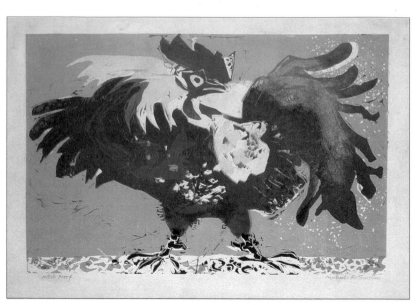

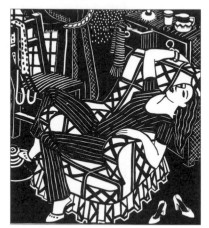

### The Model in Thea's Chair 1933
**ARTIST Amy Kingston**
**SIZE 22.8 × 20.8cm (9 × 8¼in)**

Linocut made while the artist was a student of Thea Proctor in Sydney. It is a good example of white line (her costume) in contrast with black line (her chair).

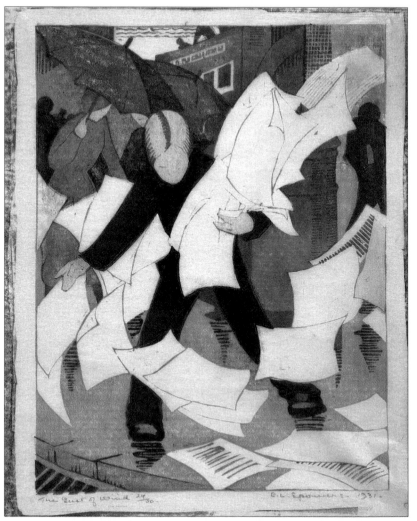

### The Gust of Wind 1931
**ARTIST Ethel Spowers**
**SIZE 22 × 16.5cm (8¾ × 6¼in)**

Colour multi-block linocut. This Australian artist studied with Claude Flight and was much influenced by him, particularly in the choice of subject matter where pattern-making in movement is reduced to simple colour shapes.

## Covent Garden Flower Market
### ARTIST Edward Bawden
### SIZE 46 × 61cm (18 × 24in)

This print is a transfer lithograph from linocut blocks. The artist uses a knife for all his cutting; the gouge is used only for clearing the non-printing lino. Note how he uses a key block for the structure of the composition and the colour keys to that.

Edward Bawden started cutting lino in 1924 and he has probably made more linocuts than anyone else. The majority have been illustrations for books, advertisements and posters but it is his fine art linocuts that have elevated the medium.

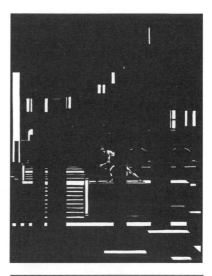

## The Labyrinth
### ARTIST Napier Waller
### SIZE 24.4 × 20.4cm (9½ × 8in)

Linocut from 1932 by a remarkable Australian artist who, after losing his right arm while fighting in Europe in World War I, taught himself to draw and cut lino with his left hand. He was the first artist to make linocuts in Australia.

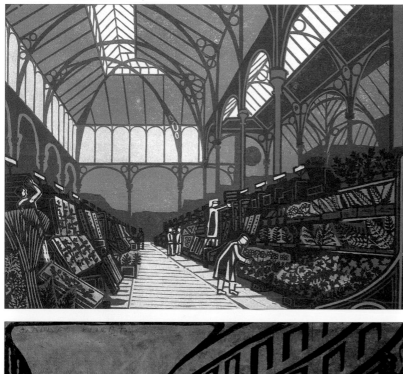

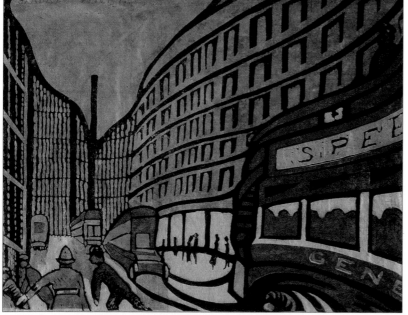

## Speed
### ARTIST Claude Flight
### SIZE 22 × 28cm (8¾ × 11¼in)

Colour linocut by a dynamic British artist who taught linocutting to so many students at the Grosvenor School of Modern Art in London during the 1920s and 1930s. His interest in Futurism led him to express movement in fluid lines. The softness of lino proved ideal for his exuberant cutting.

## WOODCUTTING PAST AND PRESENT

Originally woodblock prints were used in northern China in the T'ang period (627-649 AD) to promulgate Buddhist doctrines. The idea that text and illustration could be easily replicated spread through the Orient rapidly, and was well established in Europe by the early 15th century, when it was turned to the service of the church, the state and the universities. Each page had to be carved in wood, reversed of course, and books were printed first by burnishing as the oriental books were, then by modified wine screwpresses, and not much later by wooden presses that can be recognized as the ancestors of the presses printmakers use today. Colour was added by hand to popular items such as playing cards and ballad sheets. Scribes and illuminators became redundant.

Printing was soon organized into guilds of craftsmen, who were licensed by the ruling power. Albrecht Dürer (1471-1528) was apprenticed as a formcutter or woodblock carver, but when he wanted to cut and print his own woodcuts he was obliged to hand them over to the guild of formcutters and printers. This early monopoly affected the development of woodcutting, and very few prints were actually cut by the originating artist, though they are still

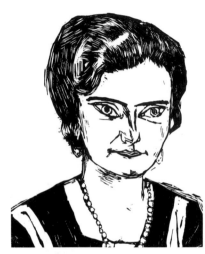

**Bildnis Frau H.M.**
**ARTIST Max Beckmann**
**SIZE 35 × 32.8cm (14 × 13in)**

The spiky cutting in this woodcut is characteristic of the v-gouge. Fragments of wood have deliberately not been cleared from the cheeks and shoulder, which gives a vital and immediate sense of the artist working on the wood in front of the sitter.

**Camouflaged Ship in Dry Dock, Liverpool 1918**
**ARTIST Edward Wadsworth**
**SIZE 23 × 21cm (9⅛ × 8¼in)**

The sharp square edges indicate that the cutting was made with a knife. The bold pattern-making in this woodcut is enhanced by the careful clearing of all the white areas.

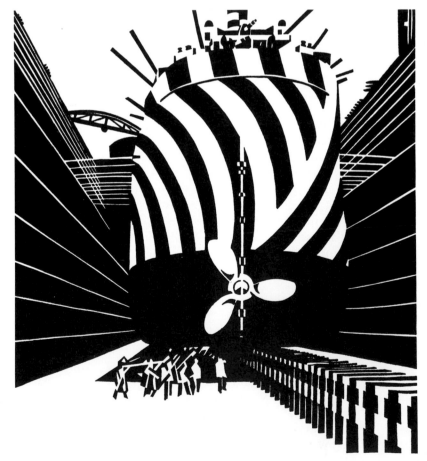

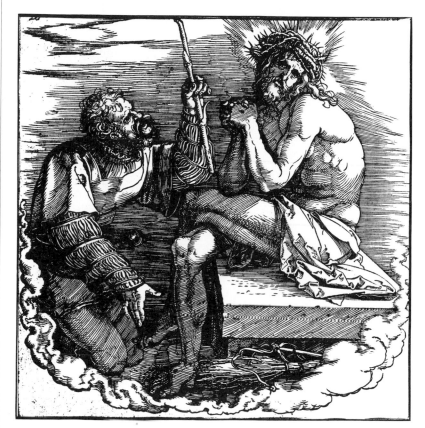

**Christ on the Throne being Mocked**
**ARTIST Albrecht Dürer**
**SIZE 20 × 19.4cm (7⅞ × 7⅝in)**

Dürer was apprenticed to a woodblock cutter and later made many woodcuts for himself as well as metal engravings and etchings. Note how the small white interstices between the black hatching have to be cut out to imitate drawn hatching.

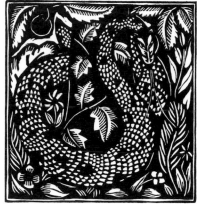

**The Serpent 1911**
**ARTIST Raoul Dufy**
**SIZE 20.3 × 19.5cm (8 × 7⅝in)**

This woodcut is one of the rejected illustrations for *Le Bestiare du Cortège d'Orphée*. The shape of the cuts suggests that the artist used a small v-gouge for the foliage and a broader one for the scales on the snake.

very often brilliant in technique. The Japanese woodblock prints that so influenced the French impressionists in the second half of the 19th century were also the product of collaboration. There, whole families were involved: one cut the design provided by an artist, then other members of the family mixed ink, dampened paper, printed and dried the prints. The organizer of the whole project was the publisher, who also sold the prints.

The use of artisans in Europe eventually led to the weakening of the medium and the initiative passed to the masters of the various intaglio techniques, who developed ever-finer methods and more delicate ways of depicting tone. The final straw was the invention of photography in the mid-19th century, which satisfied a trend towards illusionism. An alternative use of wood, engraving on an end-grain section, offered a finer effect than the side-grain woodcut, and thus what was left of the woodcutting tradition was ruined.

The woodcut was resurrected in 1893 when the artist Paul Gauguin (1848-1903) returned from Tahiti to Paris. He had been interested in the Japanese woodblock prints he had seen before he left Europe, and the impact of Maori and other art forms he saw in the Pacific was profound. He cut the plank wood as freely as the tropical vegetation grew surrounding him. Large, flat areas were often partially rubbed giving a tonal effect; Gauguin had a flawless sense of

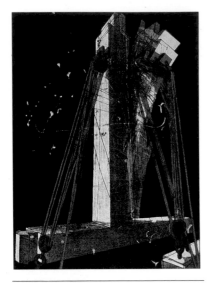

**'84 Katsura (XII)**

**ARTIST Seiko Kawachi**

**SIZE 71.5 × 51cm (28 × 20in)**

Woodblock print featuring traditional Japanese techniques but on large boards of veneered plywood. The subject of this series of prints is the manner in which large beams of timber are forced to split and crack under tension. Katsura is a high quality timber and one favoured for the veneer on plywood used for woodblocks. The artist incorporates into the print blemishes found on the surface, enlivening the textures.

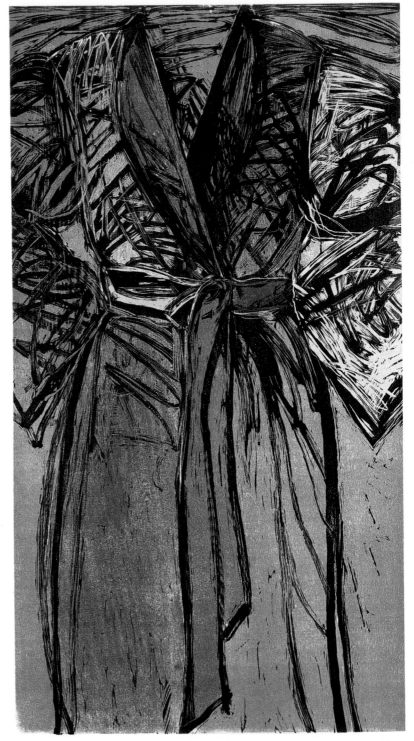

**Bathrobe**

**ARTIST Jim Dine**

**SIZE 165.4 × 90.2cm (65 × 35½in)**

This large 14-colour woodcut is printed from two plywood blocks. One block prints the black, the other block carries 13 colours abutting to each other, necessitating very careful inking by hand.

visual balance which included combining primitive symbols and heroic figures. The Norwegian artist Edvard Munch (1863-1944) saw these prints in Paris and, inspired by them, made the first of many woodcuts in 1898 in Paris. He believed in participating totally in each stage of making a print, from choosing the wood, to the inking and printing of each colour. He insisted in hand-printing everything, and experimented ceaselessly with inking blocks in different ways. For example he cut up blocks and applied ink by brush to adjacent parts.

These two artists used wood because of its challenge. The difficulty of cutting and the character of each individual piece seemed a metaphor for their personal struggles and explorations. These prints were the very opposite of the dull reproductive woodcuts made by artisans, and they had a profound influence on a new generation of German artists who were seeking new ways of expression in the new century. To them the power of the woodcut was the ideal means to express the social turmoil of their times.

In the late 20th century expressionism is again particularly significant, and the woodcut is popular with the new younger generation of printmakers

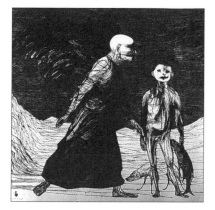

**Tobias and the Angel**
**ARTIST Leonard Baskin**
**SIZE 36 × 38cm (14¼ × 15in)**

Wood engraving on a large scale. Baskin is noted for his use of black line, where the cutting out represents the non-printing area so that the artist is working in a negative sense. The large areas of barely worked black make the composition very dramatic and perhaps owe something to Baskin's interest in sculpture.

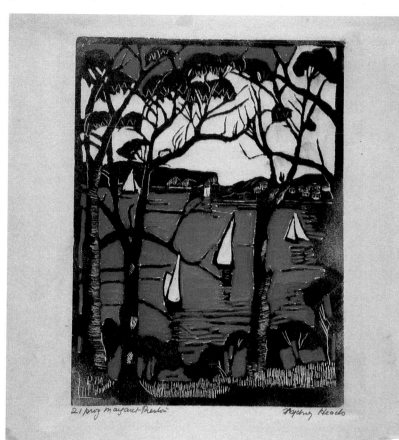

**Sydney Heads 1925**
**ARTIST Margaret Preston**
**SIZE 28 × 19.5cm (11 × 7¼in)**

Woodcut printed in black on Japanese paper with water-colour added by hand. The contrast between the cut quality of the black and the soft, fluid blue water-colour is interesting.

## WOOD ENGRAVING PAST AND PRESENT

End-grain wood had long been used to carve very hardwearing blocks for fabric printing, but it was not used by artists until Thomas Bewick (1754–1828) chose it for illustration blocks because it would print more good copies before wearing down and take finer work than side-grain wood. Bewick also pioneered white-line engraving, where the design is predominantly shown in white lines against a black background. Wood engraving is essentially a black-and-white art, although during the 19th century it was much used for three-colour illustrations, and some artists continue to use the same system today.

The traditional role of wood engraving has been in illustration, where it replaced side-grain woodcuts. Until photographic methods of making printing blocks were developed in the late 19th century, all images in books, catalogues and journals were wood engravings – lithography still tended to be used for individual prints. This multitude of wood engravings was cut by artisans who had great technical virtuosity but rarely initiated a work. Reportage drawings made on the spot of some important event were often cut up and distributed among several engravers. Each one cut his own portion, not quite to the edges. The separate blocks were then clamped together to make the full-size picture and one engraver worked the edges to make continuous lines.

**Federal Sharpshooter**
**ARTIST Winslow Homer**
**SIZE 23.2 × 35cm (9⅛ × 13¾in)**

Wood engraving after an illustration by the artist. He did not engrave his own blocks and the style of cutting is typical of the skilful interpretation of a drawing used by hack engravers. Note the use of the two-line multiple tool on the left trouser leg. You can see some of the joins between the sections of the composite end-grain woodblock.

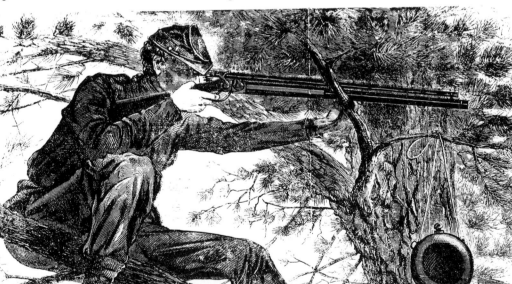

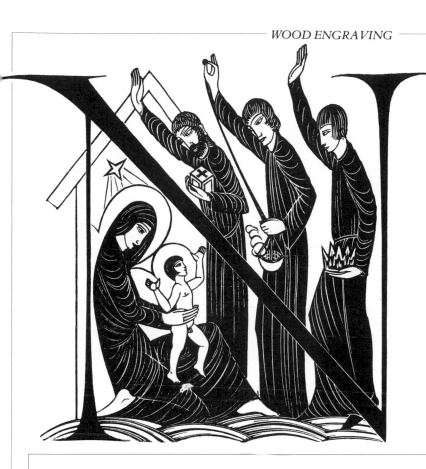

**N for Epiphany**
**ARTIST Eric Gill**
**SIZE 10.75 × 12.75cm (4¼ × 5in)**

Wood engraving to illustrate *The Four Gospels*, a private press limited edition publication. Note how Gill uses white line on the figures for decorative purpose rather than to describe form. His use of black line and white line in his wood engravings is closely related to his approach to sculpture.

**An illustration from The Hansom Cab and the Pigeons 1935**
**ARTIST Eric Ravilious**
**SIZE 6.4 × 7.6cm (2½ × 3in)**

Wood engraving done entirely in white line technique, where the cutting is positive drawing. This artist, who worked between the Wars, was noted for the pattern-making he saw in everyday scenes.

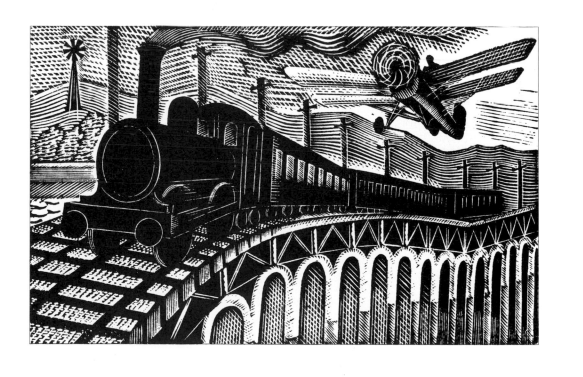

### Chalk, Flint and Bone
### ARTIST Monica Poole
### SIZE 10.75 × 16cm (4¼ × 6¼in)

Wood engraving using white line in a very subtle way to describe the different textures of the chalk, flint and bone. Note the dotted cutting on the chalk in the foreground in contrast to the hard lines used for the flint behind and the curves for the bone.

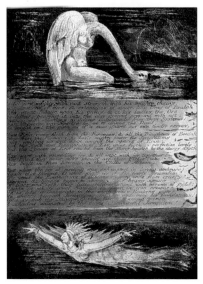

### A Page from Jerusalem
### ARTIST William Blake
### SIZE 30 × 29cm (11¾ × 11⅜in)

Relief etching hand-coloured after printing. Blake drew on copper plates with varnish, which acted as a resist when the plate was etched by acid. The plates are surface inked.

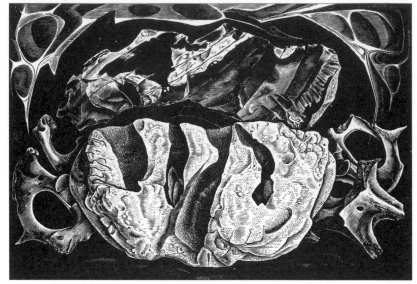

The revival of fine book production in the '20s and '30s led to a new generation of wood engravers who were artists, not artisans. Although most of the work was still essentially illustration, some engravers also made individual graphic works. The same is true today with a noticeable split between the traditionalists, who are still illustration–orientated, and those who will try new materials and alternative roles for the medium. Wood engravings are now being used photographically enlarged in advertising – something the old guard find deplorable. The mural in London's Charing Cross Station on the Underground is composed of enormously enlarged wood engravings by David Gentleman. It is very successful, although the medium is being used as a design vehicle rather than in its own right. Whichever way you look at it, wood engraving is a medium that offers a true graphic experience where all the refinement of black-and-white mark-making finds its purest expression.

## OTHER RELIEF TECHNIQUES PAST AND PRESENT

Lino and wood will, no doubt, remain the principal materials used for relief printmaking, although that is by no means the whole story. Today we associate relief printing with a wide range of materials, but such experimentation is not new. William Blake (1757–1827), who trained as a metal engraver, experimented with ways in which he could avoid paying for the setting of type for the books of words and images he published himself. He used a form of varnish to draw on a copperplate (some scholars think that he drew with varnish on paper and offset that on to the plate to avoid writing backwards). The varnish acted as an acid-resist when the plate was immersed in an acid bath. The etch would bite around the resist leaving the writing and the main parts of the drawing unbitten. This relief etching was then surface-inked and relief printed.

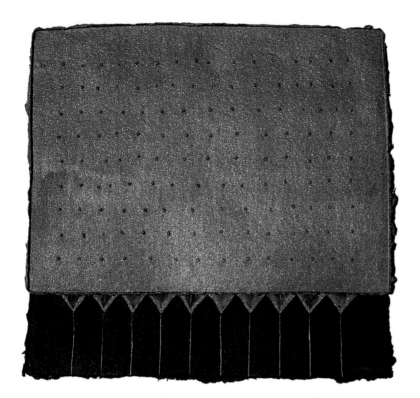

### Moonwalk
**ARTIST Judith Ingram**
**SIZE 76 × 79cm (30 × 31 in)**

Mixed media print made · from handcast paper, linocut, paint and a collage of feathers and produced in a small edition of five copies. This artist uses printmaking as just one element in her constructions.

### Cockerel with Scarlet Tail
**ARTIST Michael Rothenstein**
**SIZE 42 × 63cm (16½ × 24¾in)**

Linocut with textures made by applying gesso to parts of the lino and working it before it sets. Printed in four colours on Japanese paper.

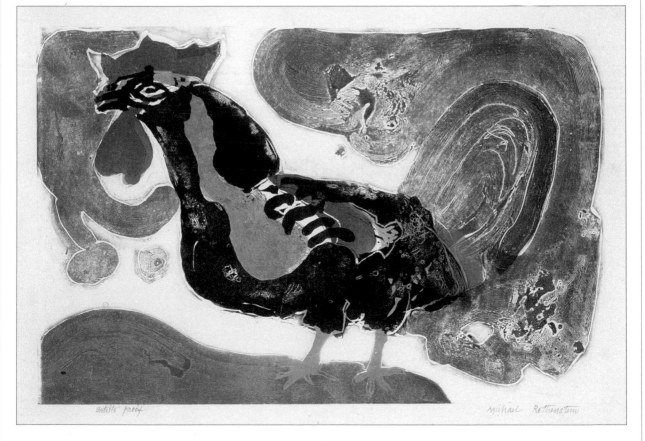

The fact is that almost anything reasonably flat can be inked and printed. Children are taught to print from cut potatoes, from paper doilies or corrugated paper. This is to be encouraged for it reveals the alter ego of many common materials, and sophisticated printmakers should not reject the vocabulary of marks. Try rolling up a pair of old jeans with ink and taking an impression – the image is surprising – and it has been used by several serious printmakers.

In addition to found objects there are many manmade materials that can be cut, torn or moulded into printing blocks. Papers and other cellulose sheets make fine blocks. Card prints have become very popular. The material is either cut into jigsaw shapes or the surface is manipulated to create areas of texture that ink-up variably.

Plastics of many kinds offer the relief printmaker interesting alternatives to the classic materials such as boxwood. Thin plastic sheet sold for the model-maker can be engraved successfully and sells at a fraction of the cost of boxwood. Other plastics that can be cut to the same thickness as box are also being used successfully.

Surface-printed blocks made by collaging or glueing materials on to a base are another element in a repertoire that, even now, has not been fully explored. Michael Rothenstein made important discoveries in the development of etching lino as well as in the use of materials to build up a printing surface. He has also held many group teaching sessions in which found objects were inked and printed to make very large-scale murals.

The printing of found objects is allied closely to the use of embossing as an element in a design. It has not been very common in the Western tradition, but is important in the superb Japanese prints from the Ukiyo-e (the Floating World); that so stunned the Impressionists in France in the mid-19th century. Japanese woodblock artists of our time have developed a remarkable synthesis between old and new techniques in a way that has enriched relief printmaking for us all. The subtle embossing that was used to ornament the "brocade" prints, so-called because of the elaborate representation of patterned surfaces, is now transformed into an important working element in the design.

A feature of contemporary printmaking is not only the use of non-traditional materials but also the mixing of media. The only criterion is to choose the material and method most suited to conveying the idea – and to avoid being seduced by new tricks. Supposing you want a large-scale print in which there are to be small areas that need great detail. Lino will give you the size but not the detail; wood engraving the reverse, detail but not space. The answer is to use both: lino for the broad areas and wood engraving for the details. Similar problems are solved by other combinations of techniques, not confined to relief printing. Intaglio may be used on top of relief, or relief on top of offset litho.

A further development in printmaking is the use of paper pulp. Most prints are still made on sheets of paper made, by hand or machine, at professional paper mills, but as the specialist mills closed in the '60s artists looked at the possibilities of making their own paper. They could not achieve the smooth, well-made printmaking papers they were used to buying, but they found that they could manipulate the pulp to create entirely new works – formed paper works. Sometimes these were printed upon and sometimes relief blocks were used as formers or moulds on which the pulp was cast.

# THE MATERIALS OF RELIEF PRINTMAKING

From earliest times the most commonly used material for making printing blocks was wood. Its advantages were obvious: it was plentiful and therefore cheap, it was soft enough to cut, yet hard enough to print many copies before wearing down. The size of early woodcuts was limited more by the rather small sheets of paper made in Europe and by the size of printing presses than by the size of woodblocks available. In China, Japan and Korea, where there were many artists highly skilled in making woodblock prints, much larger sheets of paper were made, and their method of printing by burnishing did not restrict the size of the print.

## Woodcuts and woodblock prints

These terms are used to differentiate between Western and Oriental traditions. Woodcuts are printed in the West using oil-based inks and a press; woodblock prints are printed in the Orient using water-based inks and hand burnishing. However, Western print-makers sometimes employ burnishing and water-based inks, so you cannot always rely on the usage of words.

## Wood engraving

When the end-grain section of wood is carved it is called a wood engraving because the very fine tools used were originally bor-rowed from metal engraving. Some scholars call a finely worked side-grain woodblock a wood engraving, claiming that if the tools are engravers' tools the result is an engraving, but the usual association is between side-grain and woodcut, end-grain and wood engraving.

   End-grain woodblocks are usually small in comparison to those used for woodcuts, and the grain, running at right angles to the cut surface, has little or no influence on the cutting of the design. As the wood is so close-grained, the texture is very fine, and detailed work is a characteristic of wood engraving.

## Linocutting

Linoleum is used far more than any other material today to make relief printing blocks. It has many advantages: it has no grain or direction, and it is robust enough to allow many hundreds of prints to be taken before it wears down. It is available in very large pieces; it is inexpensive and easy to obtain. It is softer than wood to cut, and its only disadvantage is that its granular texture is too coarse for very fine cutting.

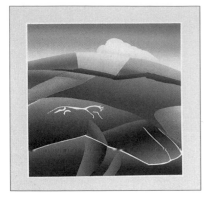

**White Horse Hill**
**ARTIST Lynne Moore**
**SIZE 45.5 × 40.1cm (18 × 15¾in)**

In this card print the thin card is cut in jigsaw-like pieces, which are inked and assembled for printing. There is no overprinting of colours. Note how the artist uses blended colours to give shape to the landscape and depth to the sky.

## Other relief printing materials

A very wide range of other materials is used today as alternatives to wood and lino. They are chosen because they provide a different surface, and the resulting print registers that difference. They may also be chosen because they are less expensive. In order of cost, prepared end-grain boxwood blocks are the most expensive, followed by side-grain woodblocks; lino and platics are about the same, and blocks made from paper, card, board and collaged blocks are the cheapest. Printing blocks made of metal or stone are also quite costly, and are not very often used in relief printing.

# PRINTMAKING TODAY

The invention of photography in the mid-19th century completely changed the nature of printing. One result of this was that the craftsmen who engraved wood and metal became redundant. The word "print" meant, by then, a reproduction that was copied by an artisan from an original drawing or painting. Indeed, the Royal Academy in London recognized a category of reproductive prints, but refused to exhibit prints actually made by artists themselves. The time had come to try to reinstate the idea of the fine art print created in its own right. The signing and numbering of prints was introduced, and in 1880 the Royal Society of Painter-Etchers and Engravers was founded in London. The exclusivity of small editions was fostered, and artists distanced themselves from what was seen as the taint of commercial printing and photography.

Over the years confusion and comparison with reproductions persisted, and in 1960 an international meeting in Vienna attempted to define an artist's original print as one that is printed by the artist and is signed and numbered. In France in 1965 it was stated that it must be "conceived and executed entirely by hand by the same artist... with the exclusion of any and all mechanical and photo-mechanical process". They were already out of date, however, because with Pop Art photography became an important feature in the new screenprints.

Screenprinting had all the vigour of a new movement and seemed to overwhelm the older printing techniques of relief, intaglio and lithography. It also became more technologically sophisticated so that artists who worked with clever printers were pressurized to produce more and more, and made many prints not far removed from reproductions. Some, however, resented losing control over their work, and started exploring the old hand methods again. Mezzotint, one of the intaglio methods, practically had to be re-invented, so far had it fallen into disuse.

Out of this came the present reappraisal of relief printmaking. The tactile and emotional qualities of materials reasserted themselves. People talked again of the beauty of a piece of wood and the delight and challenge of working it; well-worn lino blocks were affectionately compared to old leather. A synthesis between old and new technology and materials is now evident, making relief printing the most versatile and interesting printmaking medium.

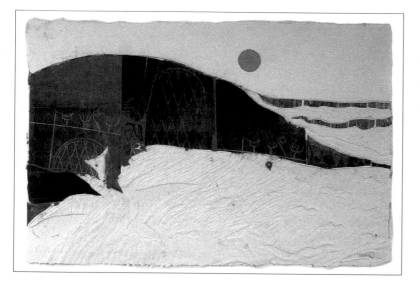

### Landscape
### ARTIST Ray Lefroy
### SIZE 60 × 90cm (23½ × 35½in)

Handcast rag paper with a linocut as a mould on which the paper fibres settle. The artist has used white and colured paper pulp. Note how the textures cut in the lino have formed the paper.

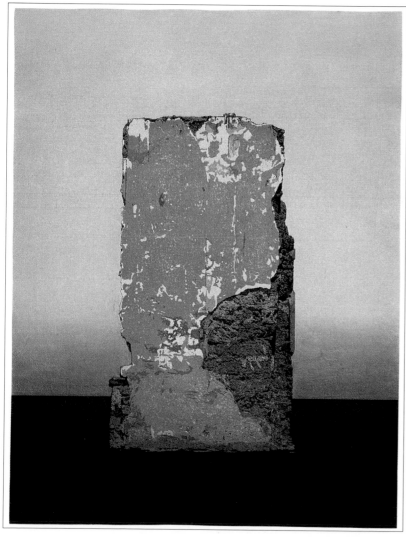

### Green Mud Wall
### ARTIST Hodaka Yoshida
### SIZE 68 × 51cm (26¾ × 20in)

The subtle colour background is printed from woodblocks and water-based inks in the traditional Japanese technique. The chunk of wall made of plaster over straw is printed in oil-based ink from a photo-relief etching. Such combinations of old and new methods are frequently seen in contemporary Japanese printmaking and are particularly an inspiration to relief printmakers.

## SELECTING THE METHOD

Whichever block material you select, be it lino, wood, plastic, card or some other material, the actual organization of the blocks falls into five basic categories: single block, multiple blocks, single reduction block, multiple reduction blocks and jigsaw blocks.

A monochromatic image printed from boxwood, plywood, lino or another material presents no great problems other than inking, placing the block in the correct position in relationship with the paper and printing it well. Colour prints, which are in the majority today, immediately introduce the analysis of the number of colours required and pose the question of how best to realize the print.

It would be possible, for example, to do any reduction print as a multi-block print by cutting a separate block for each colour rather than adopting progressive cutting and printing. The use of masks laid on a single block during inking makes it possible to apply ink selectively and to extend the potential number of colours without the necessity for cutting other blocks. This and hand-inking with

**Still Life 1928**
**ARTIST Ben Nicholson**
**SIZE Unknown**

Single block linocut in which the granular texture of the material is deliberately used as an integral element in the composition. This comes from a period in his work when he used relief prints as a means of designing patterns for fabrics.

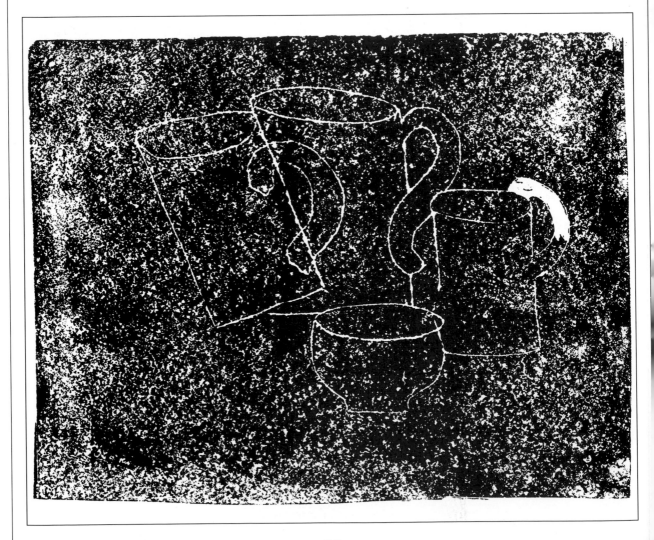

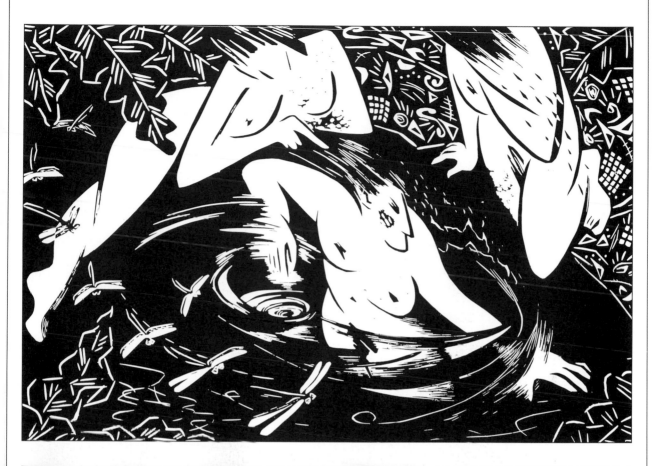

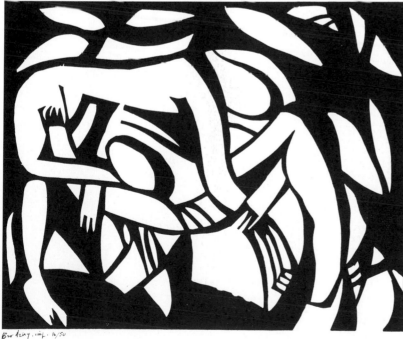

## The Bathers 1
### ARTIST Tsugumi Ota
### SIZE 76 × 58.5cm (30 × 23in)

Woodcut printed on an Albion press using oil-based ink. Note how the edges of the white areas have been cut with a knife, the foliage cut with a v-gouge and the white areas cleared with a u-gouge. The shape of the marks indicates which tools have been used.

## The Wrestlers 1913
### ARTIST Henri Gaudier-Brezeska
### SIZE 22.5 × 28cm (8¾ × 11in)

Horace Brodsky introduced Brezeska to lino-cutting and he made this monochromatic linocut and one other called *The Boxers* just before his early death. They reflect his semi-abstract sculptural style.

small rollers or dabbers means that a single block can still be used to produce a multi-coloured print.

There is not necessarily only one way to make a print. The choice may depend upon cost – one reduction block may be used to print five or more colours which is obviously cheaper than five separate blocks. But the reduction method presupposes that you will be able to print the full number of copies all the way through. If you can only print a part-edition for the moment then you can not destroy the blocks by progressive cutting. Relief printing offers several alternative methods.

**Pryde-Pierrot**
**ARTIST Eduardo Paolozzi**
**SIZE 40.5 × 40cm (16 × 15¾in)**

Woodcut from a suite of six prints called *For Charles Rennie Mackintosh*. This print was pulled with brown water-based ink. Note how it is made up from many small square blocks that have been cut with mechanical tools.

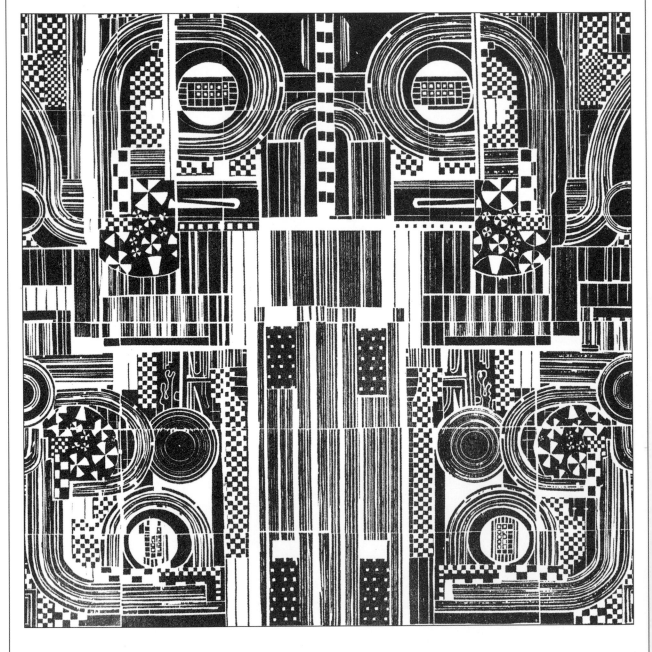

## Single block methods

The majority of single block prints are monochromatic but multi-colour inking on one block extends the range of possibilities considerably.

Monochromatic prints are somewhat out of favour with the general public – it seems that the demand for colour continues unabated. Connoisseurs, however, have always recognized that black and white prints represent some of the greatest achievements in printmaking. It is necessary to consider the white as well as the black for it should play an equal part in the design. This relationship is, perhaps, most noticeable in wood engravings where the use of white-line and black-line engraving is a more obvious part of the repertoire. This counterpoint is in fact an essential part of all monochromatic work and gives wide scope for interpretation through marks made by various tools.

Multi-colour inking on a single block requires some planning in advance. The commonest method is to cut the block so that each colour area is sufficiently separated from its neighbour to avoid colours mixing during application. This can be done by means of small rollers, brushes, dabbers or even the fingertip. If the colours are very close it can take considerable time to ink up for each impression.

**Loch a Clachan**
**ARTIST Gladys McAvoy**
**SIZE 33 × 51cm (13 × 20in)**

Single block linocut printed using water-based inks applied by roller. Some parts of the block are etched with caustic soda and some of the inking was done through masks on to the block.

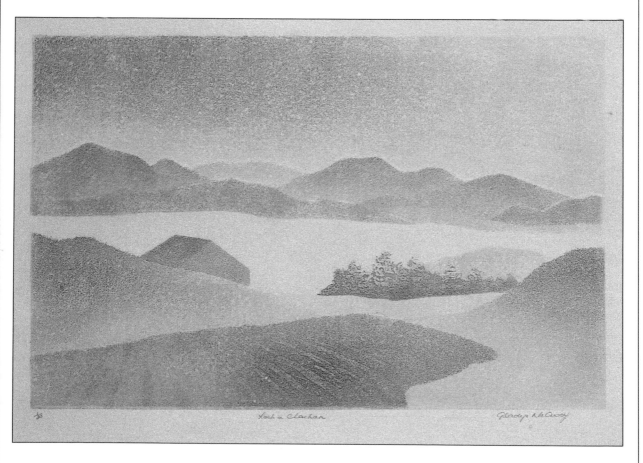

The second method is to cut all the non-printing areas away and to cut one or more masks (stencils) from stiff paper or acetate sheet. The mask can be placed on the block and ink rolled through any apertures on to the block beneath. Alternatively the block may be fully rolled up with ink and the mask placed on the paper or rather between the block and the paper. If the block is cleaned it can be used again with another mask and another colour. Taking this to its logical conclusion the lino or other block material need not be cut at all but merely act as a support for the ink, which is entirely controlled by a series of masks.

**Joel**
**ARTIST Simon King**
**SIZE 11.5 × 11.5cm (4½ × 4½in)**

Wood engraving designed to illustrate a text. Note the different sorts of marks made by different tools and the variety within each passage.

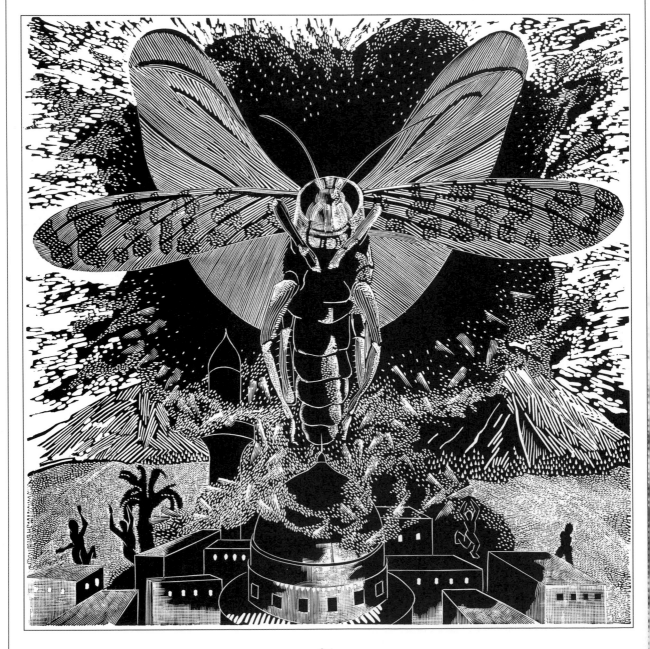

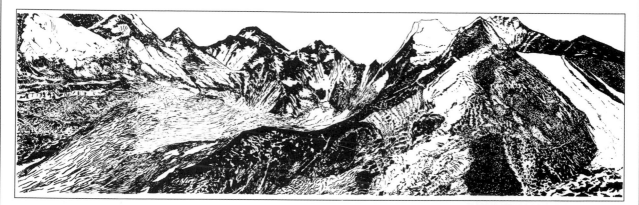

## Himalayan Trek
### ARTIST Katie Clemson
### SIZE 76 × 305cm (30 × 120in)

Very large monochromatic single block lino-cut printed in black and white by burnishing on paper mado in a roll. It won the linocut prize in the Ninth British International Print Biennale at Bradford in 1986.

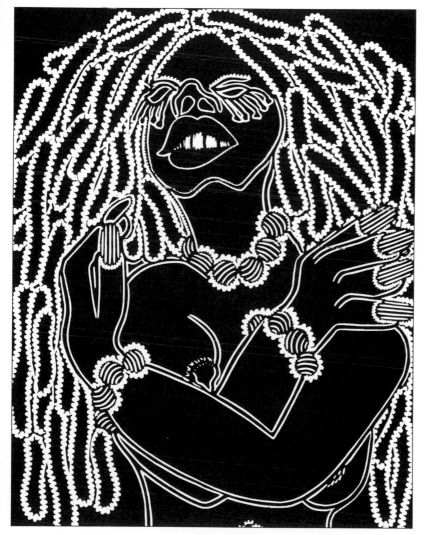

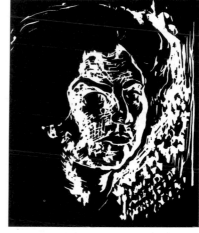

## Kopf im Doppellicht 1906
### ARTIST Emile Nolde
### SIZE 29.5 × 23.5cm (9¼ × 8¼in)

Woodcut in the Expressionist tradition featuring an almost abstract balance between black and white areas for drama. The v-gouge has often pulled off fragments of wood emphasizing the haste of the cutting.

## Lady Caroline
### ARTIST Peter Daglish
### SIZE 75 × 60cm (29½ × 23½in)

Linocut showing how the soft material is good for the vigorous cutting of fluid lines entirely in white-line technique using gouges.

## Banner
### ARTIST Rosemary Simmons
### SIZE 170cm (70in) each side

The motifs along the bottom were printed from lino on to canvas. This was later stretched and painted for use as an exhibition banner.

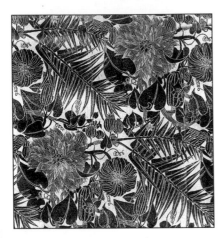

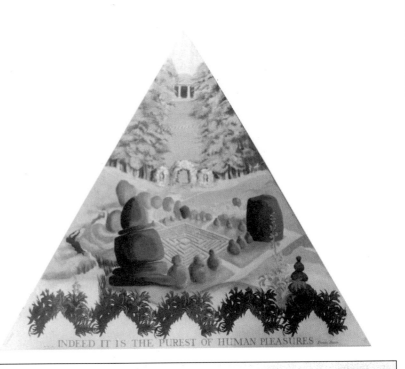

## Wallpaper design
### ARTIST Marthe Armitage
### SIZE 56cm (22in) wide

Single block linocut printed in one colour in repeats to cover lengths of wallpaper. The artist prints some of her wallpapers by hand and others on a modified offset lithographic press.

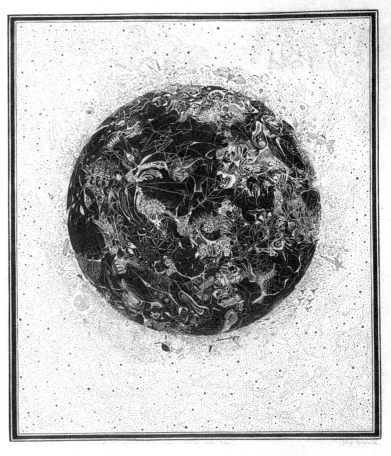

## Improvisation, Lubrication, Humorous and Fanciful
### ARTIST Josef Gielniak
### SIZE 34.9 × 29.8cm (13¾ × 11¾in)

The Polish artist spent most of his life in a sanatorium suffering from tuberculosis. He was often very weak but was just able to make very finely worked linocuts using wood engraving tools and working very slowly.

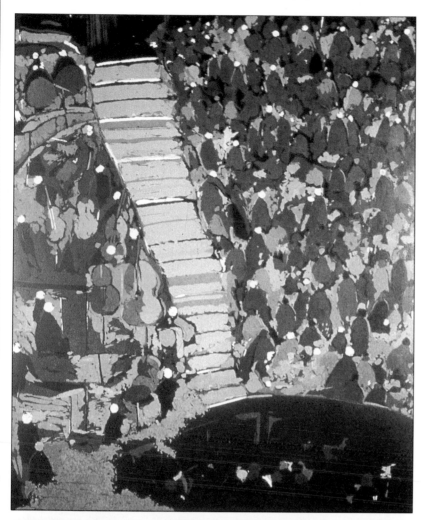

### Night at the Proms
### ARTIST Katie Clemson
### SIZE 61 × 35.5cm (24 × 14in)

Multi-block linocut printed in seven colours in which the pattern made by the banked-up audience is contrasted with that of the orchestra in the Royal Albert Hall in London.

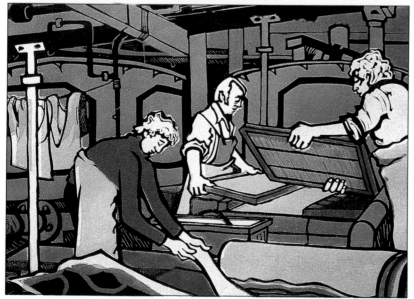

### Papermaking at Hayle Mill
### ARTIST Carol Walklin
### SIZE 33 × 46cm (13 × 18in)

Combined key block and reduction block linocut. The key block prints the black outline and structure of the design and the colours are printed from one reduction block with some masking of areas during inking.

## SINGLE BLOCK REDUCTION METHOD

The single block prints shown in this section demonstrate the power that can be generated by using one colour and the simplest of materials and tools. All the energy of the printmaker can be directed into the cutting of the block without the need to consider the balance of the colours and their registration during printing or the behaviour of inks together.

Many printmakers, however, think in terms of colour rather than monochrome and therefore must explore more complex ways of making an image. The print by Gladys McAvoy on p.35 is a transitional method. She uses a single block but by inking only parts of it for each colour she produces a multi-colour print. In the reduction method a single block is also used to obtain a multi-coloured print, but the most common method is still to use one block for each colour and it makes a very good starting point for the beginner.

**Veronica Wipes the Face of Christ**
**ARTIST Paul Peter Piech**
**SIZE 30.5 × 30.5cm (12 × 12in)**

Reduction block linocut. One of a series of 14 Stations of the Cross made specially for an exhibition held in West Germany.

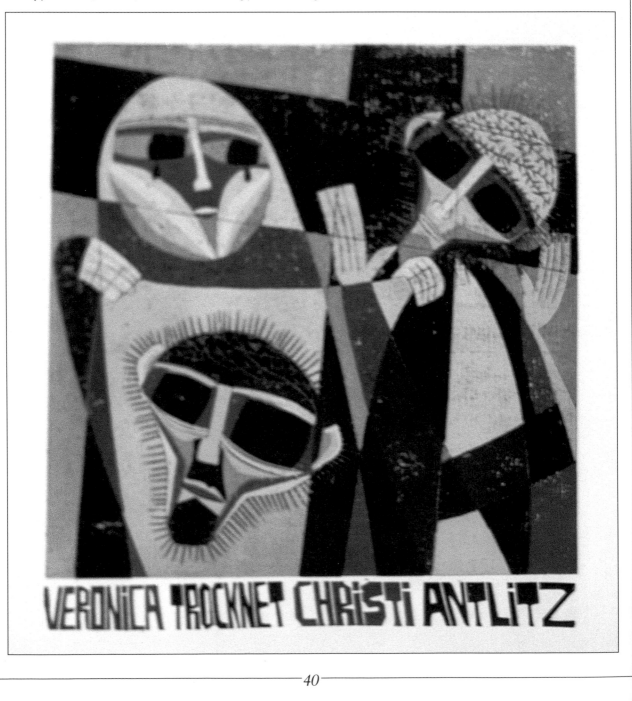

VERONICA TROCKNET CHRISTI ANTLITZ

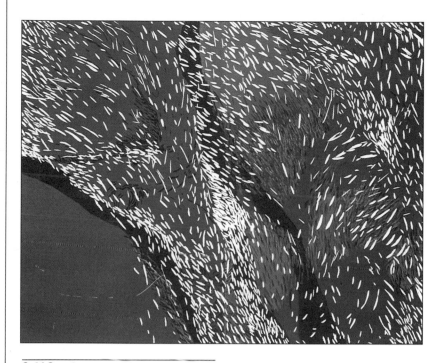

**Gold Coast**
**ARTIST Ann Conner**
**SIZE 92 × 123cm (36⅛ × 48½in)**

One woodblock and one lino block are used for this large image which is printed on two sheets of paper to form a diptych.

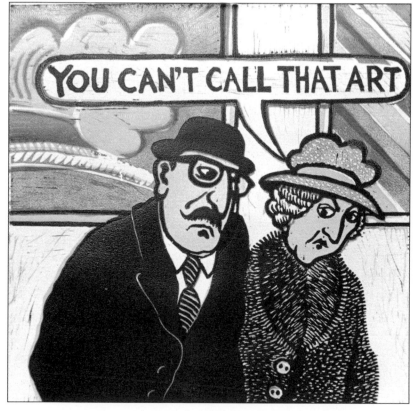

**You Can't Call That Art**
**ARTIST Peter Ford**
**SIZE 25.5 × 25.5cm (10 × 10in)**

A colour linocut with lettering that speaks for itself. This British artist works within the honourable graphic tradition of social comment.

## Multi-block methods

Traditionally each separate colour has always been printed from its own block. It is a faster way of printing because the inking of the block is straightforward and there is no question of having to laboriously paint in an area of colour here and one there. Instead the block is quickly rolled all over with one colour. It is also easier, particularly for the beginner, to work out how many colours and therefore blocks will be needed rather than to plan the more intellectually demanding reduction method. Its disadvantage over

### MULTI-BLOCK PRINT WITHOUT A KEY BLOCK

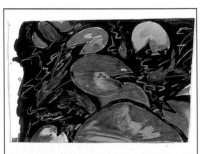

**1** Coloured drawing of a goldfish pond with waterlilies done in paint and chalk on paper.

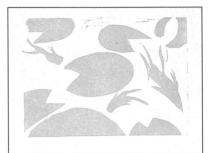

**2** A proof of the yellow block, which prints beneath all the colours except the pure blue in the water.

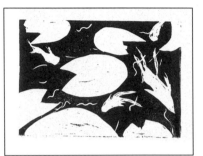

**3** A proof of the black block, which goes over most of the water except the blue lines that show through as ripples.

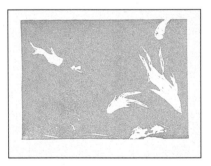

**4** A proof of the blue block showing how some of the yellow and all the red areas have been cut away from it.

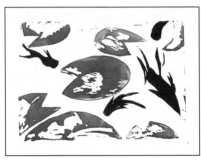

**5** A proof of the green and red block. The colours have been inked using small rollers – they are far enough apart.

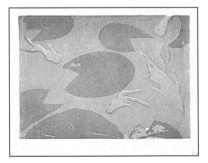

**6** A proof of the blue printed over the yellow. Oil is used to make the colours transparent so that a light green is made.

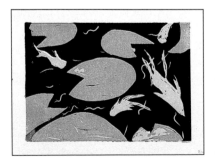

**7** A proof of the black printed over the blue and yellow blocks. The blue is seen only in the ripples but contributes to the green.

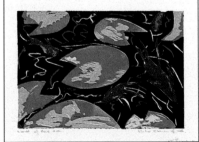

**8** The finished print of *Waterlilies* by Katie Clemson. Highlights to the goldfish were added to the inked red block by brush.

the reduction method is not only the extra block material required but the registration of one colour with another, which needs to be carefully planned and executed. Since the blocks remain intact it is possible to print just part of the edition at first and complete it at another date.

One advantage of the multi–block system is that the materials can be varied to produce different effects. Lino might be chosen where the design calls for a large flat colour area but the same material could be too coarse for a very detailed passage. In that case cut the fine

## MULTI-BLOCK PRINT WITH A KEY BLOCK

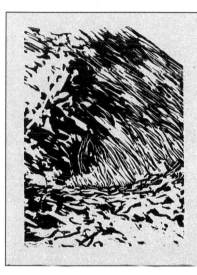

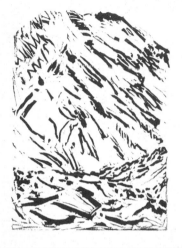

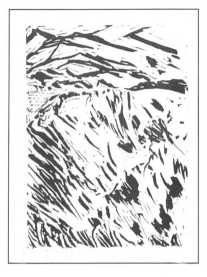

**1** A proof of the black block, which is also the key block. All the other colours are printed to fit this colour.

**2** A proof of the second block printed in cadmium red. This colour was printed last in the final print (see p. 171).

(see p. 171)

**3** A proof of the third block, which was printed in a warm orangey red. This was the fourth colour to be printed.

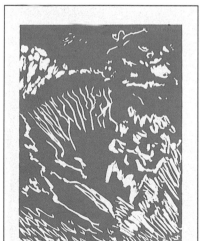

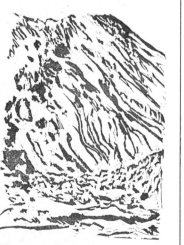

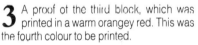
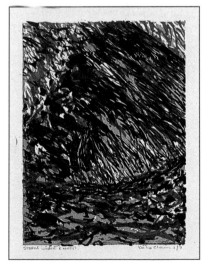

**4** A proof of the blue block, which was printed first during the final printing because it underlays most of the black block.

**5** A proof of the mauve block, which was printed third in the final print. The order of printing is decided during proofing.

**The Finished print**

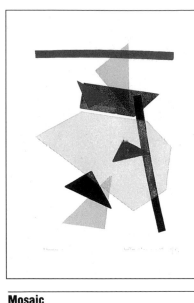

### Mosaic
### ARTIST Katie Clemson
### SIZE 51 × 40.5cm (20 × 16in)

Free form multi-block linocut. The position of the blocks is determined by using acetate sheet (see p.175). The same method can be used to check registration if the ink on the acetate is allowed to dry so it can be laid on a proof.

### The Black Flower of Night
### ARTIST James Burr
### SIZE 80 × 57cm (31½ × 22¾in)

Mixed media relief print from woodcut block, linocut and a block made from crumpled paper glued on to a base (see the blue circle). This free form print emphasizes the whole area of paper as part of the image.

### Convergence
### ARTIST Ann-Marie Le Quesne
### SIZE 102 × 66cm (40 × 26in)

This large scale card print (far right) is not a jigsaw type but uses overprinting. The cutting is unusually fluid for this material. Light colours have been printed first and dark colours on top.

work on an end-grain wood block. Likewise if you require the pattern and texture of crushed fabric or perhaps of corrugated cardboard you can make the blocks from those very materials.

Multi-block prints are in the majority for the method is more flexible than any other. There are two basic ways of approach. If you have a very clear idea of what you want the print to look like then you can make a tracing paper plan for each colour as a guide for cutting the blocks. You may, however, prefer to let the cutting of the blocks remain fluid and not cut a block until you have proofed the previous one, thus allowing the design to be influenced and modified as it progresses.

Two further basic approaches to the realization of the design then come into play: to use a key block or not? A key block is cut first and it contains all the major work often in linear form to which subsequent colours are fitted. Key blocks are seen in most pre-19th century coloured woodcuts and woodblock prints. Later the use of the key block has often been dropped as the deployment of colour has become more dynamic. Multi-block prints today tend not to employ a key block system but it is most helpful for the beginner in organizing a multi-block print.

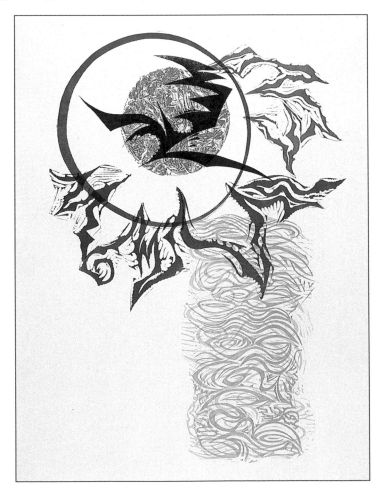

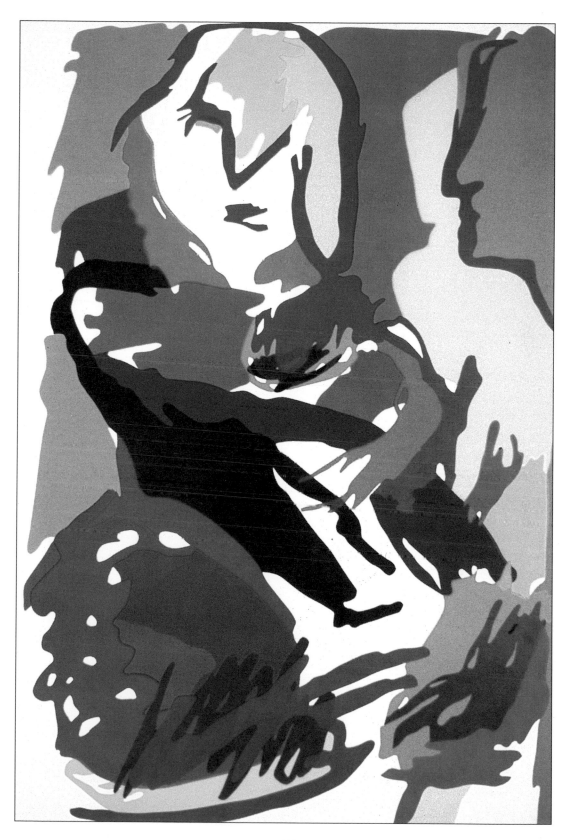

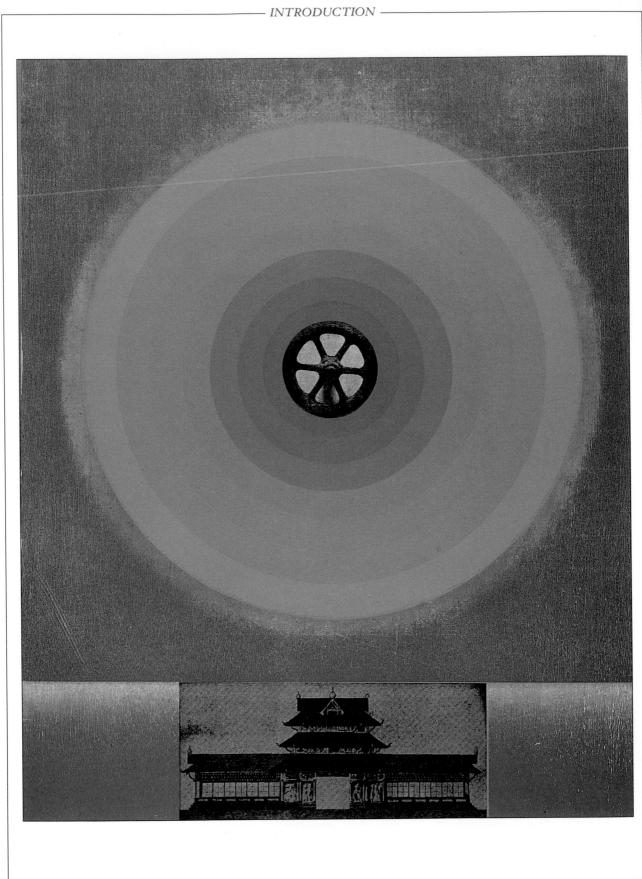

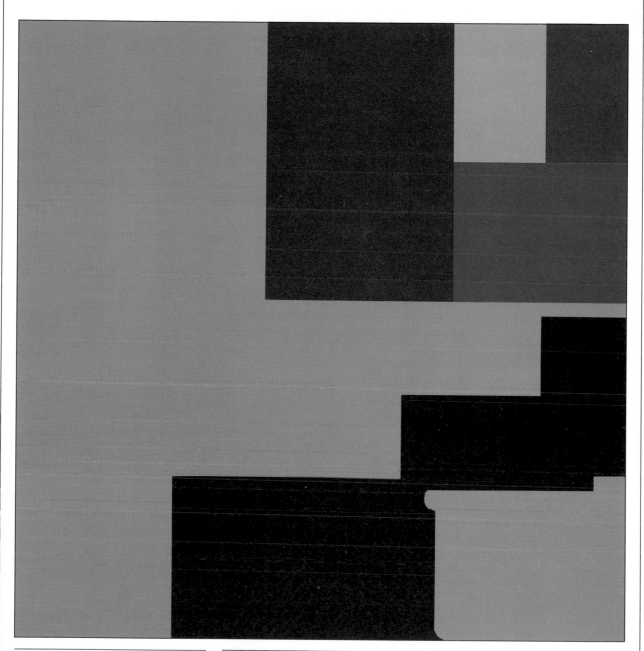

**Black Pagoda**
**ARTIST Michael Rothenstein**
**SIZE 73 × 58cm (28¾ × 22¾in)**

Mixed media relief print from plywood, lino and photo-etched metal relief. Note how the background and two bottom rectangles have been sparely inked so the vertical grain of the plywood is exaggerated. Smooth lino is used to print the central target shape from seven different rings.

**Untitled**
**ARTIST Paul Huxley**
**SIZE 48 × 48cm (19 × 19in)**

This colour multi-block linocut is from a portfolio published by the Mark Rothko Foundation Trust. Linocuts often are associated with expressionist work so when this linocut was done it was mistaken for a screenprint – relief printmaking had a lower profile at that time and screenprinting was at its height.

## Reduction methods

Pablo Picasso is sometimes credited with the invention of the reduction block method – it is also called the suicide or elimination method – but it seems to have been in use by small-scale commercial printers for some time before he made it his own. It was one such printer of posters who suggested to Picasso that he might find it an easy way of keeping the various colours in registration with each other.

The method consists of taking a block and starting by cutting out the highlights – those parts which will show as unprinted areas of paper. The block is rolled up with ink and printed on every sheet of paper; the whole edition number plus extra sheets for artists' proofs etc. The block is cleaned and further cuts are made; the block is printed in the second colour. More work is cut and the block is printed until all the colours are printed, by which time there will be very little of the original height block material left. The order of printing the colours is usually from light to dark. This all requires some mental agility because you have to think in a reverse order to when using the key block system. It is all too easy to cut away a crucial part and ruin the whole lot – hence the name suicide print.

Beginners will find their first reduction print less than suicidal if they have a fully worked-out design to the correct scale and in colour so that reference to it will solve most cutting problems. The advantages of the reduction method are two-fold: a full colour print can be made from one piece of lino or wood and the registration of all the colours will be correct as long as the block and paper are always in the same relationship to each other. The disadvantage, apart from the suicidal element, is that you must print the whole edition before you can see what the finished print will look like. You cannot take progressive proofs of each colour and go back to make modifications to the blocks.

Blair Hughes-Stanton developed an even more exacting system by using several reduction blocks. His prints often have seventeen or more printings from three or four reduction blocks. He tended to use one block for all the yellows and related colours, one for the blues, one for the reds and one for the greys to blacks. This gave him an enormously wide range of colours.

## Free form blocks

Some registration methods presuppose that all the blocks used will be rectangular and of exactly the same size – this is particularly so if a fixed system such as the frisket on a Columbian or Albion press is used. It is not necessary, however, to have regular blocks when using registration systems such as base sheet or modified Kentō. Free form or shaped blocks are necessary when using irregular materials such as driftwood, but it is also an economical way for using up offcuts of wood or lino. The only real problem comes in printing when the block position on a press bed is not central, which will make the pressure uneven. Small non-printing blocks of the same material must be placed at the opposite sides of the bed to even out the pressure.

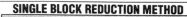

**SINGLE BLOCK REDUCTION METHOD**

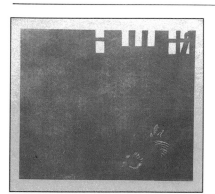

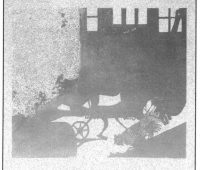

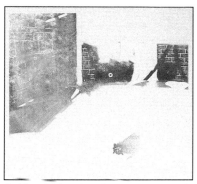

**1** The first colour to be printed is a background of light ochre with the white areas only cut away on the block.

**2** The second colour is light blue-grey. The upper left has been temporarily textured with a sand and glue mixture.

**3** The third colour is terracotta but is applied to parts of the block only. More lino has been cut away by this stage.

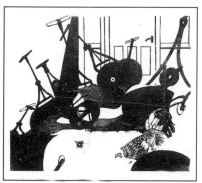

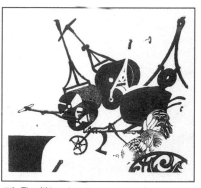

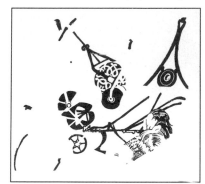

**4** The fourth colour is charcoal grey. The foreground wheel is partially inked and a lot more lino has been cut away.

**5** The fifth colour is mushroom brown. The background has been cut away as well as the shadows of the garden implements.

**6** The last colour is blue-black, which picks out the darkest tones. There is very little uncut lino left on the block.

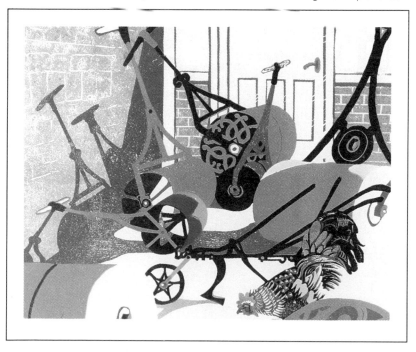

*Edo and Heavy Metal (West Dean)*, the finished print, by Carol Walklin, was inspired by the sight of a garden shed at West Dean College full of antique lawn rollers and other garden implements. The passing cockerel reminded her of a beautiful bird seen at the *Great Japan Exhibition* then being shown in London.

## SINGLE BLOCK REDUCTION

The pictures on the previous page show a proof of each stage of cutting a single block reduction print. You can see how the block material is gradually cut away. The print also utilizes some partial inking and the application of texture to the block surface.

The pictures on this page show the progressive proofs taken of a single block reduction print so that you can see the effect of overprinting each colour. The design gradually builds up but is only completed when the last colour goes on. There is no partial inking on this print – each part of the remaining lino is inked at each stage.

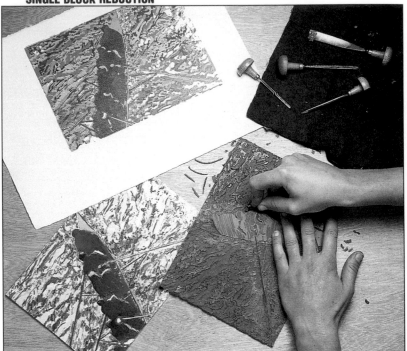

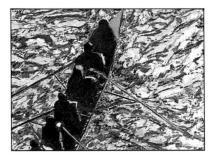

**1** A coloured drawing of an Eight seen from above as it rows under Hammersmith Bridge in London.

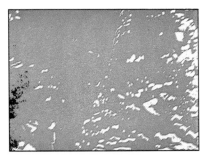

**2** A proof of the first colour, a blue-grey. Only the white areas have been cut from the lino block.

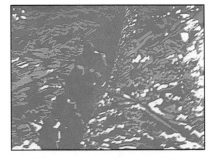

**3** A proof of the second colour, a turquoise, printed on the first. More of the block has been cut away to show the first colour.

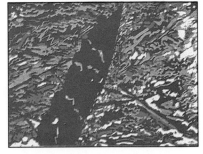

**4** A proof of the third colour, sap green, printed on the first two colours. More work has been cut away to show the turquoise.

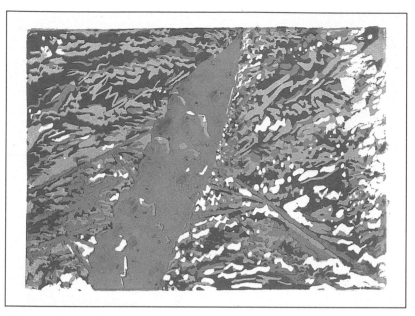

**5** A proof of the fourth colour, opaque yellow ochre with white, printed on the first three colours. The water has been almost completely cut away.

### The final image
*The Eight* is completed when the fifth colour, black, is printed on top of the four previous colours. There is very little uncut lino now left on the block. The overprinting of the transparent inks has made several more very subtle colours.

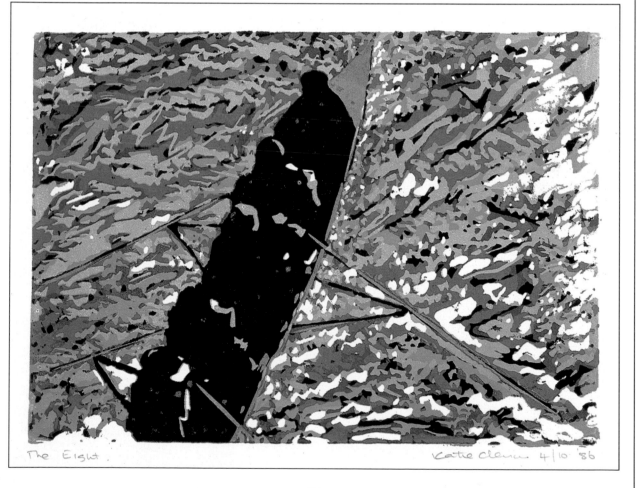

The Eight.                                    Katie Clemson 4/10 '86

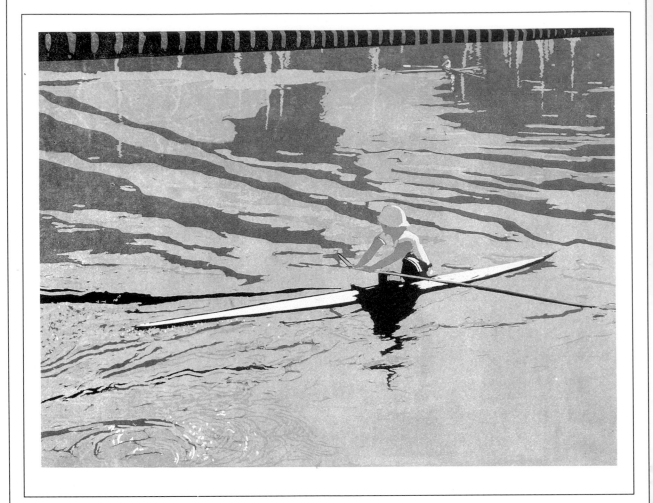

**Rower**

**ARTIST Katie Clemson**

**SIZE 35.5 × 61cm (14 × 24in)**

Single block reduction print. Five colours printed from one piece of lino are used for this print.

## Jigsaw blocks

In this system the blocks are cut out like a jigsaw. Each piece is inked separately, the pieces are assembled together and the composite block with many colours on it is printed just once. The advantage is that you can produce a multi-coloured print at one impression. The disadvantage is that inking for each impression can take a long time and ink could start drying on parts of the block before the last section is inked. It needs careful control of temperature and the consistency of the ink.

Another problem is that if you cut up one block into pieces there will be fine lines between each section when it is reassembled – just the thickness of a bandsaw blade or even a scalpel blade. Artists such as André Derain and Philip Sutton have used these lines as a deliberate structural element in the design. Other artists such as Lynne Moore cut each part separately allowing just enough at the edges so that the printed colours abut each other without lines showing. This is made easier if each inked block is printed separately rather than assembled with the rest but it also makes the printing process very long.

## MAKING A JIGSAW BLOCK

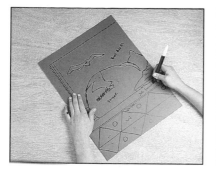

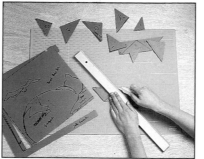

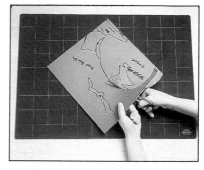

**1** The design is drawn directly on the block of lino, colour-coded as a guide for proofing each colour unit.

**2** The block is cut into pieces using a sharp knife and a straightedge on a rubber cutting mat, to protect the bench.

**3** Scissors are used to cut round curves. Only thin, pliable lino can be cut this way but it is quick and neat.

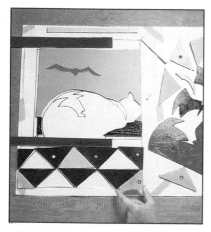

**4** Each section of lino is inked in its own colour and the pieces are re-assembled into the complete design.

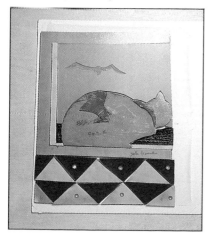

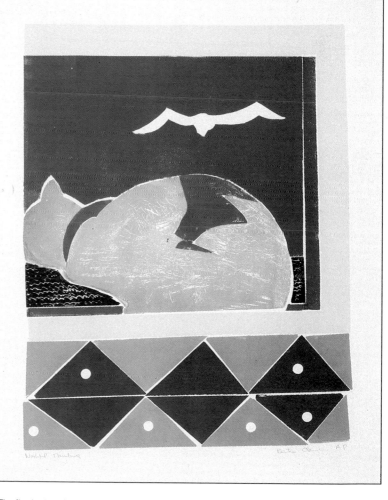

**5** The inked sections of lino are almost all in place. All the colours on the re-assembled block will be printed simultaneously.

**6** The final print of *Ziggy on Holiday* by Katie Clemson makes use of the white lines between the colours as part of the design.

## Variation and ingenuity

The techniques described in this book are widely used but are not necessarily the only ones practised by printmakers. Local conditions often demand special methods; an example is the dampening of paper. A simple plastic-wrapped bundle may suffice in damp Britain but be inadequate in a very hot or dry climate. Some ingenuity will be required to construct an insulated box in which the correct humidity can be maintained over several days. Another example is found with printing presses. The basic principles are the same but manufacturers in different parts of the world introduced their own modifications. Available materials vary and problems may have to be solved in different ways in different places. Use this book as a source for ideas, not as a dogmatic programme.

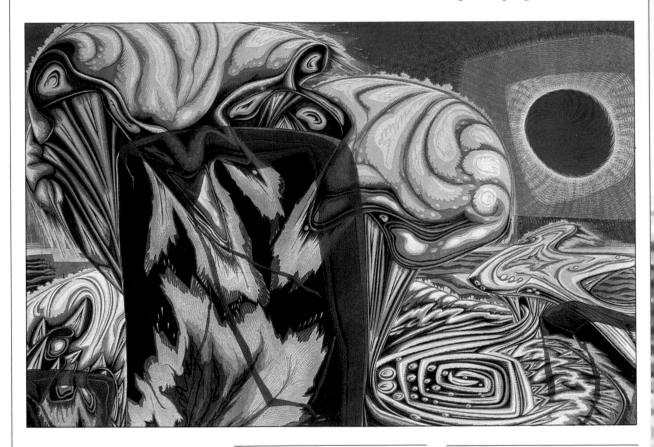

**The Wave**

**ARTIST Blair Hughes-Stanton**

**SIZE 48.5 × 72cm (19 × 28½in)**

Colour linocut using three reduction blocks. Each block is cut and printed several times giving a large number of colours. Hughes-Stanton was a successful wood engraver until a disability forced him to work on a larger scale. His linocuts and his teaching have been important in the revival of interest in the medium.

**Reflections**

**ARTIST Simon King**

**SIZE 61 × 43cm (24 × 17in)**

Colour linocut featuring the use of several reduction blocks to build up a subtle range of colours that describe the landscape. This artist uses a frisket on a platen press for very accurate registration. He was a pupil of Blair Hughes-Stanton at the Central School of Art and Design in London and was taught both wood engraving and linocutting by him.

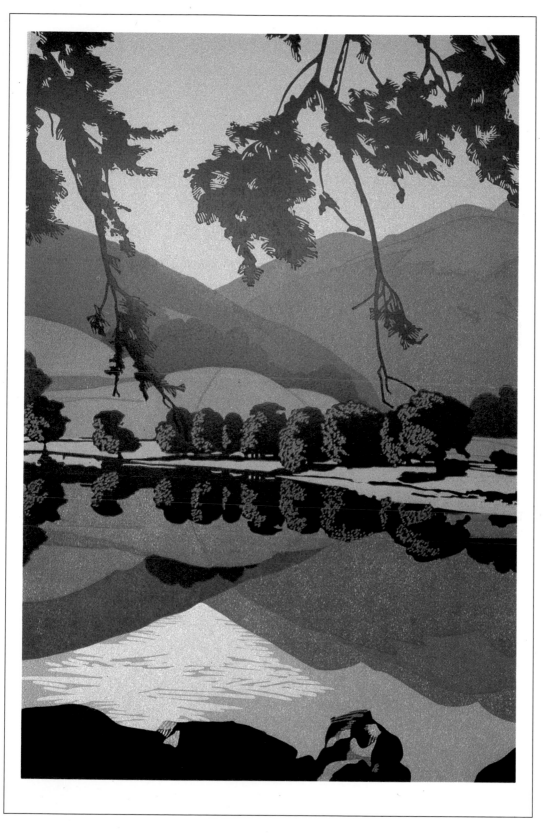

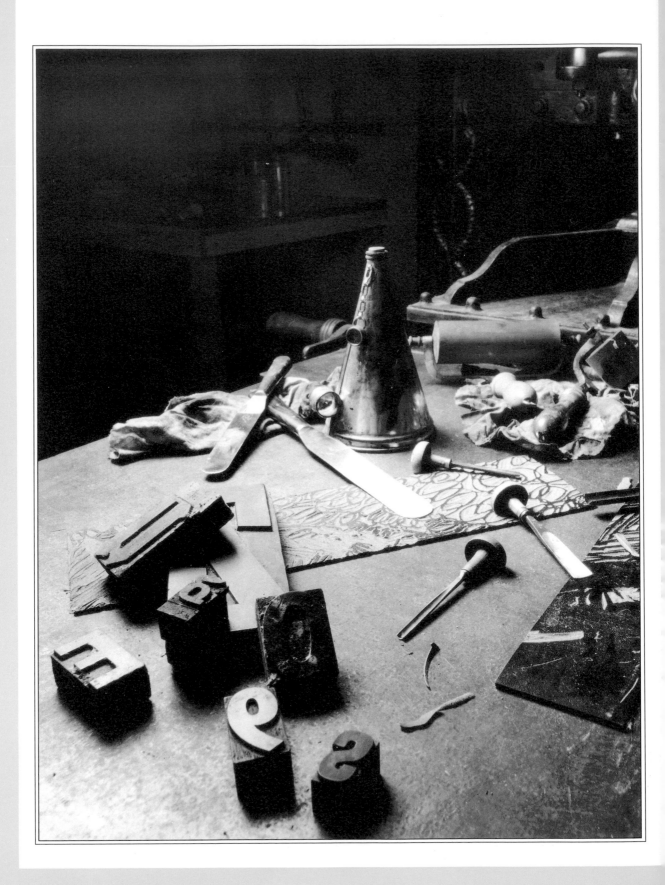

# CHAPTER TWO

# Materials, Tools & Cuts

Lino is probably the most popular material of the wide range to choose from for use in relief printmaking. It is an attractive medium for the beginner because it is easy to work with, but its appeal does not stop there. Lino is far more versatile than is generally thought, and has been the chosen medium for many of the most important 20th-century prints. Because it has no grain, it can be cut in any direction and to any size and shape. It invites spontaneity as swooping curves are just as easy to cut as straight lines. Its smooth surface gives the artist a free hand; etching can provide texture and contrast.

Wood has always been the traditional material for relief printing. One of the pleasures of working with wood is that you can let the design grow out of its natural grain and markings. Also, the feel of the wood and an awareness of the time it has taken to grow are both important factors in the artist's relationship with the medium.

The use of plywood and other manufactured boards is now widespread, and printmakers are constantly experimenting with other materials such as card, plastic sheet, sheet metal, formed paper pulp and found materials.

This section of the book explores the printmaker's media, discusses the tools used and the cuts that can be made with them, and tackles the crucial issue of translating the design in the mind's eye into practical reality.

**Full Moon**
**ARTIST Richard Bosman**
**SIZE 96 × 122cm (37¼ × 48in)**

This large, expressive colour woodcut is by an Australian-born artist who lives in the USA. The blocks were cut by hand and with electric gouges and printed on a large intaglio press at the Experimental Workshop, San Francisco.

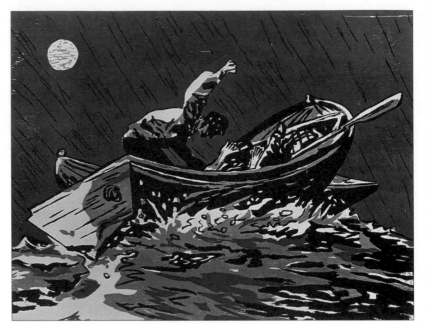

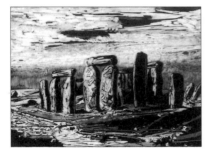

**Stonehenge**
**ARTIST Gertrude Hermes**
**SIZE 25.5 × 36cm (10 × 14in)**

This unusually large and dramatic wood engraving is closer in style to the artist's colour linocuts. The tonal handling of the sky produces the drama of sunrise and stormy skies. The stones, which are dramatically lit, appear dark and moody.

## WHICH MEDIUM?

The present revival of interest in relief prints marks the artist's return to direct working and personal involvement in printmaking.

The powerful, rhythmic linocuts of the '30s display a most important feature of the material – it can be cut in flowing lines in any direction. The design may have been carefully worked out with regard to balance of line and colour, but there is a liveliness in the cutting of the flowing lines – you can see how the artist worked – which makes a strong link between creator and viewer. The same potential for fluidity and boldness attracts artists to this medium today; lino is still an important printing material on its own or used with other printing methods in mixed media.

Woodcut, the oldest printmaking method, is now storming international print exhibitions and demanding reassessment. Today's images are very large and usually done on plywood boards, but the character of the wood is still evident. The same principles that made wood suitable for the powerful woodcuts done between the wars again attract artists: wood is more resistant to cutting than lino; it has grain and direction; it imposes itself on the artist and demands a positive attack. Images that are dramatic in size, subject and colour bring out the best in wood. Woodcuts look as if the artist has confronted the material and fought a battle: there is a tenseness and power here that is unique in printmaking.

Wood engraving is a much more traditional art and has not undergone the same dramatic revival. The characteristics of end-grain wood determine the nature of the images the engraver produces. It is fit for quieter statements and requires greater technical mastery: ideas become condensed and purified in this

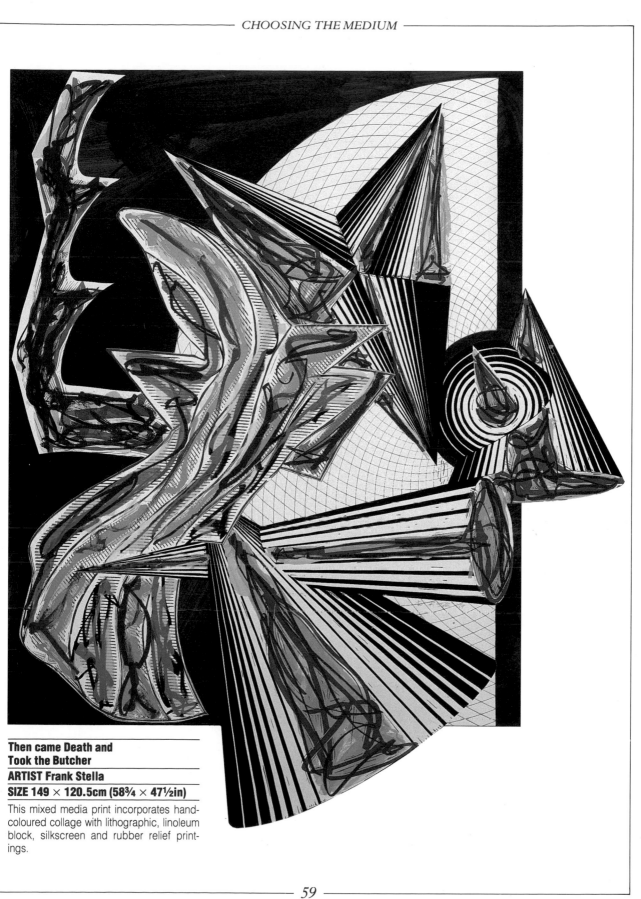

**Then came Death and
Took the Butcher**
**ARTIST Frank Stella**
**SIZE 149 × 120.5cm (58¾ × 47½in)**

This mixed media print incorporates hand-coloured collage with lithographic, linoleum block, silkscreen and rubber relief printings.

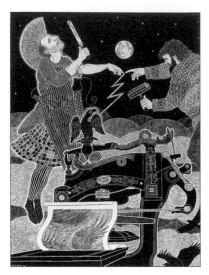

microcosmic world. Nevertheless, wood engravings of our time reflect life today in subject matter and manner of drawing. Generally colour is excessive, although it is more often used than previously, and to some extent wood engravers are also experimenting with new materials.

## LINO

Lino is a floor covering made by laying a mixture of linseed oil, resin, powdered cork and pigments (for colour) on a backing of woven jute (also called burlap or hessian). Linseed oil is pressed from flax, and the word "linoleum" comes from the Latin *linum* (flax) and *oleum* (oil). Lino is manufactured in long rolls up to 3m (9ft) wide, and in various thicknesses from 3–6mm (⅛–¼in). Exact thicknesses in millimetres are 3.2mm, 4.5mm, 6mm and 6.7mm. Battleship lino is the thickest and most hardwearing type, and is particularly good for printmaking because of the depth of cutting it allows.

### Choosing and preparing lino

When buying lino, choose a plain colour as a pattern will distract the eye and get in the way of your design. The surface of the lino should be flat and without blemishes, unless these are to form part of the design. Printed lino has an uneven surface and flakes when cut. Lino hardens with age, and old lino can be brittle, which means it will cut unevenly. On the other hand, very new lino may crumble when cut; if this happens, keep the piece for six months to harden. You will need lino at least 3mm (⅛in) thick to get a good cutting surface, and this may rule out the use of lino tiles. Offcuts of lino from flooring shops are often a cheap buy. Good quality artists'-grade sheets are available in artists' supplies shops, but in small standard sizes only – for large sheets of the best quality lino you should visit a specialist printmakers' supply shop.

**Northern Enlightenment**

**ARTIST Bob Bain**

**SIZE 76 × 57cm (30 × 22½in)**

This linocut, produced as a poster for the Peacock Print Workshop in Aberdeen, Scotland, shows the workshop's director projecting the spark of life into a young kilted punk. The artist used parallel cuts and cross-hatching to emphasize tone, contrast and detail.

**STYLES OF LINOCUTTING**

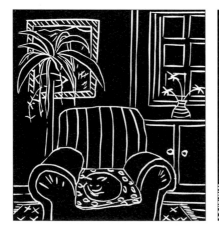

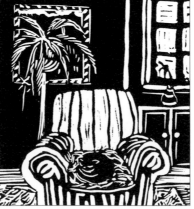

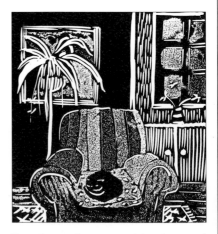

**Three different approaches to a single colour linocut**
Shown above is a linear image that has been created by white line cutting.

A strong three-dimensional approach. Here, line has been ignored; bold cutting emphasizes form through the use of negative and positive areas.

The print now has tone and therefore more depth. This was achieved by using caustic soda etch and some tonal cutting with a small u-gouge.

Good preparation of the block material is the first essential in making a successful print. Good preparation of the surface will ensure an even ink film every time and reduce the amount of ink you use.

## Flattening lino
A large sheet of lino that has been stored in a roll must be perfectly flat before work begins. If the lino is too stiff to be flattened immediately, you can make it more pliable by warming it. Stand it in a warm place to soften, then lay the lino flat and weight it with a heavy board topped with bricks or books. Be prepared to leave the lino for weeks as it gradually relaxes.

## Cutting lino to size
Mark out the shape you require, using a set-square and ruler if it is to be regular. Score along the line, against a straightedge if appropriate, with a sharp knife, cutting half way through the lino. Bend the lino back away from you along the cut – it will break cleanly – and then cut through the hessian backing with a knife or scissors (thin lino is useful for making irregular shaped blocks, as it can be cut straight through with strong scissors).

### MOUNTING LINO BLOCKS
Mounting lino on to hardboard or plywood gives additional support and makes cutting easier. It can also raise the printing surface to type high ( page 62), and makes hand- ling easier when inking and printing the block. The margins around the sides can be used for attaching registration devices; the diagrams below show three such variations.

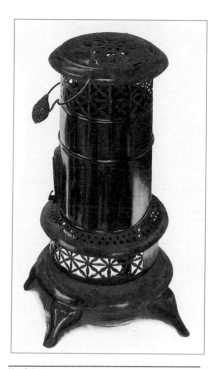

### Extended mount for handling

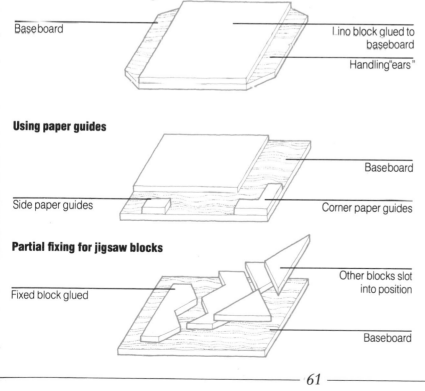

Baseboard

Lino block glued to baseboard

Handling "ears"

### Using paper guides

Baseboard

Side paper guides

Corner paper guides

### Partial fixing for jigsaw blocks

Other blocks slot into position

Fixed block glued

Baseboard

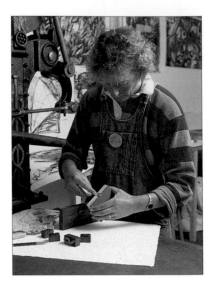

## Mounting type high

Although metal type is now redundant in commercial printing, it is prized by artists making their own 'private press' books and other publications. Old secondhand type can still be found at printers' closing-down sales. When wood or lino blocks are to be printed alongside text they must be exactly the same height as one another, or one will print more strongly. Lino and wood that is less than type high will need to be mounted on the right thickness of wood to bring it up to the same height as the type. In Britain and North America type is 23.32mm high, in France and Germany 23.56mm, in the Netherlands 24.85mm and in the Soviet Union 25.1mm. Mount the printing material on blockboard, thick plywood or printers' composition board, glued and weighted as above. Make the mount up to the exact height required with one or more sheets of fine card, cut to size and just placed under the block.

## Preparing the surface

The surface of lino can be smooth and waxy or rough and grainy, depending on its age and how it has been stored. You can make positive use of scuffs by incorporating them into the design; otherwise it is best to work on as smooth a surface as possible.

All lino is slightly greasy owing to its linseed oil content, and some types are coated with varnish or a similar sealing agent, which will make the lino accept water-based inks only patchily. The first step in preparing the surface is therefore to de-grease it by wiping with household ammonia or methylated spirits on a soft cloth.

You may now have an acceptable working surface. If not, abrade it by scraping with a razor blade which will produce a glassy surface that is ideal for detailed work. Otherwise the surface can be rubbed down with fine sandpaper, or you can use water to lubricate the rubbing action with either 240 or 320 grade wet-and-dry paper (waterproof silicon carbide paper) or fine steel wool and scouring powder. Avoid getting the lino too wet in case you soak the hessian backing. Work consistently all over, going right into the corners. Wash, wipe or brush the surface clean, then examine it under a magnifying glass and rework any uneven patches.

## Mounting lino

Mounting a lino block is not essential, but it can be useful for several reasons. It makes the lino firm and strong, which helps if you are going to cut it deeply or extensively or if you are intending to print copies in quantity. Also, a mount can bring the block up to type height for printing alongside metal type (see left). Mounted lino is convenient to handle when you are inking and printing, and the mount can also provide space for registration marks.

Lino blocks are usually left unmounted if they are irregularly shaped, or for jigsaw printing, where several sections are to be inked in different colours and reassembled before printing. It is possible to combine mounted and unmounted blocks in a jigsaw system – mount the main block on a spacious board so that you can fit the unmounted blocks around it once you have inked them.

The mount can be hardboard, plywood or stout card. If the mount is for strength only, cut it to the same size and shape as the block. For ease of handling, cut the mount to the same size as the lino block top and bottom, but add on about 5cm (2in) in width to give a 2.5cm (1in) margin at either side. You can then lift the block by the mount to avoid the danger of smudging. An extended mount like this can be useful where the block is not fixed in the press so that it can be lifted out for recharging with ink between printings. A mount for registration can be cut to extend beyond the registration marks.

Glue the lino to the mount with shellac, wood glue or PVA, bearing in mind that the glue should not be water-soluble if you are using water-soluble inks. Coat both lino back and mount thinly with glue, bring the two sides together and weight until completely dry, preferably overnight. If the mount is of hardboard, glue the rough side to the lino backing.

## PREPARING THE SURFACE OF LINO

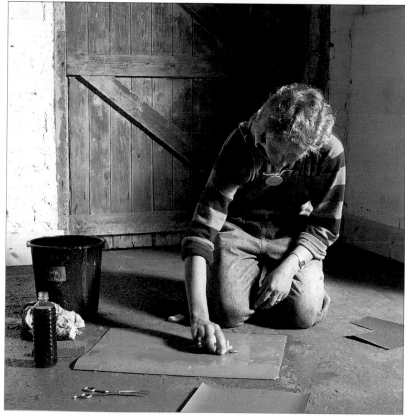

**1** Wetting the block. Keep the surface wet and try not to saturate the hessian backing.

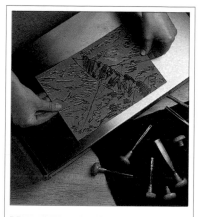

**PREPARING THE SURFACE OF LINO**
An old food warmer keeps the lino warm and soft and easy to cut. Be careful not to overheat the block.

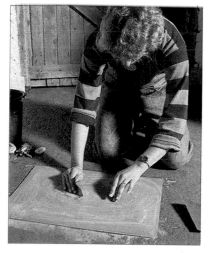

**2** Sanding the block. Thoroughly rub down the wet surface with a medium grade wet-and-dry sandpaper. Test for smoothness and then finish off with a finer grade.

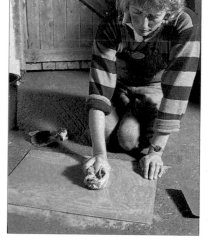

**3** Cleaning after sanding. Use a cloth and water to wipe away the residue from the surface.

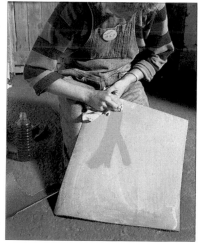

**4** Removing the dried surface film. Use methylated spirit on a dry rag to wipe away any filmy dirt. The surface is now smooth and clean.

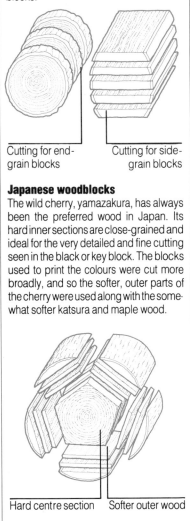

## METHODS OF CUTTING THE WOOD

Side-grain or plank wood blocks are cut from the tree trunk along its length in the same direction as the grain. Woodcuts are made from side-grain blocks.

End-grain blocks are cut from sections across the trunk so that the fibres of the grain are at right angles to the surface. Wood engravings are made on end-grain blocks.

Cutting for end-grain blocks | Cutting for side-grain blocks

## Japanese woodblocks

The wild cherry, yamazakura, has always been the preferred wood in Japan. Its hard inner sections are close-grained and ideal for the very detailed and fine cutting seen in the black or key block. The blocks used to print the colours were cut more broadly, and so the softer, outer parts of the cherry were used along with the somewhat softer katsura and maple wood.

Hard centre section | Softer outer wood

# WOOD

A section through the trunk of a tree reveals a pattern of rings: the light coloured rings are spring growth and quite soft, and the darker rings are summer growth, which is much harder. The age of the tree can be determined by counting these rings. Knots in wood form where a branch starts to grow out of the trunk.

Wood is sawn in two ways, along the grain (side-grain or long-grain), or across the trunk (end-grain or cross-grain). End-grain wood is the preferred cut for wood engraving as it has a denser texture, which makes it suitable for fine work on a small scale. For woodcutting on a large scale, plywood and other manufactured boards are ideal, and they have the added advantage of being quite cheap. Printmaking blocks need not be regular in shape, but they should be as flat as possible, unless the warp of a piece of wood is to form part of the design.

## Side-grain wood

There is a great variation in texture between different woods cut along the length of the trunk. Softwoods have quite wide bands of soft spring growth between the narrow bands of hard summer growth. In cutting the surface the tool passes quickly through the spring growth and bites up against the summer growth. Hardwoods have a closer texture and most cut evenly right through.

The markings on side-grain wood can be used to advantage in a design. Wood that has been weathered by sea or sand often shows pronounced patterns of this sort because the soft spring wood has been eroded by the elements, leaving the harder wood standing proud. Such features can be used in the studio.

Planks are usually sold in standard widths of 15cm (6in), 23cm (9in) and 30cm (12in). The larger a block of plank wood, the thicker it needs to be to prevent warping. Wider blocks can be taken from a piece of old furniture, such as a table top, the back of a cupboard or the base of a drawer – unless of course you have the considerable expertise in carpentry necessary to join planks together. The wood in old furniture is mature and will not warp, but woodworm, though decorative, may have weakened the board.

## End-grain wood

End-grain wood is best for wood engraving because of its close texture. Box is the wood most favoured because the grain is so tight that it cuts like butter. It is very expensive, however, as it is slow-growing and rarely gets large enough to cut a block more than 7.5cm (3in) in its largest dimension. Larger box blocks are made by glueing several pieces together, which is a highly skilled job and best left to the professional blockmaker. Boxwood blocks are traditionally made type high for wood engravings to be printed alongside type in the same chase. Old blocks are often reused on the underside or sent back to the blockmaker to be planed down to a fresh surface. Holly and pear are cheaper alternatives to box.

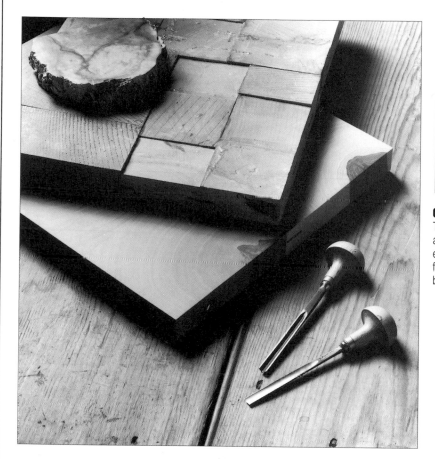

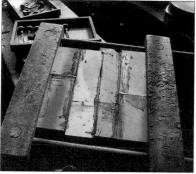

**Composite blocks for engraving**
The strips of end-grain boxwood are glued and cramped up using special cabinet makers'cramps. The jaws of the cramp are made from softwood which does not damage the blocks.

Chunks of end-grain wood need not be made into perfectly smooth and symmetrical blocks – some people prefer to use the free shape and natural texture of the wood as elements of their design.

## Manufactured boards
Man-made boards are widely used by printmakers because their manufacture prevents warping and they are available in large sizes at a reasonable price. Laminated and block boards should preferably be cut to size on a circular saw so that the layers do not split and drag, leaving an uneven edge.

## Plywood
Ply is made by revolving the tree trunk against a blade to peel off a continuous sheet of thin wood. The sheet is cut into pieces and the layers are glued together with one grain set at right angles to that on the layer below. Ordinary plywood has three layers, the middle one usually being thicker than the outer two. Multi-ply is thicker, with five or more equally thin layers. Plywood is generally of pine, and has a strong directional grain of open texture. Plywood, multi-ply and veneered boards come in thicknesses of 3-22mm ($\frac{1}{10}$-$\frac{4}{5}$in). Artists generally prefer 4-12mm ($\frac{1}{5}$-$\frac{1}{2}$in) boards, with 6mm ($\frac{1}{4}$in) being the most commonly used.

**Method of joining sections**
The pieces of boxwood are joined together with small wooden fillets. The grid is not perfect, but offset slightly on purpose to strengthen the block. The surface will be planed down until the joins are smooth and even.

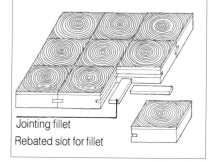

Jointing fillet
Rebated slot for fillet

## Veneered boards

Veneered boards, in which the outer layers are made of better quality wood, are very popular for woodcutting. The Japanese favour shina (Japanese lime), which is light, soft to cut and has an almost invisible grain, and lauan (Philippine mahogany), which is a little harder and has a more evident straight grain. In North America birch-faced boards are much used because they are light and a pleasure to cut. Another advantage is that because the veneer is usually applied to both sides of a board for stability, it is possible to make two woodcuts from one board.

### Seasoning and storing wood

Precious woods in short supply such as cherry and box which are particularly suitable for woodcutting and engraving must be treated with great care. They can not be kiln-dried as ordinary wood is today; such rapid drying in gas-fired kilns under pressure results in much warping and splitting of the wood making it useless for the printmaker.

In the heart of London T.N. Lawrence & Son have been supplying blocks, tools and other printmakers materials for over 100 years. They have tools specially manufactured for them and they offer a sharpening service, they are the only makers of composite wood blocks for engraving in Britain and their stock of fine grained wood is matured naturally for three to four years before selected pieces are made into blocks.

The picture, top right, shows sections of cherry wood stacked ready for shelving when it is graded according to type and age. As you can see the diameter seldom exceeds 15cm, 6in and the thickness is about 2.5cm, 1in.

The picture, far right, shows the wood stacked with fillets of wood between, which allows the clear circulation of air around each block of wood. These too are stacked by type and age. In the foreground you can see large old-fashioned cabinet makers' G-cramps which are used to clamp the parts of the composite blocks together. The making of these box wood blocks is a highly skilled business and now a very rare one. T.N. Lawrence & Son keep a stock of the smaller commonly used sizes and will make up larger blocks to order though these are very costly. They will also re-surface blocks that have been damaged or where the edition is complete. Their highly skilled craftsmen will also re-surface old blocks which used to be used to print catalogues and advertisements. The specialist machines which they use can be seen in the bottom right picture.

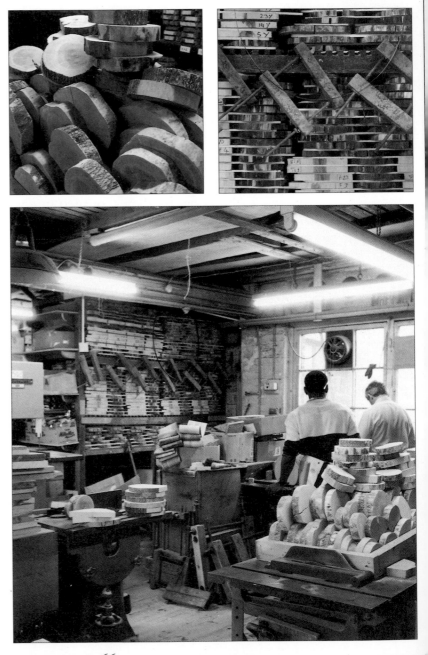

## Laminated and blockboard

Both laminated board and blockboard are made of strips of wood (generally pine) laminated or glued together and faced with sheets of ply. Laminated board has a thin core; blockboard is considerably thicker. The cutting surface is the same as plywood, but because the board is consolidated it is extremely stable, which means it can be cut on both sides.

## Chipboard

As the name suggests, chipboard is made from chips of wood bonded together with resin and pressed to make a very dense board. The uneven woodchip surface and the high glue content make it difficult to cut, but the textured surface can be used to create an interesting pattern.

## Preparing and storing wood

In printing from a woodblock you may want to use the natural shape of the wood, including any warping, in which case the printing should be done by burnishing, a technique similar to brass-rubbing. Only blocks of uniform thickness can be printed in a press, as uneven blocks will mean uneven pressure, which may damage the equipment. The surface of the wood is another consideration: the grain can be smoothed down so that it hardly shows, or used to give texture to a design.

Allow newly purchased wood to acclimatize to the temperature and humidity of the studio for several days before beginning to work on it. To avoid warping, do not store wood near a radiator or other heat source. It is possible to prevent wide side-grain blocks from warping by mounting them on thinner board at right angles to the grain.

## Making the block

If you require an even surface, plane it flat and sand it smooth before cutting the block to size. Thinner blocks may need to be mounted on board (see "Mounting Lino", p.62). Stick the block to the mount with wood glue or PVA and weight or clamp until perfectly dry.

## Bringing up the grain

A wire brush, hand-held or used with an electric drill, can wear away the soft spring wood leaving the grain more prominent. Steel wool and hot water can also do the job, or the soft wood can be etched away with a solution of nitric acid, which should always be used with great care. First roll up the block with a thin coat of oil-based printing ink, then brush the acid over the areas where you want the grain to show most strongly. The more concentrated the solution and the longer you leave it, the greater the definition. Light charring will also reduce soft wood.

**HARDENING THE SURFACE**
Hardening the surface on both sides of a block of soft or open-textured wood by oiling with boiled linseed oil helps prevent warping due to humidity, and means that oil-based inks are accepted more easily without soaking into the wood. This should be done about a month before work begins.

## Preparation sequence

Rosemary Simmons uses a variety of materials in her relief prints. The print, shown in colour on p.107, began as a drawing in a sketch book. The next stage was to take a number of reference photographs for the main pictorial element – the old apple tree with a few fruits still clinging on in winter. Next, a drawing in black ink was made on tracing paper to show the position of each block. The background block – plywood with vertical grain – was printed first using two shades of yellow water-based inks blended on the block in the Japanese manner. Three lino blocks formed the side and top edges; they were printed with oil-based inks. The tree was first drawn in Indian ink on paper and sent to a process engraver to make a photo-etched plate. The plate was printed next in black oil-based ink. Finally, the tree shadow was printed from lino and the apples touched in with a brush.

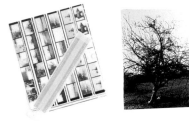

photo-reference

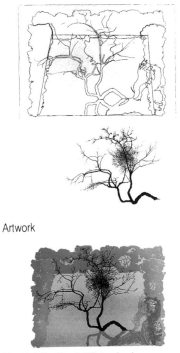

Artwork

Proof of *Peakland: Winter Apple*

# PREPARING THE DESIGN

For your first relief print you should use only one colour just to get the feel of the material and the tools. If you already have an idea, draw it on paper to the correct size and make a tracing of this to transfer to the block as a guide for cutting. If you don't have an idea for an image, try making a random cut in the block and see what it suggests – one mark often leads to another, and the design will gradually emerge. Many printmakers start by drawing directly on the block with a fibre-tipped pen or marker in a free fashion and use this drawing as a starting point, allowing the actual cut lines to suggest further work. Such free cutting has a natural spontaneity that is particularly suitable for lino and softer woods.

Consider how the printed design is to be positioned on the paper. It is usual to leave a margin of unprinted paper around the design, which allows the sheet to be handled without the print being touched. There is also a very important second reason for the border – an aesthetic reason. Look at various prints and see how margins isolate the image from its surroundings. A frame has the same effect, but as many printmakers like to keep the deckle on handmade paper visible, you often see prints framed without a window mount and the placing of the image on the paper must stand as it is. Look at prints that have very wide margins or where the image is deliberately placed off-centre – the effect is to make you look at the whole sheet of paper as the work of art, not just the image in the middle. Some printmakers take the printed image right to the edge of the paper – this is known as a "bled" print. Compare Michael Rothenstein's bled print *Black Pagoda* with the irregular space around *Loquito* on p.97 and his early *Cockerel Turning Round* on p.18 with its regular border.

## Colour prints

It is wise to make your first colour print on the basis of an accurate coloured design worked out on paper to the correct size. You may need to get references for details in the form of photographs or sketches. Make thumbnail sketches to try out the placing and balance of the composition.

Your full size design can be worked out in water-colour, gouache or poster paint, or coloured crayons, markers or chalk. The next stage is to select one of the five basic ways of making colour prints described in the introduction. Whichever method you adopt, it is important to analyse your design into its colour components. Although we describe complex methods of multicolour inking, your first colour print should be one colour only per block. Will colours overprint to make other colours? Will areas of colour butt up to each other without overlapping? Will the colour of the paper play a significant part in the design? Remember that you cannot get lighter than white paper – white ink is never so bright. Look at those same three Michael Rothenstein prints on 97 and 18 and try to work out how many colours were used.

Make a tracing of each colour element in your design, each colour on a separate sheet of tracing paper and with differently coloured ball–point pens so there is no confusion. The tracings are a helpful guide and need not be very detailed – leave some scope for spontaneity while cutting. Each tracing can be transferred on to its own block as a guide.

## Registration of colours

One final decision has to be made before you are ready to cut the blocks: how are the colours to be registered one with another during printing? The systems of registration are described in detail on p.140-45, and depend on your method of printing. Some systems have guides for the position of the paper integrated into the block itself, so if you are using this type of registration it must be drawn on the tracing sheets at this point.

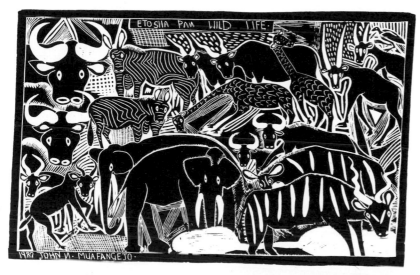

**Etosha Pan**

**ARTIST John Muafangejo**

**SIZE Unknown**

A hand-printed linocut by a Namibian artist depicting village life and current affairs in Africa. The graphic drama is emphasized by lively white-line cutting. Muafangejo often uses lettering with his images.

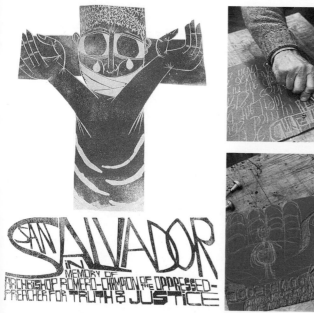

Paul Peter Piech makes linocut poetry posters and prints that incorporate words. He just draws a rough guide directly on to the blocks, and then cuts the lettering free-hand (it must, of course, be cut in reverse).

## TRANSFERRING THE DESIGN

A fully worked out design for single or multiple blocks has to be transferred from paper to the prepared block(s). There are various methods for doing this, but the most important point is that the work on the block must be reversed for the final printed version to appear the same way round as the original design. It is useful to check in a mirror to see what it will look like.

### Transfer by tracing

The simplest way of reversing the design on to the block is to draw it on tracing paper. Turn the paper over on to the block, fixing it in position at the top with tape. Slide a sheet of carbon or transfer paper underneath and go over the drawing, which will show through, with a ball-point pen.

Art supply shops sell carbon paper in large sheets and in other colours besides black, but if you are using water-based inks for printing, use non-greasy red transfer paper, specially made for lithography, instead of carbon. Use a coloured pen if your design is drawn in black so that you can see what you have missed tracing. In a multicoloured print where the different colours are all indicated on

### Photographic transfer

In the latter part of the 19th century photographs or photographs of drawings were often transferred to boxwood blocks as a guide for engraving. This process is still used occasionally today. The block surface must be very smooth. Waterproof it by coating it two or three times with liquid egg white, smearing each coat across the block with your fingertips to eliminate air bubbles and waiting until one coat is completely dry before applying the next. Mix a little zinc oxide for whiteness into the final coat, and smooth it down very gently when dry with the finest sandpaper.

Pour a proprietary brand of photographic emulsion over the surface of the block and allow the excess to run off. As soon as the emulsion dries it becomes light-sensitive, so it is essential to work in the dark. Put the photographic negative on the block once the emulsion has dried, then expose it to a light source and develop according to the manufacturer's instructions. The resulting image will provide a guide for cutting.

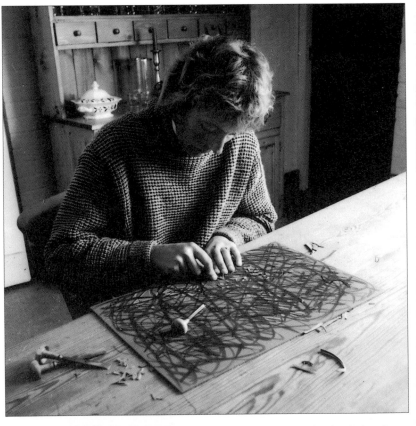

**DIRECT DRAWING ON TO THE BLOCK**
Direct drawing on to the block allows spontaneity of expression. Here Katie Clemson is cutting an abstract design that she has drawn roughly on the block in felt-tipped pen.

the one tracing, as might be the case with free-form or jigsaw methods, use a different coloured pen for tracing each colour.

If the tracing has not transferred clearly, go over the outline on the block again. Use water-soluble or spirit-based pen if you are going to be printing in oils, and Indian ink if you are going to use water-based inks for printing, so that the design is not dissolved. This is important if you want to take a proof of the block before you finish cutting, or if you are using the reduction technique.

Another way of making the tracing easier to see is to paint the surface of the block beforehand with one or two thin coats of white poster or emulsion paint. Add a few drops of detergent or liquid soap to the paint if the block is slightly greasy.

The traditional way of transferring is to draw the design on thin, fine paper with waterproof black ink. The paper is coated with thin gum and reversed on to the block. When it has dried, the paper is dampened and gently rubbed off with the finger bit by bit, leaving the ink design on the block surface. An alternative is to oil the paper once it has been gummed on. This makes the paper transparent and you cut right through it while cutting the design.

## TRANSFERRING THE IMAGE USING CARBON PAPER

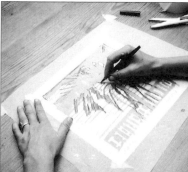

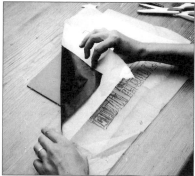

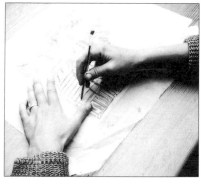

**1** Detail or tracing paper is taped over the original and the image is traced with a soft pencil or a felt-tipped pen.

**2** Place the reversed tracing over a piece of carbon paper on top of the block and secure with tape.

**3** Trace over the image from the back of this tracing paper using a hard pencil or a ballpoint pen.

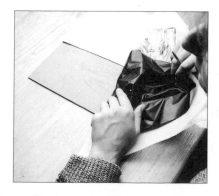

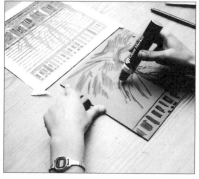

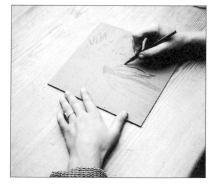

**4** Check that the image is transferring clearly on to the block by lifting one corner; if any areas are missed retrace.

**5** Draw over the carbon image with a felt-tip pen or Indian ink, which won't wash off with solvents used after the printing process.

**6** Drawing the design straight on to the block. In this case the print will produce a mirror image.

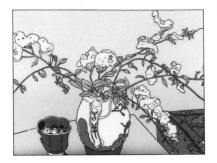

**Blue Cup**
**ARTIST Trevor Allen**
**SIZE 59 × 47cm (23¼ × 18½in)**

Colour linocut with a key block. This print has a background blend, and the artist uses acetate to register the colour areas with the key

## THE KEY BLOCK SYSTEM

This is the simplest system to use when making multicoloured prints. A key block contains all the elements of the design and can be used to print a black outline. A further block is then made for each individual colour to key into the design. Trace the relevant sections only on to as many blocks as required. Keep the shapes simple and use only two or three different colours to start with.

Traditionally the key block was printed first, in black, to give the exact position for subsequent colours to be added, but this is not necessary if you use an efficient registration system (see pp.140–45). If colours overprint the key block they may spoil its crispness: for example, yellow on a black key block turns it greenish, and a colour with white mixed in will turn a black key greyish.

The answer is to print all the colours first, having determined their exact positions at proofing stage, then print the key block last.

The key block need not, of course, be black – it could be any colour. Another option is not to print the key block at all – when you have proofed the colour blocks you may decide that the image looks complete without it.

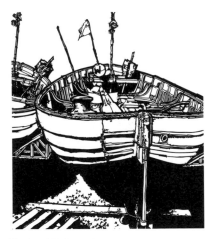

The key block used

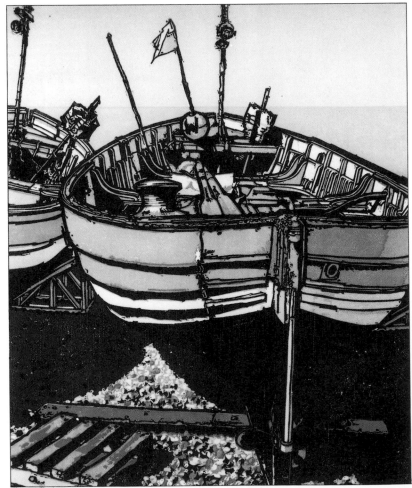

**Beached**
**ARTIST H.J. Jackson**
**SIZE 41 × 53cm (16 × 21in)**

Coloured linocut with a key block. The artist always uses key blocks, which give the scene dramatic presence. The linocut is printed by hand, using a metal tobacco tin.

**TAKING AN OFFSET**

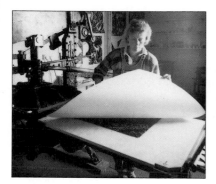

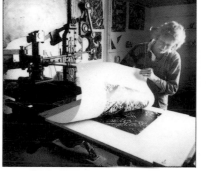

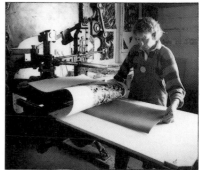

**1** The key block has been inked generously in a dark colour. A sheet of smooth white paper is lowered on to the block.

**2** Checking the offset print. After pulling a print lift back the offset, checking that it is a good strong even print.

**3** Printing the offset on to the second block. Replace the key block with another cut to the same size and lower the print on to it.

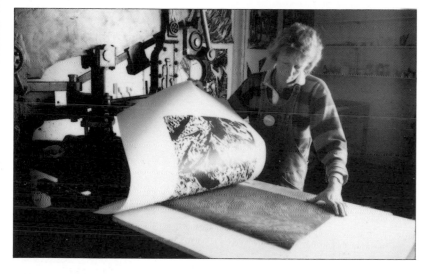

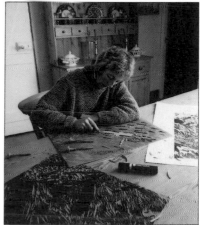

**4** Pull the print as normal. This time tho paper prints on to the blcok. Let this dry and you have an exact imprint of the key block on block two.

**5** Working from an offset with the key block and a copy of the print so far, it is possible to incorporate block two in the print by drawing and cutting.

# MAKING OFFSETS

A quicker and more accurate way of marking out colour blocks than by making several tracings from the original drawing is by offsetting the design from the key or first block, once this has been cut. An offset is a print that is applied while wet to a fresh block, giving an image identical to that on the master block.

When you are satisfied that no more major work is required on the block take an offset. Roll up the block with black ink and take a pull on non-absorbent paper – a shining coated surface will stop the ink from sinking in too much. Immediately place the offset face down on a new prepared block, using whatever registration system you have adopted. Apply pressure by burnishing, or use a press. Peel off the paper and you will find the master block image repeated on the second block. Allow the ink to dry before cutting the block to print your second colour. Repeat offsets for all extra colours.

## Linocutting tools

A good basic set of linocutting tools is shown below and right. Tools are sold in sets or individually to suit the artist's requirements.

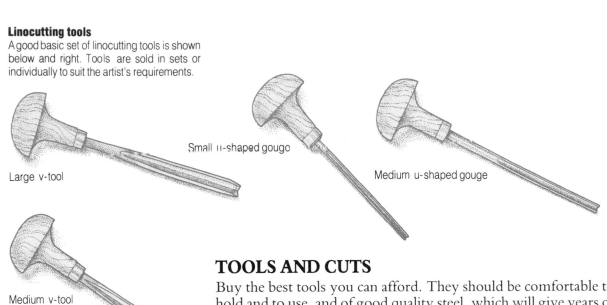

Large v-tool

Small u-shaped gouge

Medium u-shaped gouge

Medium v-tool

Small v-tool

Extra large flat u-shaped gouge

Large u-shaped gouge

# TOOLS AND CUTS

Buy the best tools you can afford. They should be comfortable to hold and to use, and of good quality steel, which will give years of life and sharpen well. Two or three good tools are a better investment than a cheap set.

## Tools for linocutting

Knives and gouges are the basic linocutting tools. Gouges come with either v-shaped or u-shaped cutting heads. All three types of tools can be used for drawing a design; in addition u-shaped gouges are used for clearing away areas of lino not to be printed. One knife or v-shaped gouge for drawing and one medium sized u-shaped gouge for drawing and clearing are often sufficient.

### Knives

There are no knives made exclusively for linocutting. Penknives, snap-off bladed knives and hobbyists' knives with exchangeable blades are all suitable, as are Japanese and European woodcutting knives. Because lino is easy to cut, it is generally enough to hold the knife in one hand while you guide the block with the other. Japanese woodcutters traditionally use a two-handed 'dagger' grasp – they mount the block and fix it to the bench with clamps first.

### V-shaped gouges

A v-shaped length of steel is set in the handle and sharpened at the point. About 10 different sizes are available, varying in acuteness of angle as well as in broadness of blade. The blade makes a v-shaped cut and is used for drawing, and is particularly for curved lines. You can also make textural marks with it, such as dots and pick marks.

### U-shaped gouges

The blade can be a tight 'u' shape or a shallow dish shape. There are about 10 sizes of decidedly u-shaped gouges ranging from 1·5mm (1/16in) to 9mm (3/8in) wide, and the same number of dish-shaped gouges from 1·5mm (1/16in) to 2cm (3/4in) wide. Generally, the true u-shapes are used like the v-shaped gouges for drawing freely, and the shallow tools are used for clearing away lino not to be printed. A carpenter's gouge can also be used for clearing.

## USING LINO CUTTING TOOLS

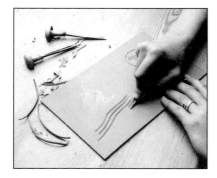

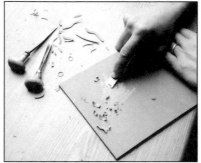

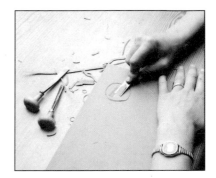

Using a u-gouge. A medium u-gouge is a versatile tool used to cut bold lines and shapes typically associated with lino. It is also invaluable for clearing out unwanted areas.

The flatish, slightly curved u-gouge is not such a common tool and does not always appear in standard tool sets. It is used here for making shallow marks, which, when inked, will print with a hazy, half-tone effect.

The flat gouge is used for clearing. It is useful too as a backup to the smaller u-gouge for removing the ridge lines between cuts.

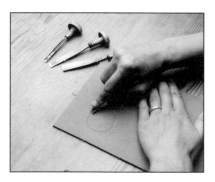

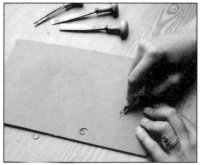

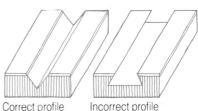

Correct profile     Incorrect profile

The v-gouge. This tool is used for everything from very fine tonal cutting to continuous swirls, dots and free cutting. Here a circle is being outlined ready for clearing with the shallow u-gouge.

The v-gouge. This tool makes very fine, controlled lines resulting in an effect similar to an engraving. See *Northern Enlightenment* by Bob Bain, p.60.

### Undercutting: something to avoid
Remember to leave the area to be printed wider at the base than at the top, as under-cutting can cause the lino to break when pressure is applied.

## KNIVES FOR CUTTING LINO

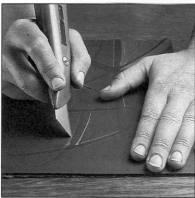

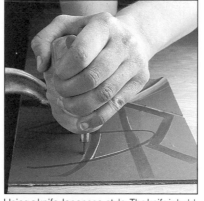

Using a knife Western-style. With the knife slightly angled, the two cuts forming a "v", a cut is made along each side of the line. The strip will lift away. See *Covent Garden* by Edward Bawden.

Using a knife Japanese-style. The knife is held upright and gripped with two hands, this is called the "dagger grip".

### HINTS ON BUYING TOOLS
Be wary of buying cheap sets of tools. Tools made for schools usually have inter-changeable cutting heads, but they are made of soft steel, which is almost im-possible to sharpen. Also with wear the aperture on the handle gradually widens until the tool becomes useless. Most pro-fessional tools are fitted with mushroom-shaped handles, although straight 7cm (3in) handles can be fitted if you prefer.

# POSITIVE AND NEGATIVE CUTTING

Relief prints are produced by the transfer of ink from a raised surface on to a sheet of paper or other material. The word "relief" comes from the Italian *rilievare*, meaning to raise. The raised surface on the printing block is achieved by cutting away areas that are not to be printed. If you want to make a black or coloured line on a white ground, you need to cut away either side of a ridge that will carry the ink. This is a positive line. A negative line is a channel cut through an area left proud – the surrounding area will pick up the ink and print black, and the line will be white.

## Practising linocutting

One of the reasons lino is so popular for relief printing is that the medium has no fixed tradition, which encourages experimentation. Feel free to use as many tools, conventional and unconventional, as you like. The thing to bear in mind is that you want to keep the ink off the areas that should not print, so clear these to as great a depth as possible – without exposing the hessian backing.

Start by experimenting with a sharp knife and cut positive and negative lines, both straight and curved, making two cuts, one either side of the line. Tilt the blade slightly so that the area to be printed is wider at the base than on the surface – an undercut area will break under the pressure of printing. For a negative line the two cuts will form a 'v' shape at the base; for a positive line the 'v' will be inverted. Pull the knife towards your body, holding the block with your other hand behind the cutting area and turning it as required (always keep your non-cutting hand out of the path of the knife in case it slips). Then, with a flat u-shaped gouge, remove the material either side of the positive line. Practise making single cuts with the knife and removing the lino up to the cut edge with the gouge.

Now make the same cuts using a v-shaped gouge. Push the gouge away from your body and note how the line is more fluid than a knife cut – the tool goes round corners easily. Make the same cuts with a medium u-shaped gouge and note that the cut is shallower and its beginning and end rounded.

Try all of the different tools you have, varying the pressure to deepen and widen the cuts. Make textures with small cuts, by picking at the lino, and by rotating the tool point. Sandpaper the edge of a line to soften it. Try making a design without lines, but entirely with textures. Make holes with a hammer and nail, or dents by rocking a chisel end. Achieve a more delicate effect by wire brushing an area or working on it with fine wood engraving tools.

### WARMING LINO

Old lino can be hard; new lino can be hard in the cold. It cuts like butter when warm (Henri Matisse compared cutting lino to playing the violin). There are various ways of warming up cold lino blocks. Repeat the process as soon as the lino cools to the point where it resists the tool again.

- Put the block on a radiator.
- Lay a hot-water bottle on it.
- Lay a damp towel on it and iron it with the iron on low.
- Warm it with a hair dryer or an electrical heat gun.
- Put the block on an intaglio hot plate set to the coolest temperature.

## Cuts made with v-shaped tools

V-tools are extremely versatile for cutting precise, sharply defined lines with simple fluidity. The sides of the v can vary in angle, thus affecting depth or width of cut.

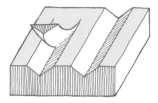

## U-shaped gouges

The round gouges are used for cutting broad free-flowing lines, and also for clearing out the spaces between two cut lines where they border a large clear area.

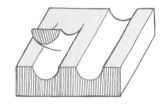

## Flat gouges

Flat or wide shallow curved gouges are ideal for cleaning out large clear areas. They can also be used to make shallow scrapes and shaves on the linoleum surface, which, when inked, will print with a half-tone effect.

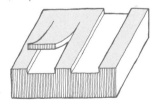

## Other mark-makers

The smallest pin scratched into linoleum can produce a fine printed result. Wire brushes can make exciting and varied marks. Knives produce slick sharp cuts. Ink will collect in very shallow marks and the results will vary from print to print.

# CATALOGUE OF CUTTING TECHNIQUES AND EFFECTS FOR LINO

### Positive and negative cuts
On the left the shape is defined by negative outline made by free cutting with a small v-tool. The same shape on the right is positive after being edged with a v-tool and having its surround cut out with a medium u-gouge.

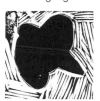

### Parallel lines
Cross hatching and parallel lines cut with a small v-tool. Tone can be varied by moving the lines closer or further.apart. (See Bob Bain, *Northern Enlightenment*, p.60.)

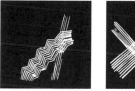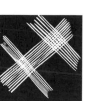

### Line variations
Different lively lines are achieved with small and large v-tools. The small marks at the bottom are caused by wiggling the tool while holding it vertical (useful for foliage and grass in landscape).

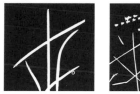

### Parallel lines
Parallel lines and cross hatching with a u-gouge create a flowing, unhindered, free image. The lines in the right hand example show the contrast between the different u-gouge sizes.

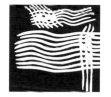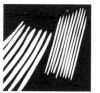

### Curves
On the left, flowing lines and tight curves achieved with a medium and a small u-gouge. On the right a larger u-gouge shows the possibilities of a free cutting approach.

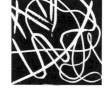

### Clearing
The shape is defined after clearing around it with a u-gouge, and then shaving further with a wider, flatter u-gouge.

### Positive and negative
These examples show a positive and a negative image achieved by chaving the unwanted areas with the flat gouge.

### Creating half tones
Careful shaving with a wide flat gouge can be used to achieve soft undefined areas (useful in landscapes). Sometimes a half-tone effect will be achieved, but the printed results will vary according to the build-up of ink.

### Depth of cut
A shape has been cut and defined with a v-tool, and cleared with a flat gouge. On the left the surface has been only partially shaved, creating a hazy tone.

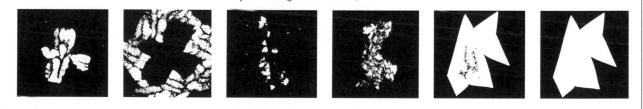

### Pins and wire
Pin and wire scratches are shown on the left. A delicate pin drawing is printed on the right.

### Wire brush
Wire brush effects made with a small brush attachment on an electric drill. On the left the brush is moved across the block. On the right the brush is held in one position.

### Broad cuts
Positive and negative cuts made with a Stanley knife. The large negative area was cleared with a flat gouge.

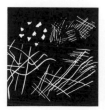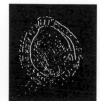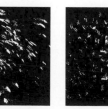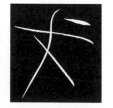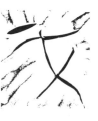

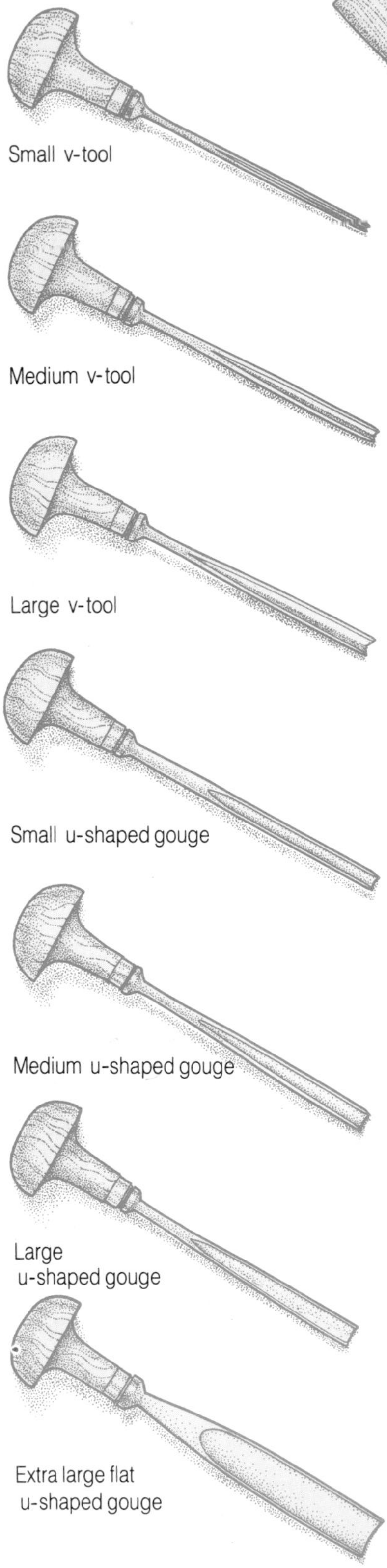

Small v-tool

Medium v-tool

Large v-tool

Small u-shaped gouge

Medium u-shaped gouge

Large
u-shaped gouge

Extra large flat
u-shaped gouge

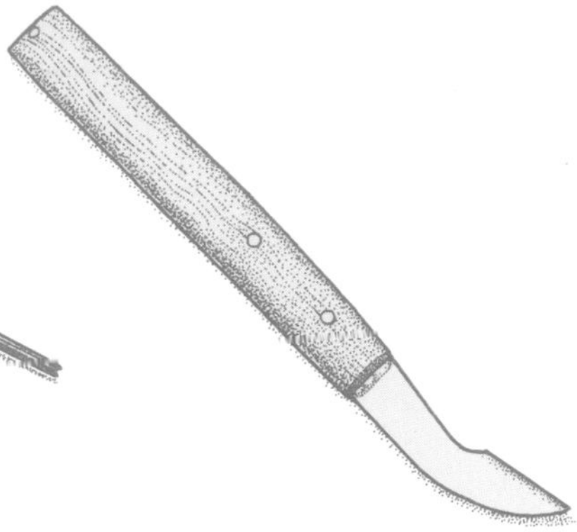

## Woodcutting tools
The tools shown here have mushroom-shaped handles, although straight handles are equally common. The latter are used with a mallet and have metal ferrules to keep the handles from splitting.

## Tools for woodcutting
Woodcutting tools are the same shape as used for linocutting, but they are made from harder steel. In addition, the woodcutter uses a flat chisel for clearing away unwanted wood from the design. One knife, two or three v-tools and a couple of gouges will be sufficient for most work.

### Knives
You can use knives with interchangeable or snap–off blades, as well as traditional European and Japanese woodcutting tools.

A European woodcutting knife has a blade of about 4cm (1½in) with a cutting edge of 2.5cm (1in) although the point usually does most of the work. The handle is straight and about 10cm (4in) long. Grip it as you would hold a pen. As you will need to use more force than when cutting lino, it is usual to clamp the block to the work bench. Use two hands, if necessary, to add power to the cut.

There are two types of Japanese woodcutting knife. One has a blade 5-8cm (2-3in) long with an angled cutting edge and a short, straight handle. The other is more commonly seen and has a lozenge-shaped cutting head sharpened on one edge. These tools are often called facsimile knives and were used for cutting very fine lines on traditional Japanese woodblocks. They are made in several sizes.

### V-shaped tools
These are also called v–cutters, scrives or veiners. They are the same as those used for linocutting, although they are more often set in straight handles about 7.5cm (3in) long to allow for the greater force needed to cut wood, which often necessitates the use of two hands. Larger tools set in longer handles are used with a mallet.

### U-shaped tools
Also called curved gouges, these are the same as those used in linocutting and come in widths of 0.3-2cm (⅛-¾in). They are designed for general work as well as for clearing. Larger u-tools are available set in chisel handles for use with a mallet.

## Chisels
Flat chisels are useful for clearing large areas of wood, particularly on ply and similar boards.

## JAPANESE KNIFE TECHNIQUE

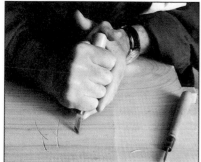

**1** Holding a knife in the Japanese grip. Hold the knife in both hands. Cut along one side of a line – note the angle of cut.

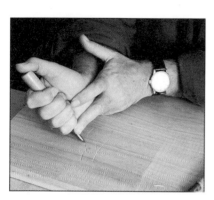

**2** Reverse the angle of the knife. This prevents undercutting. Cut the other side of the line.

## USING WOODCUTTING GOUGES

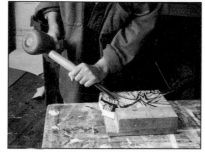

**The u-gouge with mallet pressure**
A mallet is used to exert extra pressure when the wood is hard. Note the use of the bench hook to hold the block steady.

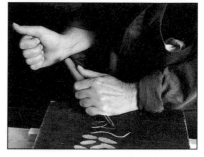

**The u-gouge with hand pressure**
The tool is guided by one hand and urged with the other. The heel of the hand drives the gouge against the grain.

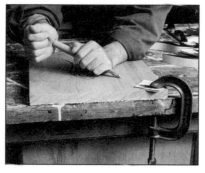

**V-gouge with hand pressure**
The tool is guided by one hand and urged with the other. Note the use of a G-clamp to secure the woodblock to the bench and prevent it slipping.

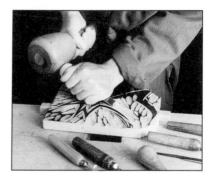

**Very shallow u-gouge**
Use to clear non-printing areas. Here a mushroom-handled tool is being used with a mallet, although straight-handled tools are to be preferred.

## OTHER TOOLS USED FOR WOODCUTTING

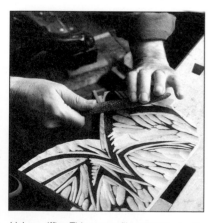

Using a riffler. This coarse file or rasp is used to shape and smooth the edges of free-form woodblocks. The tools are made in various shapes: round, half-round, flat and square, and are made with one cutting edge coarser than the other.

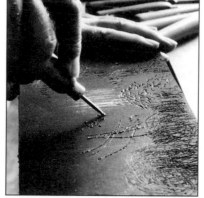

Using a bradawl. A bradawl is a small, pointed tool used for making holes in wood or leather, and can also be used for marking the printing surface of a block. Effects vary from fine holes to broad irregular scratches.

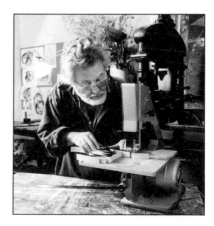

Cutting free form blocks. A band saw can take the time and effort out of producing shaped blocks and the finish is much neater. The wood is fed onto the moving saw blade.

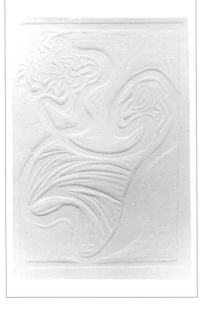

## Practising woodcutting

Wood varies enormously in its resistance to tools and in the degree to which the grain is prominent. Not only is the direction of the grain important, but the alternate soft spring growth and hard summer growth can make cutting pressures vary rapidly within a small passage.

You can discover how to handle wood only by experimenting on different types with different tools. This way you will find out which woods respond best to your style. Scale is also a factor: if you prefer working large, you will find a piece of cherry or sycamore inhibiting; if you prefer to work fast and large, try a large sheet of birch-faced ply. The very fact that it is in many ways an unpredictable material is a challenge – it is always exciting to let the wood inspire your work.

Experiment using the same knife to cut both positive and negative lines on pieces of soft wood, hard wood and boards, across the grain and then with it. Secure the wood to the bench with two clamps or a bench hook (pad the clamps with slips of card to prevent them bruising the wood), turning and reclamping the block as necessary when you change direction. Try similar experiments with v- and u-shaped gouges of varying sizes.

You can usually cut soft woods and faced boards holding the knife with one hand only. When clearing non-printing areas with a shallow gouge, you may need both hands to guide and press. Hard woods may need two hands on both knives and gouges, with the additional possibility of extra force from a mallet.

The shapes of the marks will be very like those made by the same tools in lino, but because wood is a harder and more resilient material, much finer and more delicate cuts are possible and will stand up to the pressures of printing. For example, textures made with a wire brush will remain crisp in wood.

Ply and multi-ply boards, being made of layers glued together, present special problems when you are clearing the non-printing areas. The glue in some varieties, such as marine ply, is very tough and will blunt a gouge quickly. The lighter glued sorts are easier to clear because the layers peel off neatly. Cutting through the top layer only may not give a deep enough clearance and may pick up ink from the roller; clear the next layer too.

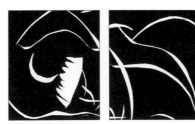

**Cutting with u-gouges**
Cherry woodblock cut with a large u-gouge, a small u-gouge and a v-tool or veiner. Note how the shallow sides pick up some ink and print lightly.

**Using knives**
Cherry woodblock cut with a Japanese knife. Each cut requires two knife strokes. In the lower left an area has been cleared up to a single cut line.

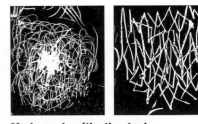

**Marks made with other tools**
Parana pine woodblock scratched with a metal scribe or stylus. The ease of scratching depends on the resistance from the grain of the wood.

## TYPES OF HARDWOOD

Trees with broad, flat leaves. The wood is mostly medium to hard to cut. The most popular woods used for printmaking are:

| Name | Weight | Cutting quality | Other observations |
| --- | --- | --- | --- |
| APPLE | medium | medium | even grain, good for fine lines, also end-grain |
| ASH | medium-heavy | medium-hard | |
| BALSAWOOD | very light | very easy | burnishing only |
| BEECH | heavy | hard | |
| BIRCH | heavy | medium | |
| BOX | medium | easy | end-grain only |
| CHERRY | medium | medium | fine even grain, traditional Japanese choice, also end-grain |
| CHESTNUT | light | medium | can be abraded to show grain |
| ELM | medium | hard | large planks, well figured |
| HOLLY | medium | medium | end-grain |
| KATSURA | medium | medium | fine grain, no knots, resistant to damp, good for water-based inks |
| LIME (LINDEN) | medium | medium | fine grain, light colour |
| MAGNOLIA | medium | medium | fine grain |
| MAHOGANY (HONDURAS) | medium | easy | crisp cuts, can be abraded to show grain |
| MAHOGANY (PHILIPPINE), ALSO KNOWN AS LAUAN | medium | easy | straight, visible grain |
| MAKORE (CHERRY MAHOGANY) | medium | easy | fine, straight grain, large plank width |
| MAPLE | medium-heavy | hard | fine grain, also end-grain |
| OAK | heavy | hard | |
| PEAR | medium | medium | as apple but even better |
| POPLAR (BASSWOOD) | medium | easy | |
| RAWAN | medium | easy | |
| SHINA (JAPANESE LIME) | light | easy | no grain |
| SYCAMORE | medium | hard | fine grain, also end-grain |
| WALNUT | heavy | hard | crisp cutting, even grain |

## TYPES OF SOFTWOOD

Cone-bearing trees with narrow, resinous leaves, older evolutionarily with simpler cell structure. The wood is mostly softer and easier to cut. The most popular woods for the printmaker are:

| Name | Weight | Cutting quality | Other observations |
| --- | --- | --- | --- |
| CEDAR | medium | medium-hard | clean cutting, grain can be shown by abrasion |
| CYPRESS | medium | medium | |
| FIR, DOUGLAS | medium | medium | not suitable for fine line work but excellent for broader treatment and large flat areas cheaper than the hardwoods. Quicker maturing. Must use sharp tools otherwise fibres pull unevenly. |
| FIR, WHITE | light | medium | |
| PINE, PARANA | light | easy | |
| PINE, WHITE | light | easy | |
| PINE, YELLOW | medium | hard | |
| LARCH | light | easy | |
| REDWOOD | light | easy | **Note** do not use common pine as it is very knotty |

## TYPES OF COMPOSITE BOARDS

Man-made boards

| Name | Weight | Cutting quality | Other observations |
| --- | --- | --- | --- |
| PLY WOOD | light | easy | three layers of softwood light glueing |
| MULTI-PLY | medium | easy | five layers or more, softwood, marine-quality has too strong glue to cut easily |
| LAMINATED BOARD | medium | easy | very strong |
| BLOCKBOARD | heavy | easy | very strong |
| CHIPBOARD | heavy | difficult | strong texture |

Fine tint tool

Large graver

Round scorper

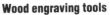

**Wood engraving tools**
The tools shown here are probably as many as you would ever require. All the basic tools come in more than one size. Beginners should start with a basic set consisting of one fine spitsticker, one medium lozenge graver and one medium round scorper.

Bullsticker

Spitsticker

Tint tool

Multiple tool

Square scorper

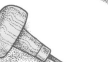

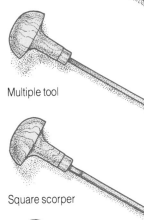

Large square scorper

Chisel

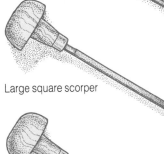

## Tools for wood engraving

Wood engravers use five types of specialist tools for engraving, as well as chisels to clear large areas of wood.

### Graver or burin

This tool cuts lines that vary in width according to the pressure applied. A steel rod, square or lozenge-shaped in cross-section, is set in a mushroom-shaped handle about 12cm (5in) long. The handle should feel comfortable to hold and to work with – choose one that is the right length for your hand. Some tools have a slight bend near the handle to lift them further from the work surface and to avoid the danger of bruising the wood as you work. The cutting edge is angled at 30° or 45° – the choice is according to preference. There are 12 sizes of cutting edge from 1.5-5mm ($\frac{1}{16}$-$\frac{1}{4}$in); the most commonly used are 2.5-3mm ($\frac{1}{10}$-$\frac{1}{8}$in). The tools are numbered from 0 to 12 according to width.

### Spitsticker

Used for cutting curved lines, the spitsticker is also called an elliptical tool because of its shape. It comes in six sizes, generally classified as fine, medium and broad. Medium is the most suitable for beginners.

### Tint tool

This tool has a much finer taper than the spitsticker. It engraves lines of uniform width, so increased pressure will not result in wider lines. It is used frequently for hatching and shading, hence its name. The tint tool comes in six sizes from 1 (very fine) to 6 (broad).

### Scorper

Also called a gouge or scampel, this tool comes with a square or a round end. Either type is used to clear broad areas, and the square one cuts neatly into corners. Scorpers come in sizes numbered 1 to 12, from fine to broad.

### Multiple tool

This tool cuts parallel lines. It is also called a multiple cutter or lining tool. The lower plane of the steel rod is cut into either 2, 4, 6, 8, 10 or 14 serrations and the cutting edge sharpened.

### Chisels

These are from 3mm-1cm ($\frac{1}{8}$-$\frac{3}{8}$in) wide, but you could use a carpenter's chisel with a cut-down handle.

## GRIP AND ANGLE OF CUT

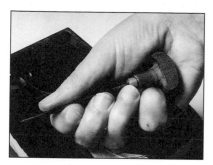

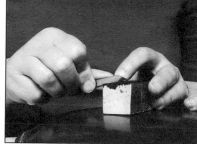

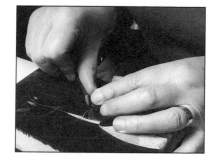

**Holding a wood engraving tool**
The flat side of the mushroom handle faces upwards. The tip is guided by the thumb and index finger, and the little finger hooks under the recessed rim of the handle.

**The angle of cut**
The tool is held at a very shallow angle to the surface of the block so that it does not dig into the wood. Always keep the other hand safely out of the path of the tool.

**Using a finger as a break**
The index finger of the hand steadying the block can also act as a break to prevent the right thumb from slipping. The tool is guided by the heel of the hand.

## USING STANDARD TOOLS

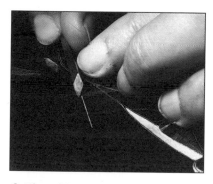

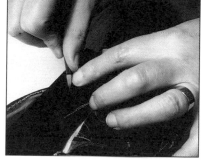

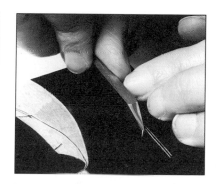

**Cutting with a graver**
Use this tool to cut straight and parallel lines. Increased pressure on the tool causes the cut to become wider and deeper, creating a thicker line.

**Using a spitsticker**
Use this tool to cut curved lines. The curved sides of the cutting face allow easy change of direction.

**Cutting with a bullsticker**
Similar to a spitsticker. The bullsticker is very similar to a spitsticker, but the whole of the cutting face is used. Used for clearing awkward corners. Also good for making stipples.

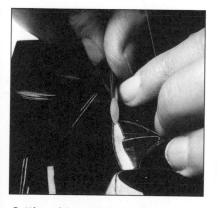

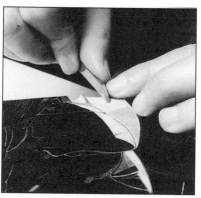

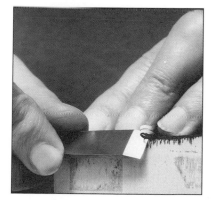

**Cutting with a round scorper**
Use this tool to cut broader marks and to clear out non-printing areas; it also cuts fine curves and dots. The square scorper is a straight line tool and will not cut curves.

**Cutting with a No 4 tint tool**
Use this tool to cut lines of equal width. It is generally used for hatching, and does not cut curves easily.

**Cutting with a chisel**
Chisels are used to remove large areas not required to print, and to chamfer the perimeters of the block, which might pick up ink.

## Practising wood engraving

Wood engraving is essentially a small-scale art; it calls for fine, delicate marks and conveys more detail than any other relief medium. It involves a controlled, intense method of working, less passionate than linocutting and more disciplined than woodcutting. It demands the utmost in inventiveness to describe the richness of a design using simple marks on such a small scale. The intellectual challenge of the medium is one of its greatest satisfactions.

Because of the fine scale, the tools used are specific to wood engraving and do not include knives. The prepared end-grain wood block should be supported on a small, circular pillow made of leather and filled with sand (a book securely wrapped in fabric is a good substitute), so that you can turn the block easily while keeping the tool moving steadily in one direction. Always hold the tool to enable you to work away from your body. End-grain wood is soft to cut and single-hand pressure is sufficient; keep the other hand holding the block out of the line of the cutting tool in case it slips.

Experiment first using the graver, which cuts straight lines whose depth and width depend on the pressure used. Note that the graver line begins with a gentle, shallow point. To end the line similarly, stop the line before you reach the end, turn the block round and start the line again to join the stopped line neatly. Then try the spitsticker, which makes the engraving of curved lines easier. Again the depth and width of the cut will increase with pressure. Try out the tint tool, which makes lines of an even width suitable for hatching, and experiment with the parallel lines made by the multiple tool. Finally try the scorper, which is generally used to clear wood from non-printing areas.

These experiments will lead naturally to the realization that it is easier to engrave a design that shows up as white lines against a solid background than one that shows up as dark lines on a white background. Looking at wood engravings it will become clear that "white-line" engravings are a speciality of the medium.

### Cuts made using gravers
This tool can be lozenge- or square-sectioned. The greater the depth of the cut the wider the line. Used for cutting straight lines and sharp diamond-shaped pecking marks.

### The spitsticker and bullsticker
This tool is pointed at the top or back and the bottom or belly – the sides are convex. The curves of the sides are wider in the bullsticker. Used to cut curved lines, dots and other characteristic stabbing marks.

### Using scorpers
The square scorper is rectangular in cross-section whereas the round scorper has parallel sides but a rounded belly. The square tool is used to clear right-angled corners and to smooth the bottom of a white area. The round tool is also used to clear non-printing areas and is more versatile in mark-making.

### Tint and multiple tools
Tint tools are very slightly tapered and cut single lines of equal width. Multiple tools are rectangular with a series of sharpened grooves along the belly to cut parallel lines.

### Combining the tools
*Tibetan Drinking Bowl* by St Claire Allen shows several techniques and uses of tools. Compare the marks on the block with the printed example. The techniques are various: the dark middle ground is cut with a very fine No.3 tint tool. This tool was made in Germany – tools can vary slightly from country to country. The varying tones on the stone with a hole in it are made with a spitsticker and the rim of the bowl was engraved with a No.6 spitsticker. The centre top edge has deep lines made with a round scorper. All the whites were cleared with a round scorper, but the top left-hand corner had to be deeply cleared with a wide square scorper and the edge bevelled with a flat chisel so that there was no chance of ink being picked up.

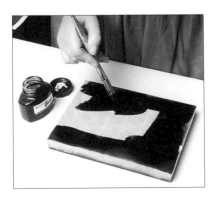

### Preparation using Indian ink
Coating the block with Indian ink gives a dark background through which the lighter engraved lines will clearly show.

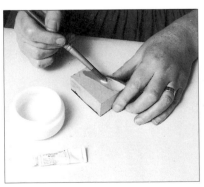

### Using water-colour
The block is coated, not too thickly, with a layer of white water-colour. The drawing can be done directly on to this surface, and the cut lines show clearly.

## CHART OF WOOD ENGRAVING CUTS

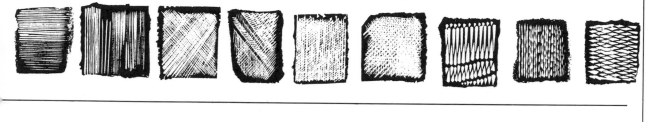

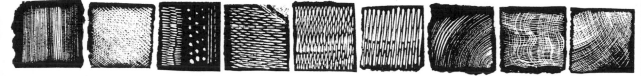

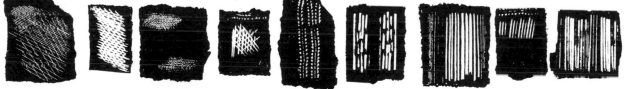

### Square and round scorpers

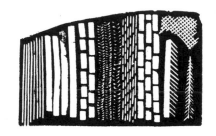

The sample section shown on the left was done entirely using square scorpers of various sizes, and contrasts with the sample on the right which was executed using round scorpers.

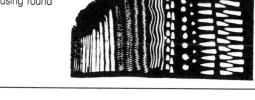

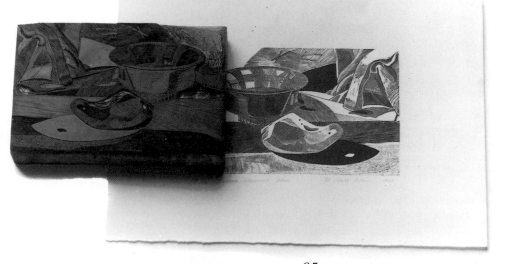

## Electrical and other tools

Hand electrical tools are widely used by relief printmakers today, sometimes for the unique marks they make and sometimes because they do a boring job, such as clearing a large area, more quickly. There are tools specially designed for the artist and for craftworking, but in reality any tools can be and are used – from dentists' instruments to the domestic DIY drill.

### Hand electric tools

There are two types of hand electric tools: those that have a rotating action such as a drill, and those that have a pecking, forward-backward action such as a gouge. Both types usually have changeable heads so that a variety of marks is possible. They vary in size from the smallest made for dentists and jewellers, through slightly larger ones used for glass engraving and engraving plastic and metal labels, up to the domestic size with its scarifying and polishing heads. A purpose-built Japanese electric gouge is designed for 'drawing' on the block as well as for clearing non-printing areas. Many of these tools are battery-driven and very flexible, but all have the drawback of vibration, with the possible loss of accuracy. Nevertheless they can be added to your list of tools and experimented with until you have confidence in their use.

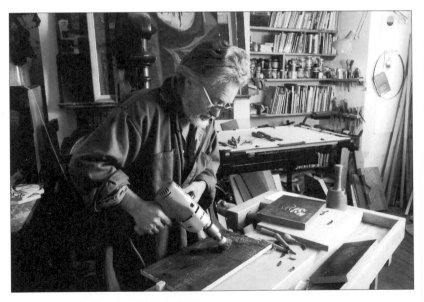

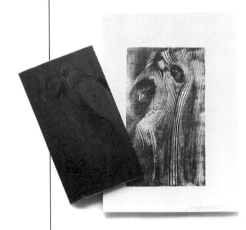

The grain of this piece of timber has been enhanced by wire brushing. The picture above shows the block and a pull from the block.

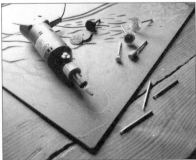

### Using a wire brush

A wire brush attachment for an electric drill marks a woodblock (above) and a lino block (left). These marks can be used as an integral part of the design, or as a method of enhancing the grain of a woodblock as shown on this example (far left) by scarifying the softer spring growth and leaving the harder patterned grain.

## Other tools

Hand–held embossing tools and punches designed for leatherwork and bookbinding can be used to impress a variety of marks in softer materials such as lino and softwood. Even a nail hammered into the block to make "white" holes can be used to build up complete designs. Objects such as a coin, metal mesh or pressing – or indeed any hard object – can be embossed into soft materials. Place the object on the block and cover it with a sheet of stiff metal to protect the press and run the sandwich through a platen or cylinder press.

Lino and wood blocks have also been "engraved" with laser or oxy-acetylene cutting tools: however, the result is an irregular edge, difficult to control.

### USING HAND TOOLS

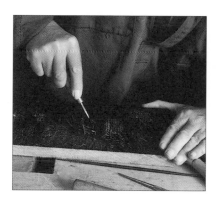 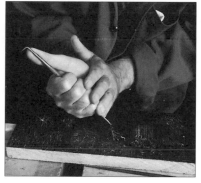 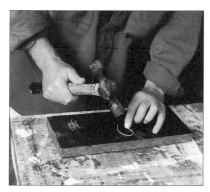

**Making holes**
Use a bradawl to make holes in the block. Nails or staples can also be hammered into the block's surface to make a variety of interesting marks.

**Using a scriber**
A steel scriber makes fine indentations. Use it to make single holes or drag to produce a line. Rough edges will ink up to make irregular marks.

**Hammer wire into a block**
Form wire into a shape and hammer into the block. Wood will take a sharp impression; lino a softer one. Large shapes need the higher pressure of a press to emboss them.

### CHART OF ALTERNATIVE EFFECTS

**Electric drill**
Use an electric drill with various cutting heads to make different marks. These examples have all been done on lino. Make sure the block is held firmly: clamp a mounted block to the bench; use strong double-sided tape or other fixative with unmounted blocks. The tool can be allowed to jump and skitter.

**Leather punches**
These tools are used to make holes in leather: the centre of the hole can be removed or left. Bookbinders' punches are similar and come in many shapes and patterns such as stars, beads, lines and points. Any hard steel edge can be used to cut regular shapes into lino or the finer woods.

**Printing from found objects**
Experiment with inking up any flat object you can find. Left, a metal bar and a curl of wire are printed directly. Right, the same objects have been pressed into a piece of lino and a print taken from the surface. The two methods have produced positive and negative images.

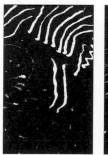 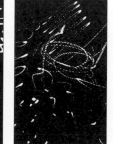 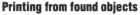 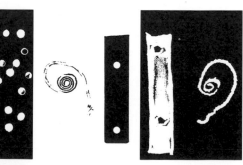

# TOOL SHARPENING AND CARE

The steel cutting heads in good quality tools will remain sharper longer and will take re-sharpening better, which means that the tool will last for several years. Sharp tools are a pleasure to work with and become an extension of the brain, down the arm, hand and fingers to the cutting face.

The traditional tools – knife, graver, gouge and so on – have always been used in conjuction with sharpening stones. Every few cuts the tool was gently touched up on the stone or stroping leather so that it never became dull and needed a major re-sharpen. The Japanese woodblock cutter expected to spend the entire first year of his apprenticeship learning only how to sharpen tools.

Knives, u-shaped gouges and wood engraving tools, with the exception of multiple-line tools, are relatively easy to sharpen. V-shaped tools are more difficult to maintain at the correct angle. Specialist printmaking tool suppliers usually offer a sharpening service that is essential for teaching institutions, but available also to the individual. Keep tools in a soft tool-roll so the tips are protected. Do not put corks on the ends as they attract damp and rust.

Because of its hard, granular constituents lino blunts tools quickly, and blunt tools lead to torn edges. Wood varies enormously from the hard but close-textured woods to those where the annular growth gives alternate hard and soft passages. Blunt tools make wood splinter and tear.

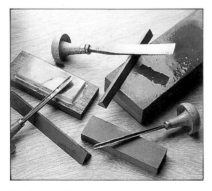

**Equipment for sharpening**
You will need an oilstone, any 3:1 oil, a bundle of cotton wool or fibrous material for cleaning, and the appropriate slip-stones. Pictured on the right is a basic flat stone, and above triangular slip-stones.

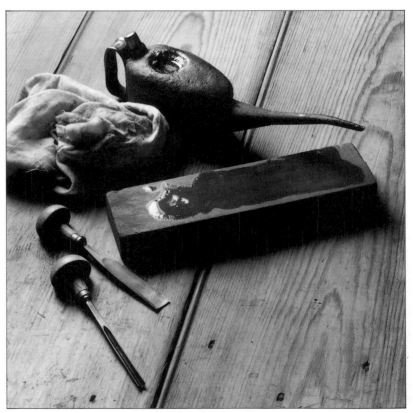

## METHODS FOR SHARPENING CUTTING TOOLS

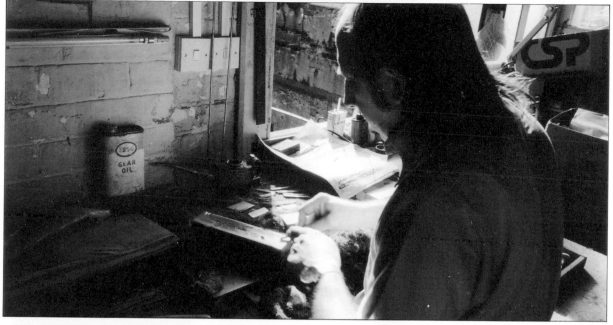

### Sharpening procedure

Have your equipment around you and be prepared to spend a long time doing the job properly. Don't rush any of the procedure, and make sure the oilstone is always lubricated with oil. Remember too, that the aim is to sharpen, not to thin the tool surface!

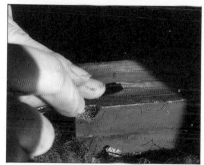

**1** Roll the back of the u-gouge steadily over the oilstone using wrist movement, to make sure the bevel is evenly sharpened.

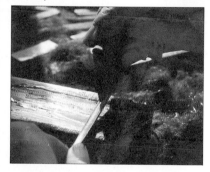

**2** Use the correct slip-stone to remove the burr from the inside of a round gouge.

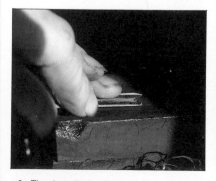

**1** The bevelled edges of the v-tool are sharpened flat along the oilstone using slow, smooth, even strokes that come from the shoulder not the wrist.

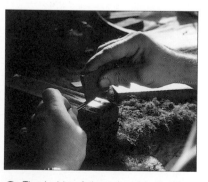

**2** The inside of the v is rubbed with a slender slip-stone, keeping both edges flat, which ensures that the tip of the v is evenly sharpened.

## SHARPENING ANGLES FOR TOOLS

### U-shaped gouge profiles

The curved cutting edges of the u-gouges vary from deep to very shallow, and can be very small or quite large. The sharpening angle on the oilstone will be the same and the bevelled edge is evenly rolled at an angle of about 18°.

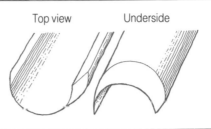

Top view    Underside

For hardwood    For softwood

Shown above are the tool angles for cutting hardwood and softwood.

### V-tool profiles

V-tools vary in size, depth and width. Both sides of the v meet in a sharp point. Each side is sharpened by pushing the tool along the oilstone at a shallow angle.

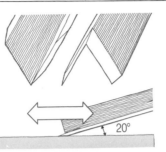

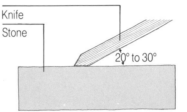

Hook    Oversharpen    Correct

### Sharpening problems

Two classic sharpening problems for v-tools are shown above. A hook of metal, or over-sharpening the centre outer bevel will necessitate regrinding and starting again.

### Sharpening knives

The knife and the flat chisel are the most simple cutting tools to sharpen because the angle only has to be established on one plane. The method used for knives is to keep the blade at an angle of between 20 and 30 degrees and sharpen using a circular motion.

Knife

Stone

20° to 30°

### Flat chisel profiles

Flat chisels are flat on the bottom and slope down at the end. They should be pushed gently along the oilstone at first, and then at the angle prescribed by the sloping end.

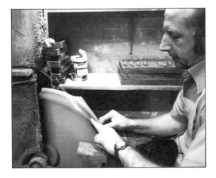

### Regrinding tools

when the cutting edge of any tool becomes really damaged, it is necessary to regrind the surface so the tool can once again be shaped and sharpened. Here a tool is being reground at the 128-year-old firm of T.N. Lawrence and Son in London, one of the few companies world-wide who offer this service.

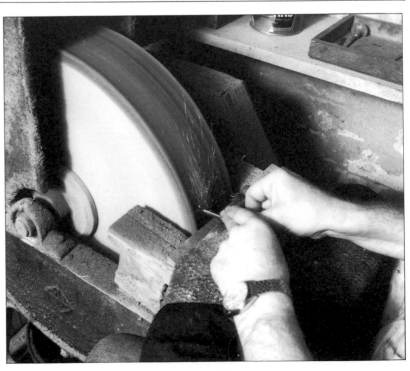

# CORRECTING TECHNIQUES

The need to make corrections arises from three main causes:

■ The tool slipped because it was not sharp or was the wrong tool for the job, or, in the case of lino, the block was too hard.

■ There was a fault in the material, unusual in lino but more likely in a natural material such as wood; for example a hidden knot.

■ You made a mistake in cutting the design.

### Small mistakes

A small slip can often be corrected quickly at the time of making it if you can find the chip of lino or wood that you cut out by mistake. Glue it back in position using woodworkers' glue or PVA. Make sure no glue accumulates on the front or back of the block – wipe it clean before drying.

If you cannot find the missing chip or have a slightly larger hole, use plastic wood or fibreglass filler. Sand flat when dry.

These repairs will probably not be noticeable in a busy passage but if the work is sparse, for example a single line describing a profile, the slight signs of joining could ruin the effect. It is better to

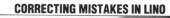

**CORRECTING MISTAKES IN LINO**

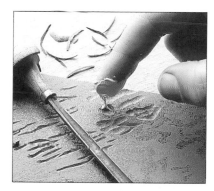

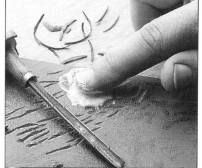

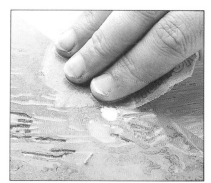

**1** Correcting using plastic filler. Add filler to the area, pushing it well into the depression to make a good bond.

**2** Smoothing the filler using a finger or a small spatula to spread and smooth the area. Remove excess filler.

**3** When the filler has set, rub with a piece of fine sandpaper to take the filler down to the original level of the block.

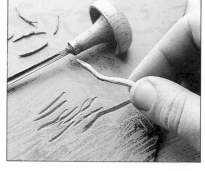

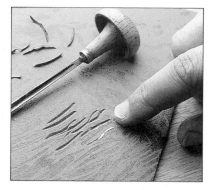

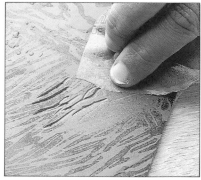

**1** A small correction using glue. Cover the underside of the small strip with PVA glue.

**2** Placing the glued strip in position. Be sure to remove excess glue from the surrounding surface before it sets.

**3** Sanding the correction. If the sides of the replaced strip are raised a little sand these areas down to the original level.

cut out a rectangle of wood or lino and replace it entirely. Lino should be cut right through the backing, and glue applied to the new, neatly fitting patch edges as well as to the edges of the hole. Fit in the patch, wipe off excess glue back and front and weight to set, preferably overnight. If the patch is so large as to weaken the block for handling, mount the whole thing on a backing (see pp.62-3).

Solid wood blocks need more skilful repairs as the circle or rectangle must be cut out well below the work with a chisel or drill, though not right through. The new piece must be of the same wood and set in with the grain going the same way. It is usual to make the plug of new wood somewhat higher than the block so it can be planed and sanded to the exact height of the rest of the block.

Ply or veneered boards are treated the same way, but if the mistake is shallow the top layer only may be replaced.

If a mistake occurs in an area of solid, flat colour where the slightest difference in the ink film shows up, all these repairs could ruin the effect desired. The only safe thing to do is to start again with a new block. If you have worked on the block for a matter of days or even weeks, and then you make a mistake, you can find yourself in a real dilemma. To tell the truth, many an artist of repute has touched up a small, unmendable fault on the pull with a brush using very slightly diluted ink – but it is not the sort of thing any printmaker should aspire to.

## Wood bruising

Wood can be easily bruised if you allow the tool shank to rest on the wood while you work (the remedy is to use tools with angled shanks); or by a clamp (the remedy is to place a thin card between the wood and the clamp); or by general mishandling. Close-textured woods can sometimes be raised by steaming: place a drop or two of water on the bruised area and hold a lit match close. The water will evaporate quickly and swell the wood grains. It may need more than one application and the result may be a coarsening of the grain, but it will no longer print grey or white due to the depressed surface.

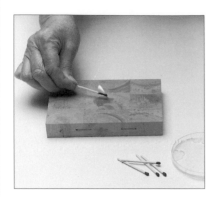

**Correcting a bruise**
A small bruise on the woodblock above was caused by the shank of a tool, and would show on the final print. The bruise was removed by placing two drops of water on it and holding a lighted match over the area. The evaporating water swells the wood grains and lifts the dented section of the bruise.

---

**REPAIRING MISTAKES IN WOODBLOCKS**

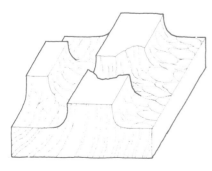

**1** The section of the line that has been mistakenly removed must be cut to a deeper, regular shape to accept a plug.

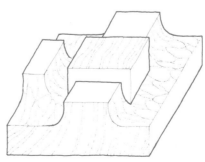

**2** The wooden plug is inserted in the prepared hole and glued into position, leaving it above the printing level.

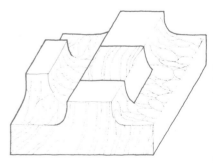

**3** When the glue is completely dry the top of the plug can be cut off with a chisel and sanded or planed down to the original level.

## Example of a corrected print

This colour linocut was made with two blocks cut by the reduction method. The final printing in black mixed with violet was planned to give the crowd scene its form. During a lapse of concentration the artist cut away a large middle ground area thinking it was grass. The choice was to begin the whole print again or execute a major repair. A section 7.5 × 18cm (3 × 7in) was cut out and replaced. After sandpapering it smooth it could be redrawn and cut. There is no trace of the repair in the actual print.

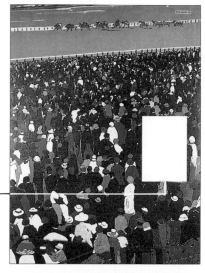

Section removed

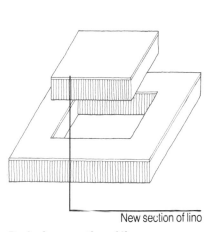

New section of lino

## Replacing a section of lino

When a large mistake is made it is often not possible to correct it by the methods previously described. In this case you will need to make a patch repair. Cut out the section to be replaced over a fresh piece of lino so that you cut out a patch that will fit exactly at the same time. Glue the patch and the edges of the hole and fit the new section into place. The surface can then be sanded with wet-and-dry to make sure there is no gully round the patch, which might show up negative when printed.

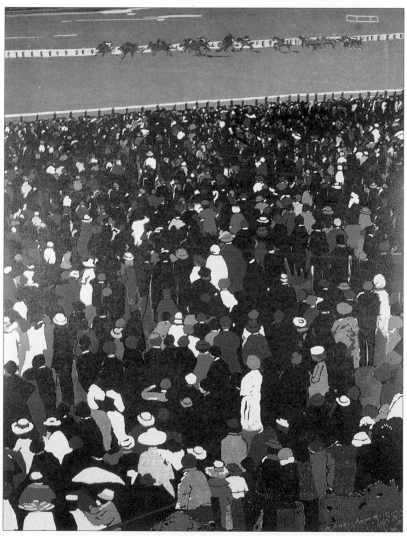

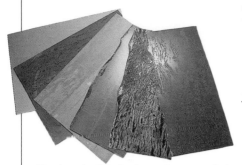

The six etched blocks shown above are rolled up in their respective inks and demonstrate that several closely related colours are needed to build up a convincing depiction of water. The first, third, fourth and fifth blocks have all been extensively etched. The second is cut with a u-gouge to give some structure to the watery passage.

## ETCHING LINO

One of the exciting properties of lino is the possibility of using an alkali solution to etch into the surface, giving areas of granular texture. The grainy effect can vary from a light breaking-up of the surface to a deeper, rougher area. It can be used all over the block or just in one part; it can be used in conjunction with all other techniques of cutting. It must be said that the method is somewhat unpredictable, but that is part of the fun. The etch is a dangerous substance and children should not be allowed to use it.

### The etch

Edward Bawden first used paint stripper as an etch and made some interesting textures. Michael Rothenstein went on to experiment with caustic soda solution (sodium hydroxide) and it has proved the more flexible etch. Caustic soda is sold in crystal form at hardware shops to clear domestic drains. It is a dangerously corrosive alkali and should be handled and stored with care.

Make a saturated solution by putting three to four tablespoonfuls of water in a glass jam jar or polythene container. Add caustic soda crystals, one spoonful at a time, allowing the crystals to dissolve before adding more. Stir with a glass rod or wooden stick. When no more crystals will dissolve, the solution is saturated. Heat will be given off during this process, so leave the solution to cool before use. Add a few drops of meths to make the solution flow easily.

### Etching lino for fluid effects

The application of caustic soda etch by brush gives a particularly fluid feeling. In the print on the right, *White Water Rafting* by Katie Clemson, the blue water area shows clearly how some parts have been etched deeper than others. It also shows how the underprinted colours are used.

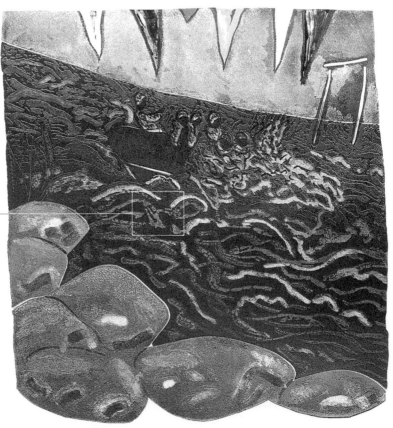

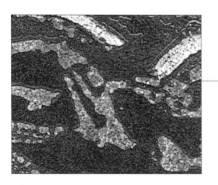

Brush strokes clearly visible in enlarged section above.

## ETCHING A TEST SEQUENCE

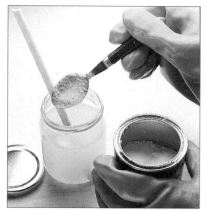

**1** When mixing the caustic soda solution wear protective rubber gloves and keep your face clear of fumes. Add the caustic slowly to a jar of cold water until a saturated solution is formed. The jar will be very hot.

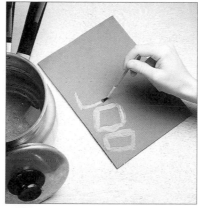

**2** Masking areas to be etched. Wax has been melted in a double boiler and is quickly painted on the block using a nylon brush.

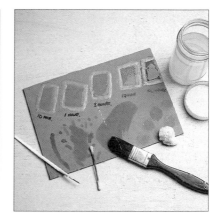

**3** Examples of etching. Caustic is applied for different lengths of time in the waxed areas. Other freer methods include application with a large brush, a sponge, a cotton bud and a fine brush.

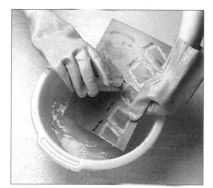

**4** Removing the caustic. Thoroughly scrub away the residue left by the caustic with a brush. Spray again with cold water.

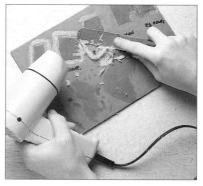

**5** Removing the wax. A hairdryer is being used to melt the wax with hot air. The wax can be scraped back with a palette knife.

### TIPS ON ETCHING LINO

- Soft lino etches faster than old, hard lino.
- Etching in warm weather or a centrally heated room will be quicker than in the cold.
- The longer the etch remains on the lino the deeper it will bite.
- Keep a container of water nearby so that should a splash of etch reach the skin it can be washed off immediately with plenty of water – otherwise a nasty burn could result.
- Wear rubber or plastic gloves.
- NEVER add water to caustic soda crystals – always caustic soda to water.

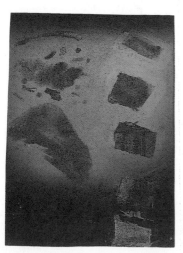

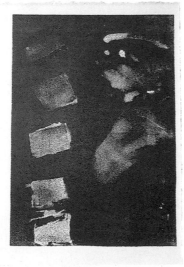

### The finished print
An example printed from the etched block used in no.3. Caustic is very unpredictable, and although here the different lengths of bites show up clearly, often they don't!

**CATALOGUE OF ETCHING EFFECTS**

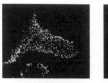 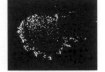 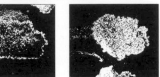 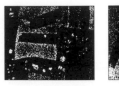

The block was etched for thirty minutes using full strength caustic soda in a saturated solution. After one hour the results are clearer.

The block has been etched for five hours. The grain is harsher and the etched areas are more tonally defined.

This block was first painted with a wax resist before being covered with caustic solution and etched for four hours. Note that some of the solution has penetrated the wax.

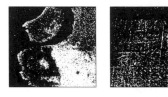 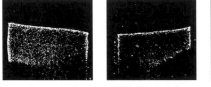

No resist was used here. The caustic was applied freely, and since the etch was not contained the edges are less defined.

An example of etching in a contained area. Blockout lacquer (resist) was used and after four hours the shape is quite hard-edged. The caustic solution tends to run towards the blocked edges, hence the stronger bite in that area.

If the caustic solution is mixed with PVA you can exercise greater control when brushing it on to the lino. Here the brushstrokes were etched for four hours. The PVA was peeled off after the caustic was washed out prior to printing.

**THE UNPREDICTABILITY OF ETCHING**
Never take experiments in caustic soda etching for granted! The effect of etching for a given period can never be estimated with any accuracy. The etch can creep through the resist and sometimes will stubbornly shrink away from areas where it is painted. Treat etching lino as an experiment in tone, and do not allow its unpredictability to discourage. Rather, use this trait for exciting results.

## Preparing the block
Rub the lino with methylated spirit to make sure there are no greasy spots. Brush the edges and back of the block with PVA or varnish as a protection in case any etch escapes to creep underneath.

## Free area etching
Brush, drip or sponge etch freely and directly on to the surface. Use a glass filament brush (or an old brush you do not expect to use again), cotton wool on a stick, a glass dropper or a plastic sponge.

## Controlled area etching
Etch can be contained in specific areas by building low walls of Plasticene or Blu-tak. Alternatively, areas of the block can be protected from the etch by means of a resist. The two most common resists are quick-drying varnish and candle wax. The varnish can be painted on with a brush and must be quite dry before etching. The wax must be heated to a runny consistency and applied hot, with a brush. If the wax is not hot it will not make a good bond with the lino and etch could creep under the wax. Oil crayons are another possibility, but they must be of a very greasy type to act as a good resist. Both varnish and wax can be scratched, which allows etch to reach the lino, creating a more linear effect than can be achieved with brush application of etch or brush application of resist.

## Etch/polymer mix
If you mix caustic soda etch with a polymer medium such as acrylic medium (made to mix with artists' acrylic paints), in the proportion of one part caustic soda solution to two parts acrylic medium, the

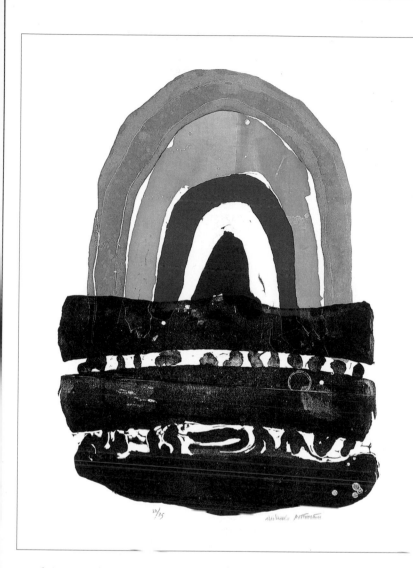

12/35

**Liquito**

**ARTIST Michael Rothenstein**

**SIZE 91.5 × 63.5cm (36 × 25in)**

This colour linocut combines cutting and etching with caustic soda solution. The artist pioneered caustic soda etching. He first noticed the effect of spilled drain cleaner on a linoleum tabletop in his kitchen. From then on he developed the use of caustic soda in his prints leading to a freer, more painterly approach.

## ETCHING TIME

A shallow etch is usually achieved in an hour or two, depending on the state of the lino and the temperature of the studio. A deeper etch will take from five to six hours, and for a very deep etch leave it overnight. As the etch works it loses its strength, so a long bite is best made by renewing the etch more than once – this also gives a chance to check progress.

After an hour or two wash off the etch under a stream of water. If there is a lot of etch lying on the surface of the block so that carrying it to a sink could be dangerous, make sure you start with the block on a plastic tray or dish before applying the etch at all.

Use a soft brush or an old toothbrush to loosen the particles of lino under the stream of water. If further etching is necessary, dry the block thoroughly and re-apply the etch.

result is a much stiffer substance. It will not flow on the block and can be applied with a large stiff brush, such as a house-painter's brush, to give bold brush effects. It should be used immediately after mixing as the polymer dries and the mix may become too stiff and lumpy. Leave to etch for five to six hours for a strong brush texture. Wash off the etch mix with plenty of water – even if the polymer has dried it will peel off with water.

## Cleaning the block

When etching is complete, remove any retaining walls or resist. Dissolve varnish with methylated spirit or white spirit, depending on the varnish. Remove wax by heating the block to melt the wax; use a hot plate or hot air source (see p.95) and then lay absorbent paper on the block to take up the wax. Alternatively, lay absorbent paper on the wax and rub a domestic iron all over. You may need more than one layer of paper to absorb all the wax. Finally, de-grease again with methylated spirit on a soft cloth.

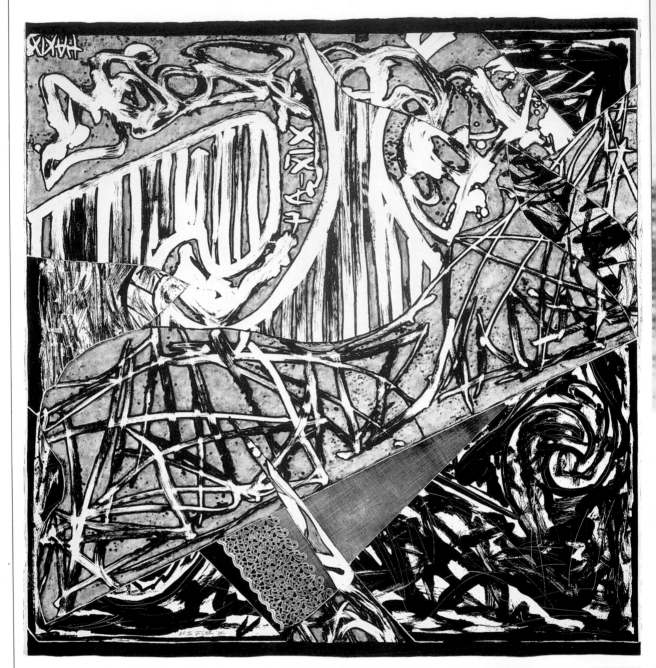

## Swan Engraving Square II
## ARTIST Frank Stella
## SIZE 137 × 131cm (54 × 51½in)

Mixed media print using collage, metal relief etching and woodcut printed and published by Tyler Graphics Ltd. The artist has fully exploited the different textures of each material and contrasted etched and cut marks.
**RIGHT** Kenneth Tyler and Frank Stella cutting the metal sections of the collage, and **FAR RIGHT** inking the various sections of the *Swan Engraving* series.

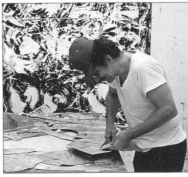

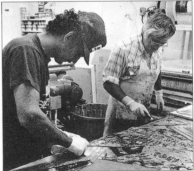

## Relief-printed collage blocks

A collage block consists of a base board, which could be a piece of lino, a piece of side-grain wood, plywood or board, on which a variety of objects is glued, or on which a substance can be modelled and sculpted. The only criterion is that the finished surface must be relatively flat. Brush a coat of glue or PVA on the base board, arrange the objects and, when firmly stuck, brush another coat of glue or PVA to seal the surface.

Gesso is a good material in which to create low-relief surfaces as it sets hard enough to withstand the pressure of a platen press. Gesso is a mixture of animal glue and plaster of paris; it can be bought ready-made or you can make your own by melting some glue in a glue pot or double saucepan and stirring in enough fine plaster of paris to make a spreadable mixture. It can be applied to the base board with a brush, utilizing the brush marks if required, or with a knife. It can be worked while still wet with a variety of tools, or allowed to dry hard and then cut, engraved, scratched or carved.

### COLLAGE OBJECTS
Found objects for collage can be string, matches, lace and textiles, metal pressings and mesh, dried vegetable matter, sand, sawdust, metallic powders, crushed paper such as tissue, corrugated board, cut-out card shapes, feathers, and anything else that catches your imagination.

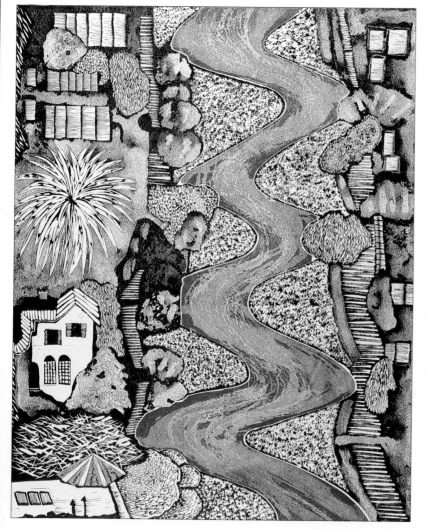

**San Francisco Road**
**ARTIST Fiona Hamley**
**SIZE 48 × 68½cm (19 × 27in)**

Two colour linocut reduction method print. Note the contrasting textures between the cut and etched area.

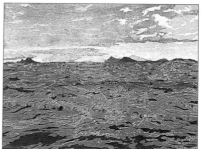

**Force 7. West Coast of Ireland**
**ARTIST Katie Clemson**
**SIZE 41 × 56cm (16 × 22in)**

Multi-block colour linocut using caustic soda etching on three of the blocks. The brushed and splashed-on etch has bitten into the lino to give the impression of fluidity to the water and a misty quality to the sky.

## MAKING COLLAGE BLOCKS

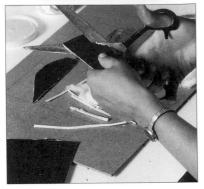

**1** Materials with different surfaces and textures have been assembled. They are cut to shape while the collage is being planned.

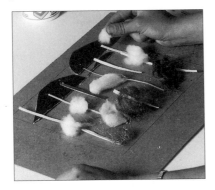

**2** The image is created on a hard piece of card by manoeuvring the materials around before any of the items is glued.

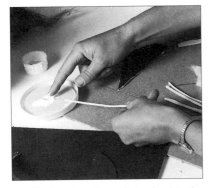

**3** Finally, the collagraph is glued to the base with a strong PVA glue. The surface can now be coated with varnish or lacquer to toughen it for printing. It can also be printed without surface treatment if the requirement is for only a few pulls.

Other materials that can be modelled include many proprietory pastes, cement, household plaster, glue on its own or mixed with sand, chalk or any other powder. It is worth experimenting.

Remember that when ink is rolled on to collage blocks only the upper areas will take the ink and print well, but large, shallow depressions will also tend to pick up ink from the roller if the roller is not supported across the block by enough work of printing height. Any extra high points will be likely to pierce the printing paper. See p.139 for the use of soft packing and offset printing to increase the area of the collage block that can be printed by standard methods.

## Plaster prints

To make a plaster block, plaster of paris is poured into a wooden frame set on a smooth surface such as plate glass. When set, the frame is removed and the slab turned over so the smooth surface can be engraved. It is easier to see the work if the surface is first rolled over with black oil-based ink and allowed to dry. The engraved lines will then show white. The plaster can be slightly softened by dampening with water to make working easier. Lino, woodcutting or engraving tools can be used. When the work is complete, brush a coat of shellac over to harden the plaster. A plaster print is inked like any relief print using oil-based ink, but it must be burnished for the block will not withstand the pressure of a press.

## Collagraphs

A collage block is printed by standard relief methods using burnishing or a relief press; a collagraph is made in much the same way but printed in an intaglio press. The base must be strong enough to withstand the higher pressure and it must be thinner than board used in a relief print, so a sheet of metal or a tough plastic is advised. The materials collaged-on or modelled-on must also be able to take high pressure. Modelling pastes or resins incorporating metal powders or fibreglass and other liquid plastics that set can be used. The block is surface-inked only, and the previous remarks on inking shallow collage blocks also apply.

## Relief etchings and engravings

Metal plates (thin blocks) are normally associated with intaglio printing, but they can also be surface printed. The techniques for creating intaglio plates – etching, metal engraving, aquatint, soft ground and mezzotint – are beyond the scope of this book. It is also possible to draw in black ink on paper and send this to a commercial process engraver to be made photographically into a line block or to use photographic material in the same way to make a screened photo-engraving. Hand inking of fine screen blocks is very difficult, so restrict the screen to 100 lines per inch.

Metal plates are normally printed using oil-based inks but early in this century there was a school of Japanese-influenced Western artists that devised a method of varnishing the metal plate and using water-based inks, brush-applied. The effect was delicate.

## Rubber and plastics

Sheet rubber, minimum thickness 3mm (⅛in), can be cut, and latex rubber casts can be taken of very fragile surfaces such as weathered wood, and used as printing blocks where the original material cannot be printed.

Many kinds of plastic sheet are used by printmakers, but since they are not cheap they do not have many advantages over lino or plywood. The exception is Perspex, which can be engraved in a manner similar to boxwood and which has the distinct advantage of being transparent, so the block can be placed over a guide design instead of tracing the design on to the surface. The major disadvantage with such materials is that they scratch easily. Wood engravers have also been experimenting with other materials such as Makrolon (a vandal-proof transparent plastic used for glazing and riot shields) and Delrin (steel substitute for turning on a metal lathe).

## Card

Card is frequently used for relief printmaking with the jigsaw method (see pp. 106-7), but it can be used for blocks kept whole that exploit the paper fibre layers that go to make up the card. Choose a thick card such as illustration board, with a smooth hot-pressed surface. Use a sharp knife to outline areas that will print solid. Peel away the top layer between these areas to expose the rough interior structure of the board. Seal the whole block with PVA or varnish and allow it to dry. When rolled up with ink the smooth top surface will take solid ink, but the peeled-off areas will give an irregular texture somewhat lighter in colour due to the lower pressure. Card is remarkably strong and will yield many copies before breaking down.

## Slate and soapstone

Soft stones such as slate and soapstone can also be cut and printed. Special stone-carving tools used with a mallet will be needed if the stone is hard, but many newly quarried stones are soft enough to be cut with a knife. The stone often hardens with exposure to the air. They are normally printed using oil-based inks and burnished, but if the slab of stone is no thicker than 2cm (¾in), it can be printed in a platen press. Thick stones could be surface-printed in a direct or offset lithographic proofing press.

## Board

Board is a vague term for a sheet of stiff construction, thicker than card, and generally made of waste wood and paper pulp. Most are of a fibrous, coarse texture that cannot be cut with much refinement.

Hardboard is the best for printmaking. The smooth side can be cut much like lino and the back has a pleasant texture. Both cut surfaces and back, if used, should be sealed with a coat of PVA, or fibres will pull off during inking and spoil both roller and slab.

Mill board, used for bookbinding, is highly compressed and can be used for large, flat areas, but should be sealed.

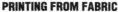

**PRINTING FROM FABRIC**

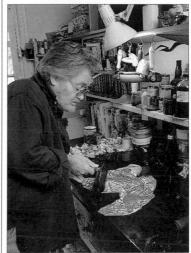

Crushed fabric is dipped in PVA solution until it is impregnated. It is then formed into shape and allowed to dry. It becomes rigid and can be rolled up with ink (below) just like any conventional block. The fabric in this case was a linen-like material, but almost any fabric can be used.

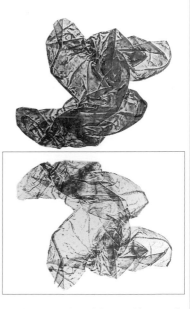

The fabric block and the resulting proof made from the block.

## Mixed media

The idea of mixing various printmaking methods is not new – the famous early 19th-century Baxter prints were made by printing one etched intaglio plate with all the fine detailed work on it and then a number of wood engravings on top for the colours. Until recently 20th-century printmakers have tended to emphasize the purity of each method and to deplore any modifications, but now we see many methods used to create a single print. At one end of the scale Frank Stella has created enormous prints working in a high-tech print studio using dyed paper specially made there for him, printed with metal relief photo-etching and woodcut (cut by laser), with the addition of stencilled and screenprinted colours. At the other end of the scale many artists working on their own combine methods and materials, without high-tech or assistants.

**RIGHT Our Lady of the Frigidaire**
**ARTIST Betty Bates**
**SIZE 81 × 56cm (32 × 22in)**

Linocut with collage. The linocut is made from separate cut-out blocks.

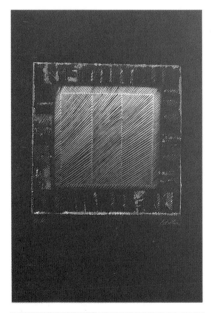

**ABOVE Untitled**
**ARTIST Betty Bates**
**SIZE 56 × 76cm (22 × 30in)**

Linocut and monoprint.

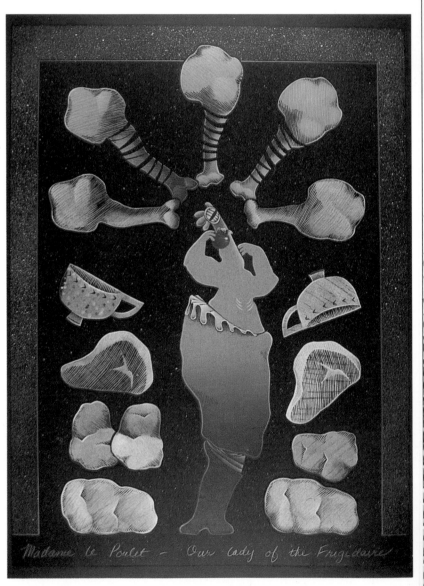

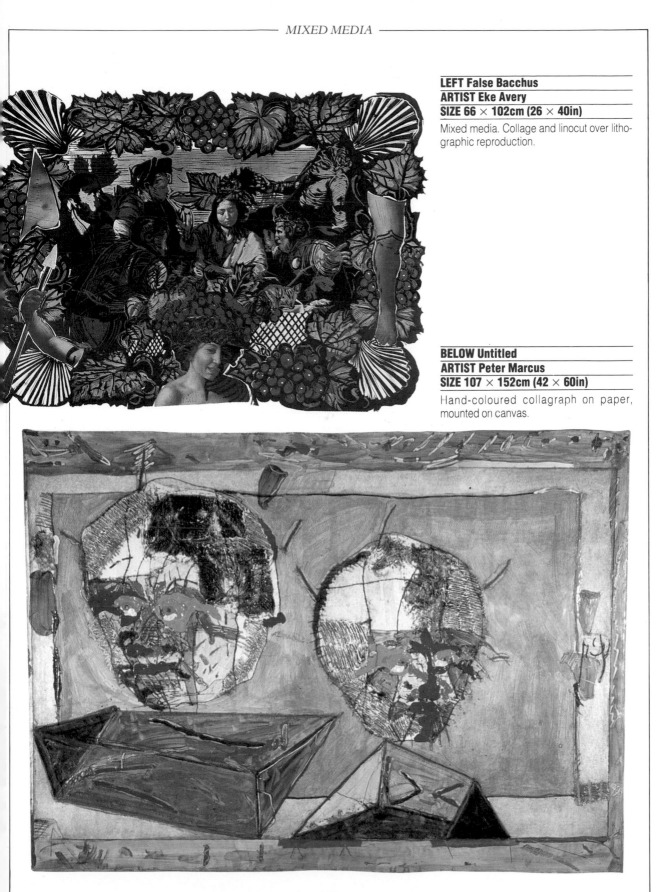

**LEFT False Bacchus**
**ARTIST Eke Avery**
**SIZE 66 × 102cm (26 × 40in)**

Mixed media. Collage and linocut over lithographic reproduction.

**BELOW Untitled**
**ARTIST Peter Marcus**
**SIZE 107 × 152cm (42 × 60in)**

Hand-coloured collagraph on paper, mounted on canvas.

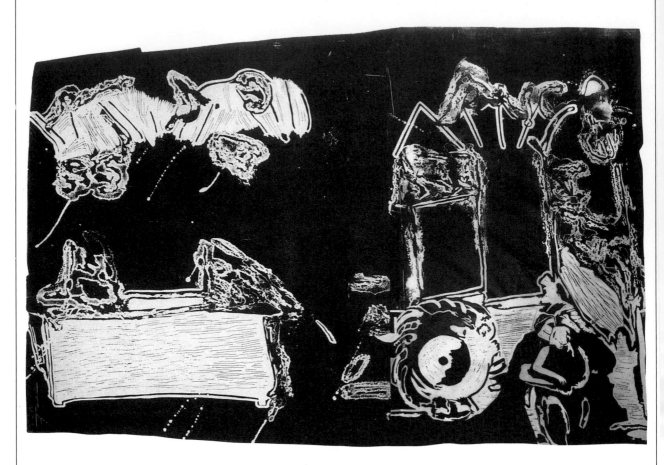

**Tyre Shop**
**ARTIST Yolanda Christian**
**SIZE 58.5 × 89cm (23 × 35in)**

This monochromatic linocut was cut with three sizes of woodcutter's u-gouges and a very fine wood engraver's v-gouge. The artist also used caustic soda etching.

Each method has its advantages and disadvantages, so it makes sense to use the best of each technique. The most common combinations are:

- Lino for flat areas of colour with wood engraving for fine detail.
- Lino for areas of fluid cutting with wood for its natural pattern.
- Metal relief etched block for detailed drawing and collage of photography with woodblock for colour.
- Flat printing with embossing.
- Smooth woodcut with found driftwood.
- Lino for etched texture, wood for natural texture and screen-printing (not covered in this book) for flat colour or photo-based images.
- Card for easily cut jigsaw shapes with lino or wood for more dynamic cutting.
- Collage or sculpted block for texture with lino or wood for flat colours and dynamic cutting.
- Lino or wood on preprinted offset lithography (commercially printed) or electrostatic (Xerox) copying for the contrast between hand and machine printing.

There are few rules, though it is worth noting that oil-based inks can be printed on top of water-based inks but not vice versa, and that embossing should be done last.

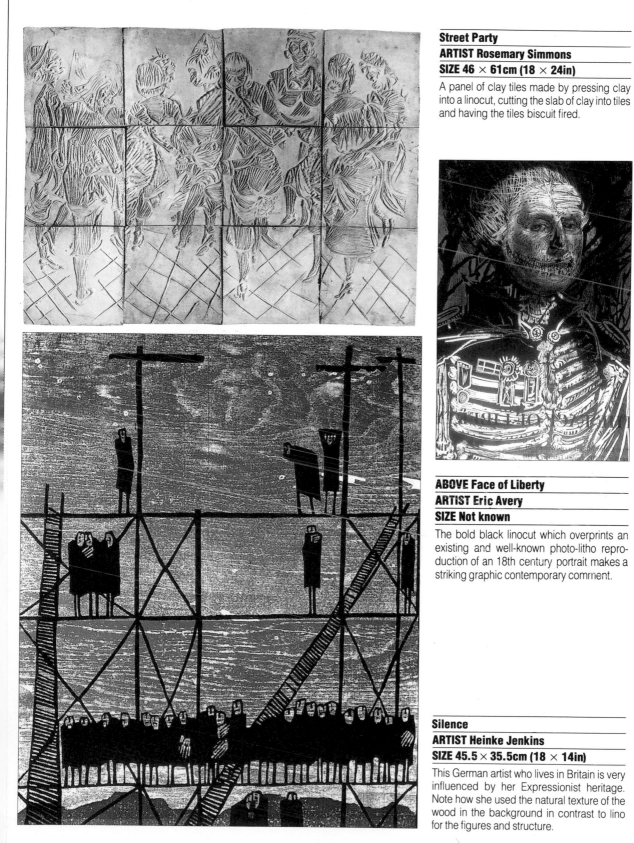

**Street Party**
**ARTIST Rosemary Simmons**
**SIZE 46 × 61cm (18 × 24in)**

A panel of clay tiles made by pressing clay into a linocut, cutting the slab of clay into tiles and having the tiles biscuit fired.

**ABOVE Face of Liberty**
**ARTIST Eric Avery**
**SIZE Not known**

The bold black linocut which overprints an existing and well-known photo-litho reproduction of an 18th century portrait makes a striking graphic contemporary comment.

**Silence**
**ARTIST Heinke Jenkins**
**SIZE 45.5 × 35.5cm (18 × 14in)**

This German artist who lives in Britain is very influenced by her Expressionist heritage. Note how she used the natural texture of the wood in the background in contrast to lino for the figures and structure.

**Collection 85-10**

**ARTIST Haku Maki**

**SIZE 13.5 × 35cm (5½ × 13¾in)**

Relief print from cement, mortar and wood-blocks. The cement and mortar was used to make a moulded block to emboss the very thick paper. This print shows the detail and subtlety that can be achieved through refinement of traditional and modern Japanese relief techniques.

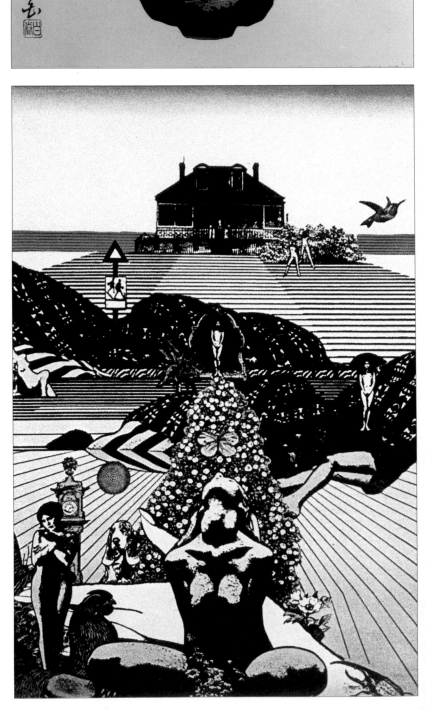

**Paradise – Landscape with a House**

**ARTIST Hodaka Yoshida**

**SIZE 41 × 32cm (16 × 12½in)**

Woodcut and photo-etched metal relief. Thirteen colours were printed from wood using traditional Japanese methods and water-based colours, with the exception of the horizon blue, which was a dye. The metal plate was printed with oil-based inks.

**Waterlilies**

**ARTIST Anne Jope**

**SIZE 41 × 61cm (16 × 24in)**

Linocut and plywood blocks. The wood has been chosen for its markings, which are exploited to give the effect of gentle ruffling of the surface of the water.

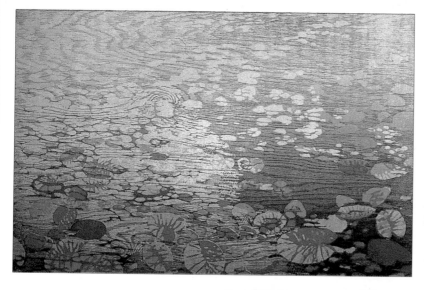

**Peakland: Winter Apple**

**ARTIST Rosemary Simmons**

**SIZE 43 × 58cm (17 × 22¾in)**

Lino, wood and one photo-etched metal relief block printed with water-based and oil-based inks. See p.68.

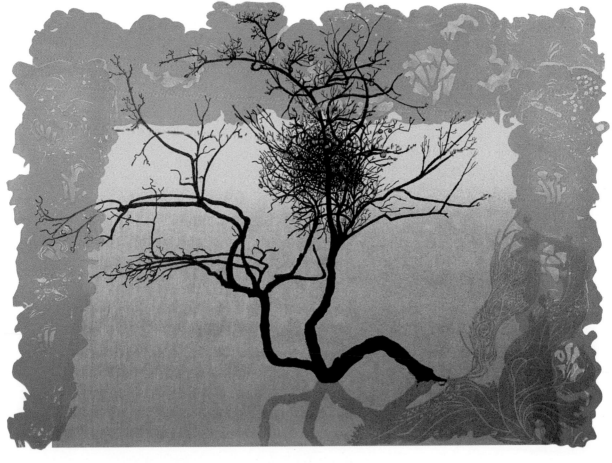

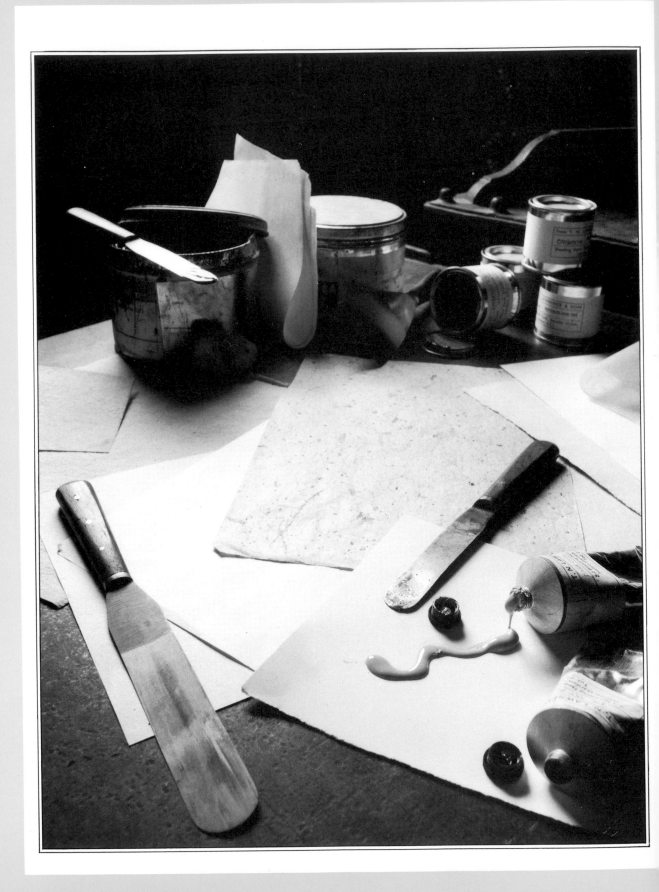

# Inks & Papers

The ink used for printmaking is not thin like drawing ink; it should not be confused with paint. All inks and paints are made from pigments. These can be derived from natural sources, such as iron ore, used to make ochres, and iron and manganese oxides, used for siennas and umbers, or they can be manufactured by chemical processes. The pigments are mixed with various vehicles to suit different supports, such as paper or fabric, and different methods of application, such as brush or roller.

There is a traditional system of describing artists' colours – whether they are used for painting or printmaking; the name does not always reflect their composition. The composition of a colour determines whether it is transparent or opaque, and whether it fades when exposed to light or is permanent. Manufacturers have always aimed to produce artists' colours that behave consistently and have managed to replace many of the older natural colours with synthetic equivalents that do not fade.

Paper is made from cellulose fibres pressed into a thin mat. It can be handmade, mould-made or machine-made. Handmade paper is best for printmaking because it is pure and strong, but as each sheet is made individually it is expensive. Mould-made paper is also made from pure materials, but is mechanically produced; it is less expensive but also loses in character. Machine-made paper is impure and not so good for an important work of art, though it is widely used for proofing and experimental work. Most papers are white or near-white, but coloured papers can be very exciting to use and you can dye your own paper before printing. Some interesting prints have even been produced from formed paper pulp made in three-dimensional moulds combined with more conventional printmaking techniques.

## TRADITIONAL NAMES FOR INKS

**Yellows:** CADMIUM, PALE AND MID, semi-opaque, light-fast; CHROME, PALE AND MID, semi-opaque, light-fast; HANSA, transparent, light-fast.

**Reds:** VERMILION, opaque, light-fast; ALIZARIN CRIMSON, transparent, not light-fast; QUINACRIDONE, PERMANENT MAGENTA AND ROSE, transparent, light-fast.

**Browns:** SIENNA, RAW AND BURNT, opaque, light-fast; UMBER, RAW AND BURNT, opaque, light-fast; YELLOW OCHRE, opaque, light-fast.

**Blues:** ULTRAMARINE, transparent, medium light-fast; PHTHALOCYANINE (MONASTRAL, THALO BLUE), transparent, light-fast.

**Greens:** VIRIDIAN, semi-opaque, medium light-fast; CHROME GREEN, opaque, light-fast; PHTHALOCYANINE (MONASTRAL, THALO GREEN), transparent, light-fast.

**Whites:** TITANIUM WHITE, opaque, light-fast; FLAKE WHITE, semi-opaque, light-fast; CHINESE WHITE (zinc oxide), opaque, not good for mixing, light-fast.

## PANTONE MATCHING SYSTEM

Pantone inks are made by most commercial ink manufacturers in addition to their own colour ranges. The Pantone book of colour samples offers a foolproof way of mixing any Pantone inks to get the same colour every time. Listed under each colour sample are the precise proportions of those of the eight basic Pantone colours needed to match the sample. All Pantone colours are transparent and artists who use them often do so in conjunction with four opaque colours: two earth colours such as yellow ochre and burnt umber, black and white.

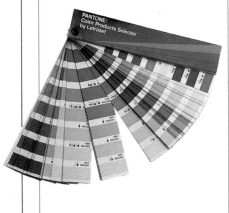

# INKS

Artists' quality printmaking inks are generally called by the same names traditionally given to colours of paint, although industrial-scale manufacturers invent names that are no guide to their composition. Ink manufacturers issue colour cards for their range that give the names of the colours, whether they are transparent or opaque and their degree of fastness to light (see left).

## The language of colour

Scientists measure colour by the length of light waves bouncing off them; artists do it instinctively. Nevertheless, theories about colour abound and they can be very inhibiting. Much the best way to learn about colour in printmaking is to look at prints, preferably not behind glass, and to contrast these with drawings and paintings.

Drawings are essentially monochrome and that single colour, be it ink or pencil, is used to portray a world that in reality is coloured. "Colour" in drawing is described by tone (shading in pencil, hatching in ink). Contrast this with painting, where every colour found in the real world can be recreated in paint.

## TRADITIONAL COLOURS

This comprehensive palette offers the printmaker the means of mixing any desired colour. With the addition of transparent oil or other reducing medium, or opaque white, the colours can be mixed or overprinted in countless combinations, giving the printmaker total colour control.

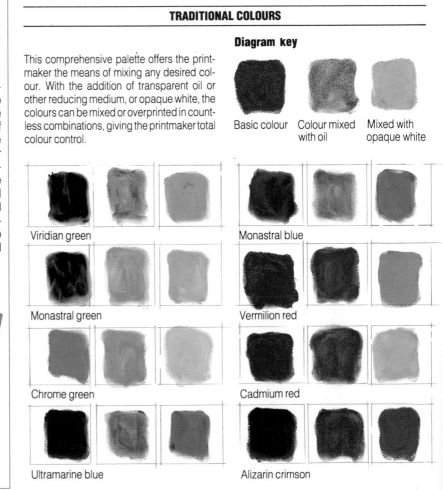

**Diagram key**

Basic colour | Colour mixed with oil | Mixed with opaque white

Viridian green

Monastral blue

Monastral green

Vermilion red

Chrome green

Cadmium red

Ultramarine blue

Alizarin crimson

Some colours seem warm and some cool – the contrast between them creates an optical illusion. Warm colours – red, orange, yellow – seem to come forward in the picture; cool colours – green, blue, indigo, violet – seem to recede. But there are subtle variations. Within the blues, for example, ultramarine has a warm tinge and monastral blue is cool; when they are placed side by side the ultramarine will seem nearer and more eye-catching. The other optical "rule" is that colours that lie exactly next to each other affect the area where they meet and the eye sees a third colour. Yellow meeting blue creates the illusion of a green strip, narrow but pulsating; blue meeting crimson makes a violet impression.

Printmaking has one foot in the world of drawing and the other in the world of painting. Look at the black and white prints by Brodsky, Dürer and van Niekirk in Chapter One: these are closely related to drawing. Then look at the multi-block print by Kurosaki and the linocut by Hughes-Stanton, which clearly behave more like paintings. Finally, look at the Munch woodcut and the Rothenstein, both of which use a restricted number of colours and combine the lessons

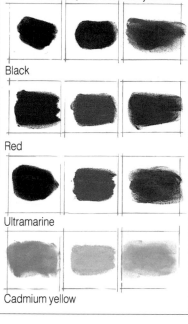

**A BASIC PALETTE**
A basic palette of four colours plus white can be mixed together in many combinations to provide a good variety of colour. A strong black; permanent or warm red; ultramarine blue; and cadmium yellow.

Black

Red

Ultramarine

Cadmium yellow

Permanent magenta

Hansa yellow

Quinacridone rose

Raw sienna

Cadmium mid yellow

Burnt sienna

Cadmium pale yellow

Raw umber

Chrome mid yellow

Burnt umber

Chrome pale yellow

Yellow ochre

learned from drawing (the character of line) and from painting (the interaction of colours).

The most striking prints are often those using three or four colours only – look at the Claude Flight linocut. It is not simply a question of the ingenuity of the artist in creating a satisfactory picture with such limited resources, it is rather that by limiting the resource extraneous detail is dropped and the essential design comes through clear and strong. This is the nub of graphic design, and thus of all printmaking, representational or abstract.

The printmaker has to juggle with the optical effects of colours and their technical properties. He or she must take into account whether a colour is transparent or opaque, what happens when one colour overprints another, and how different colours react when additives are mixed with the ink.

## Printing inks, paints and dyes

The chart on the right describes how the various types of inks, paints and dyes can be used in relief printmaking. Powder pigments and fabric dyes are bought by weight, either loose or prepackaged; other colours are sold in tubes, jars or tins. Tubed colours are more expensive than those supplied in tins. The price of colours varies according to the ease or difficulty of manufacture – for example, alizarin crimson is more expensive than burnt sienna. Some colour suppliers even out the price and charge standard amounts for small and large tins.

Artists' grade water-colours and oil paints are expensive, but a small tube of a special colour used in a limited way can be justified. Most printmakers use colours in sufficient quantity to buy direct from manufacturers or specialist suppliers, but beginners should start with readily available inks sold in tubes.

## Transparent and opaque inks

Most printing inks are transparent. This means that not only do they reflect light from the surface of the paper, but that lower layers of ink show through upper layers and optically transform them. Opaque colours are dense enough to obliterate colours beneath.

## Overprinting and order of printing

In theory the effects of overprinting are predictable; in practice they are often surprising. You might expect that yellow printed on top of blue would make green, but yellow on top of black also makes green – although a different green.

Darker colours will obliterate light colours beneath, and generally lightest colours are printed first and the darkest last. But light, opaque colours can also be printed on top of dark colours and they show strongly. They have a tendency to "float" and remain unintegrated, so they need to be used with discretion.

The first layer of colour sinks into the paper surface and has the effect of sealing it, so that the second colour when printed on top will appear somewhat darker/stronger than you might expect. This is

| WATER-BASED PIGMENTS | Vehicle and solvent | Use | Other comments |
|---|---|---|---|
| POWDER PIGMENT | water and gum arabic or rice paste; water soluble | woodcut woodblock | Powder must be ground finer with a muller before mixing for printing. Transparent or opaque according to pigment. Apply with a brush. |
| ARTISTS' WATER-COLOUR | water, gum, glycerine, syrup; water soluble | woodcut, woodblock colouring finished prints by hand | Very finely ground pigments. Expensive. Must be thickened for printing. Mostly transparent. Apply with a brush. |
| GOUACHE | water, gum, glycerine, syrup and chalk or other fillers; water soluble | woodcut, woodblock | Coarser than watercolour but brilliant hues. Mostly opaque but transparent if very diluted. Apply with a brush. |
| DRAWING INKS (soluble and waterproof) | water; shellac and borax also added to waterproof inks; water dissolves soluble only | woodcut, woodblock, colouring finished prints by hand | Very fine pigments in aqueous solution. Transparent. Apply with a brush. |
| ARTISTS'-GRADE PRINTING INKS | as gouache with retardant to slow drying, water soluble | woodcut, woodblock, lino | Good quality pigments, Mostly transparent. Apply with roller or brush. |
| SCHOOL-GRADE PRINTING INKS | as gouache with retardant to slow drying; water soluble | woodcut, lino | Coarse pigments, dull colours. Opaque. Apply with a brush. |
| **OIL-BASED PIGMENTS** | | | |
| POWDER PIGMENT | linseed oil; soluble in turpentine, white spirit or petrol | woodcut, wood engraving lino | Powder must be ground finer with a muller before mixing for printing. Transparent or opaque. Apply with a roller or brush. |
| ARTISTS' OIL PAINT | linseed oil (mainly); soluble as above | as above | Expensive. Remove excess oil. Transparent or opaque. Apply with a roller or brush. |
| ARTISTS'-GRADE RELIEF, INTAGLIO AND DIRECT LITHO PRINTING INKS | various oils; soluble as above | as above | Best quality traditional pigments with the safest modern additions. Transparent or opaque. Apply with a roller or brush. |
| SCHOOL-GRADE RELIEF PRINTING INKS | various oils; soluble as above | as above | Inferior pigment. Mostly opaque. Apply with a roller or brush. |
| COMMERCIAL LETTER-PRESS AND OFFSET LITHO PRINTING INKS | complex mixture of oils fillers, driers etc., as above | as above | Cheapest inks. Strong colours. Mostly transparent. Not all light-fast. Apply with a roller or brush. |
| FABRIC PAINTS | water until fixed | woodcut and lino | For use on natural materials. Simple heat fixing. Transparent or opaque. Apply with a brush. |
| FABRIC PRINTING INKS | oil-based, similar to school-grade relief printing inks; same solvents until fixed | as above | Mostly opaque. Steam fixing. Apply with a roller or brush. |
| FABRIC DYES (commercial) | water plus gum tragacanth; water soluble until fixed | as above | Brilliant colours. Follow makers' instructions in mixing and fixing in detail. Can also be used on paper with fixing. |

## Overprinting and order of printing

In theory the effects of overprinting are predictable; in practice they are often surprising. You might expect that yellow printed on top of blue would make green, but yellow on top of black also makes green – although a different green.

Darker colours will obliterate light colours beneath, and generally lightest colours are printed first and the darkest last. But light, opaque colours can also be printed on top of dark colours and they show strongly. They have a tendency to "float" and remain unintegrated, so they need to be used with discretion.

The first layer of colour sinks into the paper surface and has the effect of sealing it, so that the second colour when printed on top will appear somewhat darker/stronger than you might expect. This is less obvious with water-based colours. When very intense colours are required it may be necessary to print the same colour more than once – Japanese woodblock printers frequently do this because their water-based inks are somewhat diluted.

When you mix opaque colours with transparent ones the resulting colour will be opaque. You can keep a colour opaque and make it lighter by adding white, although some mixtures containing white dry a slightly different shade from the wet ink. Another curiosity is that semi-opaque colours look cold and dull when printed on a dark background, but warm and clear on a white background. Simple experiments with your basic colours will demonstrate all these points.

A colour sample showing **Pantone warm red** with and without oil overrolled with **process blue**, **yellow** and **green**, all with and without oil.

### ADDING OIL TO THE INK

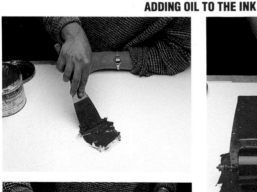

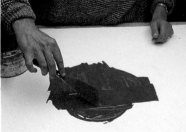

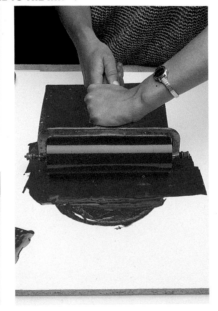

**1** Strong or medium copperplate oil is added to the ink and mixed thoroughly with it so that no clear oil streaks crop up in the printed results.

**2** The well-mixed ink and oil is now rolled out very thinly and evenly on a glass sheet using a large roller.

**Pantone green** with and without oil overrolled with **white** and **black**, with and without oil.

## COLOURS AND HUES OBTAINED BY OVERROLLING

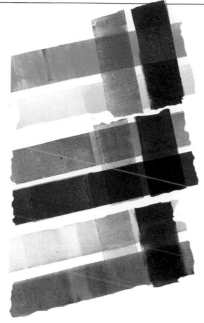

**Pantone green** with and without oil overrolled with **red**, **yellow** and **process blue**, all with and without oil.

**Process blue** with and without oil overrolled with **yellow**, **red** and **green**, all with and without oil.

**Pantone yellow** with and without oil overrolled with **process blue**, **green** and **red**, all with and without oil.

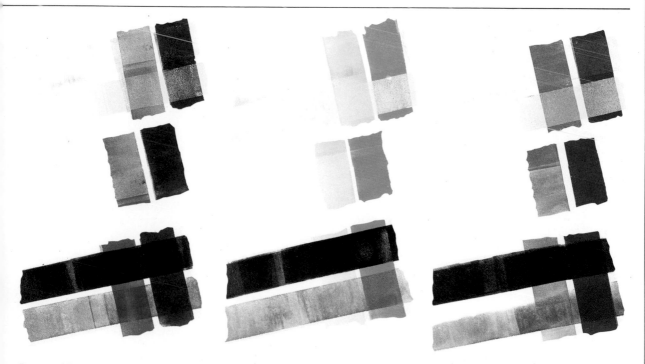

**Process blue** with and without oil overrolled with **white** and **black** with and without oil.

**Pantone yellow** with and without oil overrolled with **white** and **black**, with and without oil.

**Pantone warm red** with and without oil overrolled with **white** and **black**, with and without oil.

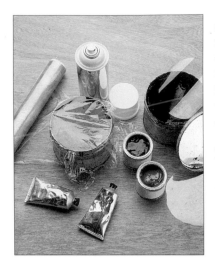

**Care of inks**
Take good care of your inks and they will last longer. Use an anti-skinning spray and put acetate or cling film under the lids of tins. Replace the caps of tubes immediately.

strength colours fade much more slowly than those that have been reduced. Reducing mediums are used to dilute water-based and oil-based colours without changing their consistency. Buy the same make of reducing agent as your inks; manufacturers vary the formula, but within their range you can be sure it will be compatible with all colours. In the '50s printmaker Blair Hughes-Stanton developed an alternative method of reducing oil-based colours with copperplate oil.

**Driers and retarders**
Adding driers to ink makes it dry more quickly, but ready-mixed inks already contain driers and adding more can change the consistency of the ink. If you add driers to the first couple of print layers this can make an impenetrable skin, so that subsequent layers of ink lie on the surface and are not well integrated. Oil-based inks dry both by evaporation and by absorbtion.

   Retarders slow the drying time. Printmakers do not usually require a longer drying time – it is more of a problem waiting for the ink to dry so that the next colour can be printed.

## USING OIL-BASED INKS

However your ink is packaged, you must keep the top or cap on firmly to prevent the ink drying. Ink in tubes has a smaller area exposed to the air, but you should still put the cap back on immediately after squeezing out some ink. An open tin exposes a much larger area of ink. A new tin has a paper or film circle on top to exclude air and the tins are usually sealed on the outside. Do not dig into the ink, but rather skim off a thin layer, raising the protective circle just enough each time. Use new protective circles of cellophane or plastic as required (large jam pot covers should fit). Putting cling-film over the top of the tin under the lid helps to make a tight seal.

   The problem of ink skinning is particularly likely in teaching situations, but it happens to everybody. Certain ink manufacturers have developed an anti-skinning spray for rollers, ink slabs and blocks that need to be left inked for a short time, and these sprays can be applied to ink in tins before the tins are closed.

   If you are faced with ink already full of hardened lumps, the traditional remedy is to spread it out on a slab and laboriously pick out each lump. A much easier solution is to press the ink through a mesh – fine curtain net works and it is cheap enough to throw away after use; metal mesh can be cleaned and re-used. You can also mix up the ink, lay the mesh on top, scrape the ink through and transfer it to the rolling-up slab.

**Ink slabs**
Ink is mixed on a smooth, impervious surface, preferably a white one so the colour can be seen easily. Traditionally marble was the preferred material, but now most people use a slab of plate glass, with the edges bevelled and polished, placed over a sheet of white paper, or, alternatively, a sheet of white laminated plastic of the kind

used for work-tops. For general use the size should not be smaller than 25 × 30cm (10 × 12in), but the wider the rollers you use, the wider the slab will need to be. You will need more than one ink slab. It is convenient to mix a colour on one slab and transfer a little at a time to another slab to be rolled out. Some artists keep a separate slab for black ink just to make sure that it does not contaminate the other colours.

## Mixing knives

Ink is mixed by folding and scraping over and over, and a flexible knife is the best tool for doing this. Painters' palette knives are too lightweight, except for taking very small amounts of ink from the tin. Printmakers' palette knives are like those sold to professional house painters – up to 15cm (6in) long and with a rounded or squared end. The round-edged knife is used to take ink out of the tin and to mix it, and the square-ended knife is better for scraping down the ink slab to clean it after use.

## Mixing the ink

Beginners always mix too much ink at first, so start with no more than a teaspoonful of the base colour or reducing medium. Then add minute amounts of any other colours needed to adjust the base colour. Most ink mixes are made up of a large amount of reducing medium and only small amounts of colour. Use one palette knife for mixing and one clean one for each of the colours added – this way you will not contaminate a tin with another colour. Mix the inks very thoroughly and keep dabbing out and comparing. The Pantone system of matching gives clear instructions for the proportions of each constituent colour in a mix, but most artists still use the traditional colours, where there is an element of trial and error. Technique improves with experience.

## Consistency of ink

Ink is applied to the block with a roller in order to obtain an even coat; ink applied with a brush, fingers, or tampons (also called dollies or poupées) will show some unevenness. Prints made in the

### OTHER INKING METHODS

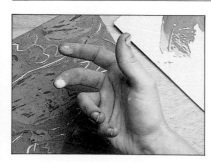

**1** Inking with fingers. Small isolated areas are difficult to ink with a roller, so ink is applied with the fingertips.

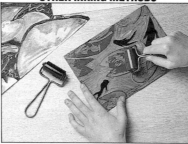

**2** Using small rollers. Two colours have been inked for printing at the same time, with two small rollers.

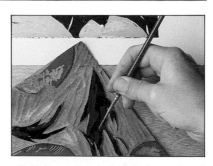

**3** Using a brush. Detailed streaks of orange ink are added with a brush over the wet red ink. Both will be printed together, causing the inks to blend slightly.

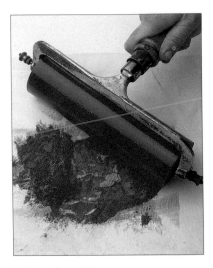

**Rolling lumpy ink**
To prevent getting lumps in ink on the roller, lay a piece of gauze over the inked slab and roll the ink through it, leaving the lumps behind.

late '60s and '70s aimed for very evenly applied ink in response to the overwhelming success of screenprints, but if you look at prints made before this time you will see that colour was often applied with a brush, and the resulting marks are an integral part of the design, often reinforcing contours and shapes. It follows that with this technique, the prints in an edition will not be identical; this runs contrary to the post-war attempt to codify "original" prints, which must be the same in all respects. Recently there has been a return to a less rigid interpretation.

Both oil-based and water-based ink must be of the right consistency for rolling, but within that stricture you will see considerable variety. Look at a selection of relief prints and note that the ink on some of them is thick enough to be almost three-dimensional; that it can be very shiny or that it can be very smooth, matt and seem to blend into the paper surface. To some extent this depends on the paper and how much ink it absorbs, but it also depends on ink consistency.

Too dry an ink mixture will not roll out easily; too liquid an ink and the roller will skid on the ink slab. There are helpful tips to do with how the ink looks and how it sounds. Ink rolled out on the slab should look like matt satin and there should be no loud squelching sound from the roller, more a gentle hiss.

### Solvents and cleaning
The most widely used solvent and cleaning agent for oil-based inks is white spirit or turpentine substitute. Use petrol to clean rollers if you need to change colour rapidly, as it dries quickly on the roller without affecting the ink. Scrape surplus ink from the slab on to newspaper and sprinkle the solvent liberally on slabs, rollers and knives. Soak up diluted ink with newspaper and finish with soft rags. A cheap solvent dispenser can be made by piercing a number of small holes in the metal cap of a small "mixer" bottle.

All solvents are inflammable, as are most inks, so it is important to keep naked flames out of the studio, including gas fires. Solvent containers should be stored within a larger container with a lid, such as a dustbin. Many people find solvent fumes irritating, so good ventilation is advised. Those people with sensitive skins should use a barrier cream and gloves during the cleaning session (barrier cream also makes cleaning hands much easier). Industrial hand cleaners are widely available and will remove ink from around fingernails, where it tends to lurk.

When cleaning rollers, make a point of checking the sides and spindle for ink splashes, which can build up to reduce the free revolving of the roller. Also note that gelatine rollers should only ever be cleaned with paraffin (kerosene). Never scrape ink off rollers with a knife.

### Rollers
Rollers, also called brayers, are made of gelatine, rubber or polyurethane, and come in various sizes from 2.5cm (1in) wide up to

about 45cm (18in). They also come in different degrees of hardness. Gelatine rollers are not used so much today because they melt in the heat and start dissolving if they get wet. Rubber rollers are very good and easy to clean. Polyurethane rollers, being uncoloured, show the ink colours up well, but they are slightly more difficult to clean. The smaller rollers have one handle, but larger ones are heavier and need two handles.

Rollers should never be allowed to rest on a flat surface because they will develop a flat strip that is ineradicable. Rollers should always be hung up, even between rolling and printing a block. Small to medium rollers can be rested on their backs or have a screw-eye put in the end of the handle and be hung from double "S" hooks on a rail above the inking surface. Large two-handled rollers need a rack that will hold them by the handles only.

Rollers made for artists are of a better quality than those made for schools: the frames are made of brass and the handles are a more satisfactory shape. Old rollers can be recovered by specialist firms.

### CLEAN HANDLING TIPS

Keep a tin of chalk powder or talc on the press or by the printing area and occasionally dip your hands in the powder and dust off. This prevents the hands getting too greasy and keeps fingermarks off the paper. Another way of preventing finger-marks is to use "fingers" of paper. Cut out a strip of paper and fold in half to use as "tongs" between your fingers and the printing paper.

## CLEANING UP AFTER PRINTING

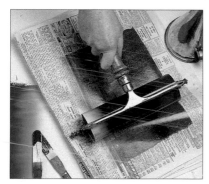

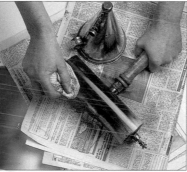

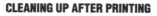

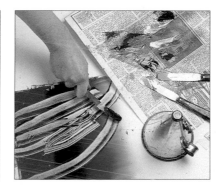

**1** Cleaning the roller. Roll excess ink from the roller on to newspaper several times.

**2** Using solvent. There is now less ink on the roller so not a lot of solvent will be needed. Sprinkle it on and rub with a rag, taking care to clean the edges and ends.

**3** Cleaning knives and inking slab. Scrape all excess ink from the slab on to the paper with a knife. Scrape the knives clean on the paper.

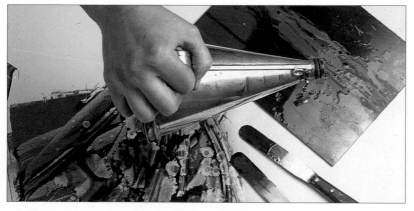

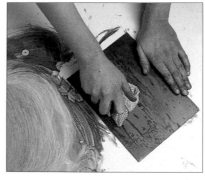

**5** Rub thoroughly with a rag until all surfaces are clean.

**4** Shake solvent on to the knives and the block. The solvent can in the picture is designed so that the solvent does not gush out.

Soft edges can be obtained by inking through a mask or stencil cut out of thin but strong paper. The block does not have to be cut at all, it simply acts as a bearer of the ink, which of course saves block material. The mask can be hinged on to one side of the block so that it falls in the same place each time for inking and flips back for printing. The suction of the inked roller tends to pull the paper mask, so fine work will tear off; broader areas are more effective. Ink will build up on the mask and should be regularly blotted with a sheet of absorbent paper such as newsprint.

Medium–hard rollers should be bought initially for general use, but you might want to experiment with soft rollers that press into the cuts of a block, or hard rollers that ink the highest points of the block surface only. Hard and soft rollers are used particularly in inking collage plates or unusual surfaces.

## Rolling up the block

Take up a small amount of the mixed ink, or ink straight from the tube or tin if it is the correct colour and consistency, on a clean palette knife and scrape it across a clean ink slab. Begin rolling this out smoothly in one direction, lifting the roller at the top of the slab and starting again at the bottom. This coats the roller with the maximum ink in an even layer. Roll the ink-charged roller on to the block surface with several rolls, again in one direction, re-charging the roller if the block is large. Then use the roller to spread the ink all over the surface, rolling firmly yet lightly to avoid leaving roller marks. A new block will take several chargings and printings before an even print is achieved because some ink is absorbed at the beginning. The same tests of eye and ear apply to the film of ink on the block: spare inking will mean a dry, light, uneven result; over-inking leaves a squashed halo that thickens each mark.

While it is general practice to roll up a block with one colour overall, variations in small areas on the same block extend the number of colours that can be printed at one time.

Rollers of 2·5cm (1in) and 5cm (2in) wide are used to roll up small areas that are sufficiently isolated from each other so that the roller will not touch another colour. Even smaller areas can be touched in with a brush or tampon. The tip of a finger is equally useful.

## Oil-based blended colours

Inks rolled on to the block should create an even film, but it need not be of a single colour. The idea of blending colours reached the West via the traditional Japanese woodblock prints that flooded Europe at the end of the 19th century, yet its use outside Japan, although still in modified form, is very recent. Blending extends the number of possible colours available without the need of further blocks, and adds a softness not usually associated with relief prints.

## Oil-based roller blends

The method is extremely simple, although it needs to be planned and may take some practice to master. The most important point is to use a roller wide enough to cover the area on the block that is taking the blend. The direction of the roller should not be changed while rolling on the ink slab, nor when rolling the block. There can be no rolling of ink in all directions to disperse it.

The ink slab must also be large. Place a small amount of mixed ink of one colour on the left-hand side of the slab, and an equal amount of the second colour on the right-hand side of the slab. By moving the roller from front to back a number of times the two colours will gradually merge at the centre. Stop as soon as the ideal blend is reached, and transfer the ink to the block, maintaining strict directional rolling. Whenever the ink on the slab is exhausted, another blend must be rolled using exactly the same proportions of each colour. Getting the same blend every time over a long edition takes considerable experience.

Blends do not have to be restricted to two colours; a third colour can be added in the centre, or a single colour can range from solid at one end to transparent, colourless extender medium at the other; both are successful alternatives.

A word of warning: do not over-blend with the roller because the centre blended colour becomes dominant and the effect is murky rather than sparkling. The base colours should be the dominant ones. Use a blend sparingly so that it really contributes to the composition and is not merely an example of dexterity. Too many blends look contrived; they should be in contrast to simpler surrounding passages.

## WATER-BASED INKS

The water-based inks available in shops are designed for children, and so are made from coarsely ground, cheap pigments that are opaque. Even diluted with water or extender they are opaque and unsuitable for overprinting, and therefore of little use to artists. They can be applied with a brush only, as they dry too quickly and are of the wrong consistency for roller application.

There are, however, artists'-grade water-based inks that are very good but available only from the manufacturers or specialist printmakers' suppliers. They come in a good range of colours that are intense and mostly transparent, and they have their own extender or tinting medium. They are sold in tins, and it is advisable to transfer the ink to glass screw-topped jars as the tins tend to rust. These inks are mixed in exactly the same way as oil-based inks, and they can be applied with a roller. If the ink is to be left on the ink slab for some time it tends to become runny: the solution is to mix in a small amount of one of the gels sold for thickening water-colours enough to create an impasto.

The solvent for all these inks is water, which makes them suitable for people allergic to oil-based inks and their solvents.

### Printing with water-based inks

All the oil-based roller techniques, such as blends, small-area inking, blotting, rubbing and masking can be used. Because of the inherent oiliness of lino it must be particularly well de-greased: try acetone instead of methylated spirit, and give the surface a good scrub with soap and water. Any of the abrading methods can also be used. Lino tends to print with a rather attractive speckled texture, which is effective where very transparent colours overprint. Etched lino will print more strongly as the exposed lino core absorbs more ink. Woodblocks will print more smoothly, as the wood absorbs the water easily. The grain is revealed more if the ink is kept thin.

### OTHER EFFECTS AND GRADATED TONES

Some artists literally paint with the roller, putting ink on only selected parts of the block. Another possibility is to lift one side of the roller slightly, thus putting a variable film of ink on the block, which can give the effect of a gradated tone. Such shading of colour – to make a highlight or soften an edge – can also be achieved by sanding or abrading certain parts of the block by other means.

Once a block has been inked up it is possible to remove some ink by rubbing with a rag, blotting with tissue paper or using a finger to pick up a little ink. At the same time, small areas can be spotted in and blended with the finger.

## Blue Shade
### ARTIST Trevor Allen
**SIZE 54 × 40cm (21¼ × 15¾in)**

This key block colour linocut has a background with a two-colour blend.

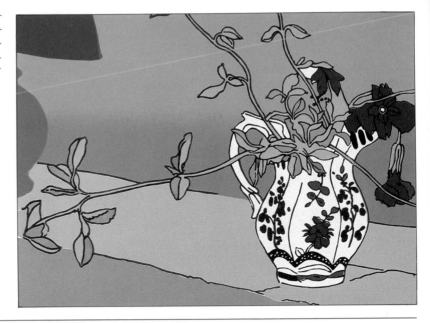

### PREPARING AN OIL-BASED BLEND

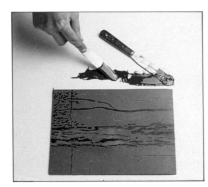

**1** Preparing for a four-colour blend. Spread the inks next to each other to the same length as the block and the roller.

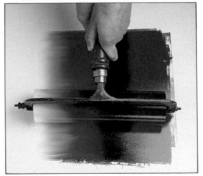

**2** Rolling out the blend. Roll in both directions, taking care not to move the roller to either side. Each colour will begin to merge with the one next to it.

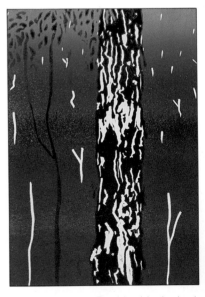

The finished print. The blend in the background emphasizes the heat generated by the bush fire. The gum tree in the foreground that has been masked-out is stark and clear and the final printing of black has accentuated the detail.

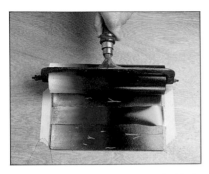

**3** Transferring the blended ink to the block. A strip of acetate is masking the area where the blend is not wanted. The ink is rolled on to the block and care is taken not to roll off the original line.

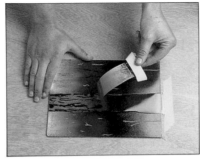

**4** Peeling off the mask from the blended block; the block is now ready to print.

Unreduced inks will print brilliantly, but the ink film will be thick and unsubtle. A more interesting surface quality will be achieved by printing intense colours in two or even three thin coats on top of each other. Best results with water-based inks are obtained by printing on good-quality waterleaf, or very lightly sized paper that is dampened (see pp.128-9 for instructions on dampening paper).

In order to maintain registration between printings, the paper must not be allowed to dry and so to shrink. It is advisable to print an edition in batches of, for example, 10 copies at a time, completing all the colours on all the sheets, before the paper is allowed to dry. This means setting aside enough time without interruption and having everything ready. The partly printed sheets are kept between sheets of damp newsprint and the whole package wrapped in polythene sheet. While printing, the package is opened at one side to allow the printing paper to be slid in and out. Ordinary newspapers can be used instead of clean newsprint, but they should be fairly old – the ink smudges for days after printing.

If the printing session is to last as long as a week, which it could well do if many colours are involved, signs of mould will appear on the paper. The way to prevent this is to mix in 10 drops of formaldehyde to every 0.5l (1 pint) dampening water. Should the package start drying out at the edges re-dampen with a fine spray (the hand sprays for plants are ideal). Where mould has already developed, it can be eradicated by drying the paper thoroughly and exposing it for two or three days in a closed space to the fumes of thymol dissolved in alcohol.

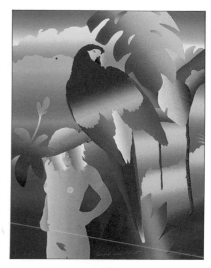

**Edward Lear's Parrot I**
**ARTIST Lynne Moore**
**SIZE 65 × 51cm (20 × 25½in)**

Card print with several areas of colour blends. The artist sometimes takes a day to ink one card print, such is the complexity of the blends. Here they are used for the parrot, figure, foliage and background.

**Painted Desert Landscape Study**
**ARTIST Fiona Hamley**
**SIZE 36 × 37cm (14 × 14½in)**

Colour lincocut with free form edges and a two-colour background blend.

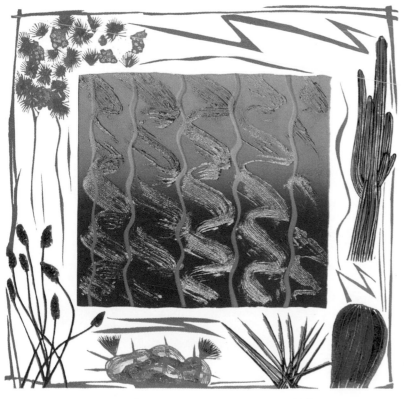

## TRADITIONAL JAPANESE WATER-BASED TECHNIQUES

Japanese techniques have always fascinated Western artists and in the early years of this century there was a flourishing school of American and British artists who made woodblock prints of Western subjects in the Japanese manner. Since 1946 many American artists have studied in Japan and Japanese artists have studied in America, with the result that modern relief prints often show a successful marriage of technique.

Maple, cherry and sycamore used to be the preferred woods in Japan, but today most woodblock prints are made on plywood and blockboard. The cutting techniques are similar to Western methods, with the exception of the manner of holding the knife. The Kentō registration system (bottom and corner stops integral with the block) is still used, and the traditional baren is the burnishing tool.

The subtleties of the finest Japanese prints are not easily matched without specialist training in the tradition, but knowledge of the basic techniques can stimulate any printmaker and lead to viable experiments.

### The baren

The baren is a circular pad held in the hand and used for burnishing the back of the print when it is laid on the inked block. Barens are imported from Japan and they can vary greatly in price and quality; beginners should invest in an inexpensive students'-quality baren. They vary slightly in size, the average being about 13cm (5in) in diameter. They are constructed in three layers: there is a coil of twisted bamboo fibre or sometimes metal, on top of which is a circular pad of laminated paper, and then the whole thing is wrapped in a piece of bamboo sheath (a leaf-like growth at the base of the leaf stem) abut 60cm (24in) long by 15cm (6in) wide. This is wrapped round and twisted to form a handle.

Barens should not get wet, but they need to be given a drop or two of camellia oil before and after printing, and it is not unusual to see a printer rub the baren on the hair or skin during printing. The bamboo sheath needs replacing after a lot of printing, so buy some spare sheaths to keep to hand. Barens have an advantage over Western burnishing tools, as they are large enough to cover a substantial area without causing hard edges during the circular motion of printing. Baren substitutes can be made from a circular piece of wood with a handle attached but they cannot mimic the subtlety that can be achieved with a baren.

### Water-based inks in Japan

Traditionally vegetable and mineral powder pigments were finely ground and mixed with gum and water. Today many Japanese printmakers use good-quality gouache paint, although they continue to prefer traditional sumi, the lovely, dense black used for calligraphy and painting.

**OTHER TECHNIQUES**

The Japanese traditionally use a form of embossing in which the damp paper is laid on an un-inked block and a small pointed stick (often the handle end of a brush) is used to form the paper into the cut work of the block. The paper will usually be left there to dry before it is peeled off.

The Japanese have always been fond of the subtle effects of mica and metallic powders. The block is printed using clear varnish or glue and powdered silver or gold (aluminium is the cheap substitute), or mica is dusted on the paper while the varnish is still tacky and the excess is blown off. Gold and silver leaf can also be applied to a light glue base, and when it is quite dry the extra foil is rubbed off.

Gouache paint is expensive, powder colour is much cheaper, though the pigments are no longer strictly traditional. Powder colour mixed with enough water to form a thick cream can be stored in airtight jars for up to a year until needed, then 10ml (2 teaspoons) gum arabic should be added to every 65ml (5fl oz) pigment. Gum arabic is made by crushing and dissolving 50g (2oz) of the dry gum in about 1l (1¾ pints) hot water. Once gum arabic has been added to the pigment it should be used quickly, but if a preservative of 1 per cent by volume of phenol (10 per cent solution) is added, it will prevent mould and the mixed pigment should last a year in a tightly closed jar. Vegetable and synthetic dyes can also be used, but will need a stronger glue such as rabbit-skin to make a workable consistency.

The pigment needs a further additive to give a little more body and stickiness so it will coat the wood easily. This is applied directly to the block and not mixed with the pigment. It is rice paste made by mixing finely ground rice (Western ground rice is too coarse, so go to a Japanese grocer) with water to make a thin cream. This is gently heated and stirred until it thickens, when it is left to cool. Make it fresh each day as it will not keep. Leaving out the rice paste leads to a spare impression and the paper tends to stick to the block.

## Paper

Japanese handmade paper is strong – due to the long fibres – and absorbent, but it is sold un-sized in Japan, and sometimes in the West too, so a light sizing may be needed to increase the strength for burnishing and dampening. Make the size by melting two table-spoons of rabbit-skin glue in one cup of water over a gentle heat while stirring. The consistency of the size should be thinner for light-weight papers and thicker for heavy papers. Use water to thin the glue and add 5ml (1 teaspoon) alum to each 1l (1¾ pints) diluted glue. The alum helps to shrink the fibres and tighten up the loose structure of Japanese papers. Use a soft, wide brush to apply the size thinly to the front of all the sheets and hang them up. Then size the other side immediately. It must be quite dry before printing. Finally trim the paper to meet the Kentō stops. The bottom left-hand corner should be a true right angle and a short strip on the bottom edge should be straight to meet the stops when the paper is turned upside-down. This is the usual position of the stops, but it can vary. The paper is then dampened.

## Inking the block

Ink is applied with a brush made usually from horsehair or badger. The length of the hair affects the flexibility, which must be just right to apply the ink, brush it out and clear excess ink off the block. Large brushes of about 5 × 10cm (2 × 4in) are used where one colour is applied over the whole block, and smaller brushes of various widths are used for details. The preparation of new brushes is important. The Japanese round off the outer edges and split each hair into two or three to increase the pigment–holding capacity.

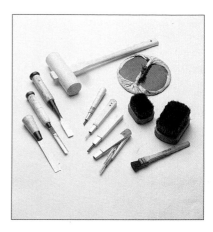

**Japanese tools**
On the top left you can see a mallet, and the flat chisel and shallow u-gouge, which are both used for clearing. Beneath is the special chisel used for cutting Kentō registration marks. Top right are a baren and three sizes of brush used for inking. In the centre at the top is a knife and below are three cutting gouges. The handle of one has been opened to show how the metal can be advanced as it wears – these tools will last a lifetime.

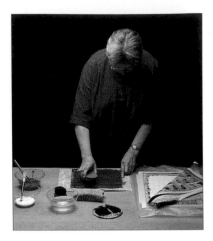

**Layout of printing area**
Place the block on a pad of dampened cloth in the centre nearest to you. Place the package of dampened paper to the left. The baren is placed beyond the block and the bowls of clean water for dampening the block; rice paste and colour are ranged on the right. Everything is within reach.

## Printing

The first step for printing each colour is to dampen the block with water with a clean flat brush kept for the purpose. Colour is applied lightly with a hog's hair-type brush and a small dab of rice paste is added. A large, square section brush is then vigorously worked all over to disperse the colour and rice paste evenly. The ink is naturally worked into the lower levels of the block too, but the paper never touches it. The dampened paper is laid on the block which rests on a pad of damp cloth to prevent warping. A sheet of thin tough paper is placed on top for protection. Considerable pressure is applied to the baren, and traditionally the block is placed on a small sloping desk at floor level so that the entire body weight of the printer can be transmitted through the arms. The baren is held in the right hand with the left hand adding pressure on top of it.

Japanese water-based inks are usually transparent and quite diluted, so that intense colours must be printed several times immediately one after another. Printing is done in batches and the paper kept damp until all colours are completed. The paper is then allowed to semi-dry, when it is pressed under weights between sheets of non-acidic white cardboard until quite dry and completely flat.

### JAPANESE PRINTING

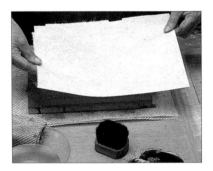

**1** Place the woodblock on a damp pad. Dampen the block with water on a pad. Brush diluted gouache on to the block.

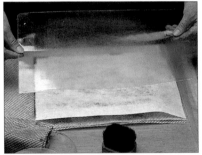

**2** Dab a few spots of rice paste on the block. Here it is being applied with the end of a brush in four or five places.

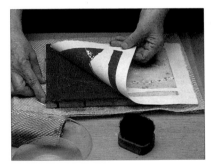

**3** Brush the colour and rice paste together. They will mix and make an even coating all over the block.

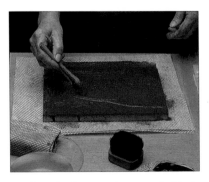

**4** Place the dampened paper on the block. Register the cut corner and bottom into the Kentō marks on the block.

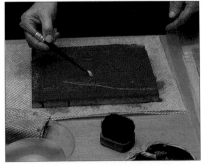

**5** Place a sheet of plastic on top. This protects the delicate paper during burnishing with the baren.

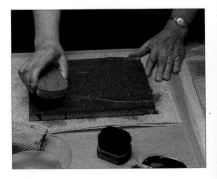

**6** The paper has been burnished all over. Peel off the print and return it to the dampened paper package.

## Bokashi – Japanese woodblock blended colour

A characteristic Japanese woodblock technique is bokashi, in which the grain of the wood is utilized: colour is carried along the grain by capillary action, but brushing will be at right angles to the grain. Most gradations use one colour only, for example, from a dark blue at the top of the sky to almost no colour at all further down. Two or more colours can be blended together, but this really is very skilful work.

The method is to dampen the wood somewhat more than for usual printing and also to dilute the rice paste slightly more. The first printing of the blend will need considerable charging of the block with colour, paste and water; subsequent impressions will need less. The brush must be the same measurement on the longest side as the bokashi area measured along the grain. A single colour blend is made by brushing a strip of colour at one end adding a dab of rice paste, and at the opposite end a dab of paste only and more water. The large brush is then moved from side to side across the grain to spread the colour and paste. After a few movements keeping a steady position, the brush is moved in a zigzag from the colour end to the non-colour end, gradually dispersing the colour in a fine, even blend. It is usual to print bokashi blends twice, one immediately after the other, to obtain the necessary soft but intense colour films.

### BOKASHI COLOUR BLENDS

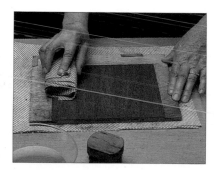

**1** Place the block on a damp pad. Wrap a block of wood in a damp cloth and use it to dampen the block.

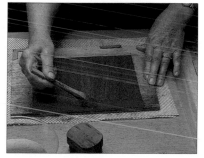
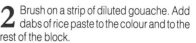

**2** Brush on a strip of diluted gouache. Add dabs of rice paste to the colour and to the rest of the block.

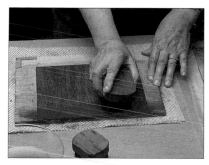

**3** Brush the block from side to side. Mix colour and rice paste and blend towards the bottom of the block.

**4** Place the paper on the blended block. Register the cut corner and bottom into the Kentō marks on the block.

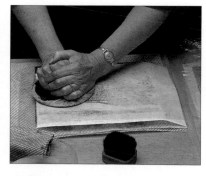

**5** Place a sheet of plastic on top. This protects the delicate paper while it is being burnished in a circular motion.

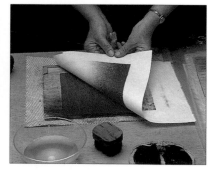

**6** Peel off the print and return it to the dampened paper package until you are ready to print the next colour.

# PAPER

Paper is an organic substance that is sensitive to humidity and temperature; it expands in damp conditions and contracts in dry ones. It is affected by the ultraviolet end of the spectrum and prolonged exposure to sunlight will gradually make it fragile and discoloured. Paper is also attacked by acid, which is present in all but the finest quality papers. Look for papers that are "acid-free" or "neutral pH" (not less than 6.5). Papers should be stored in the studio for a day or two before printing to acclimatize.

Paper is made from the fibres of plants and trees that are beaten and broken down and then mixed with water to make the pulp or furnish. Paper was entirely handmade until the late 18th century, when the first paper-making machine was invented. Most paper today is made by machine, although there has been a revival of redundant mills that are now producing handmade paper for artists once again. This in turn has led to artists experimenting with paper pulp to make their own sheets, and also to cast it in unconventional three-dimensional forms.

The ideal paper for relief printmaking is pure, strong and unsized (waterleaf). The majority of papers are sized – either glue is added to the pulp (tub sizing) or each sheet is coated at a later stage. While size makes a paper stronger, too much inhibits a good impression in relief printing. Look for waterleaf or lightly sized paper. Papers vary enormously in their capacity to absorb ink, so it is wise to start with papers recommended for relief printing, but do not hesitate to experiment with any paper that appeals to you. People feel strongly about paper just as they do about wood.

You will need two sorts of paper to begin with: newsprint and cartridge. Newsprint is useful for rough proofing, interleaving drying prints, pulling off excess ink, rough drawing and cleaning. You might also need some thick blotting paper for dampening and drying prints. You will need a smaller amount of good-quality paper for final proofing and editioning.

## Handmade paper

Each sheet is made individually by dipping a mould (a rectangular sieve edged with a removable frame called the deckle) into the vat of paper pulp. Just enough is lifted out and shaken to distribute it evenly while the water drains away. The matted fibres are already integrated sufficiently for the sheet of paper to be turned out on to a piece of felt. The pile of felts interleaving sheets of paper is pressed to squeeze out more water. Handmade paper is dried over a period of several months.

A sheet of handmade paper is distinguished by the deckle, or fringe of paper fibres, on all four sides. The fibres are randomly distributed, making for a strong sheet without direction. Handmade paper is usually available in three surface finishes: Rough, where the sheet keeps the natural fibre formation; NOT or cold-pressed, where the sheet is pressed between two boards without heat leaving a slight texture; and HP or hot-pressed, where the sheet is put between polished zinc and rolled through heated cylinders, giving a very smooth surface. Before it is sold, each sheet is inspected and those sheets with minor defects like a speck of dust or a bubble are sold separately, usually at a 10 per cent discount, under the name "retree" or labelled XX. Sheets that are more damaged, perhaps with tears or larger inclusions, are sold as "outsides" or XXX, usually at 50 per cent discount. Retree is excellent for proofing and outsides can be sorted and reduced in size for good smaller prints.

## Mould-made paper

The same high quality of raw materials is used to produce mould-made paper as furnishes handmade paper, but it is made on a very slowly revolving cylinder machine in a continuous web. It is available as a roll or as individual sheets that have a deckle on two sides (the edge of the web) and two torn or cut edges. As the paper is made very slowly there is only a slight loss of strength, although the fibres are more aligned in the direction of the cylinder rotation. It is also made in three finishes: Rough, where the still wet web is pressed on a rough felt; NOT or cold-pressed, where a slight texture is picked up from pressing on a fine felt; and HP or hot-pressed, where the sheet is smoothed between heated rollers. Mould-made papers are cheaper than handmade, they are widely available and make excellent papers for relief printmaking.

## Machine-made paper

All other papers are made on fast-running Fourdrinier machines using wood as the main raw material, and they are generally acidic, which is why newspapers and books deteriorate so quickly. Machine-made papers have short fibres set in a strong directional pattern, making them relatively weaker. Rolls of paper are cut into sheets so there are no deckles. Recently a few manufacturers have started making wood-based papers that are formulated to be acid-free, and they offer a very good alternative, much cheaper than handmade or mould-made papers.

## Furnish

The pulp mixture, or furnish, is often given in catalogues of paper manufacturers or merchants. Linen rags used to be the best source for Western handmade papers and tons of rags were collected, the buttons and waistbands cut off and the whole lot chopped up, boiled and beaten to a pulp. Today rags have too many man-made fibres mixed in so "rag" paper is now made from cotton linters (the fibres attached to cotton seed), which is very pure and used for both handmade and mould-made papers.

Other plant fibres such as sugarcane, hemp, flax, esparto grass and wood pulp are the principal ingredients for machine-made papers. Oriental papers are made from the inner bark of the kozo, mulberry and mitsumata trees, and various shrubs such as gampi. The Japanese also mix in wood pulp from Western conifers. Fine

### NAMES, SIZES AND WEIGHTS

Traditionally papers were made in a large number of different sizes, each with its special name. Handmade and mould-made papers are still made to these sizes, whereas machine-made papers conform, almost without exception, to the standard international paper sizes based on the metre.

The weight of a sheet of paper is traditionally calculated as pounds (lbs) per ream. Obviously this varies with the size of the sheet, so that the same type of paper in an imperial size (560 × 760mm, 20 × 30in) might be 140lbs per ream, and in double elephant (1020 × 690mm, 40 × 27in) 246lbs per ream.

The confusion has been resolved by paper manufacturers adopting an international measurement of grammes per square metre (gsm, $gm^2$ or $gm/m^2$). Both systems will still be found, side by side, in some catalogues. As a simple guide papers under 200gm/100lbs per ream are rather too light for printmaking and the average weight of 250-300$gm^2$ or 120-140lbs per ream (based on an imperial sheet) gives a paper of good substance for frequent handling.

## ORDERING PAPER
When buying paper for a special edition, remember to add on sufficient sheets for proofing, imperfect impressions (particularly when the block is "running-in" at the beginning) and for archival and artists' proof copies. Buying paper in single sheets is expensive. Most specialist suppliers will not sell less than a "quire", or 25 sheets; bulk paper is sold by the ream or 500 sheets.

**Commonly used sizes for printmaking**
**Royal:** 510 × 675mm, 20 × 25in
**Imperial:** 560 × 760mm, 22 × 30in
**Double elephant:** 1020 × 690mm, 40 × 27in
**Antiquarian:** 790 × 1350mm, 31 × 53in
Note that handmade papers will vary in size depending on the tradition of each mill; imperial can be 560 × 810mm, 22 × 32in.

Japanese tissue paper was always called rice paper but it is not actually made from rice. Some Oriental papers have threads, leaves, pressed flowers and coloured fragments embedded, and others are formed into lacey, decorative webs. They are very attractive on their own but difficult to use as a support for a print.

Wood pulp (called sulphite by paper manufacturers) is naturally acidic but in good quality "buffered" papers additions of calcium carbonate or magnesium carbonate neutralize the acid and they can be used for fine printmaking with confidence. Many machine-made papers have more harmful ingredients, such as optical brighteners. The paper looks very white but it will become discoloured in time. Commercial printers often have small quantities of offcuts that they will sell cheaply, or even give away when they hear of anyone still using the old hand methods of printing – there is still a fraternity amongst printers.

## Paper substitutes
Plastic "papers" have been developed for maps and documents. They are completely stable but they only accept special inks. Artists have been getting very good results on other lightweight matted fabrics such as those made for interfacing clothing. Printing on most fabrics is specialized but simple relief printing is dealt with on p.165.

## Wove and laid paper
The majority of papers when held up to the light show no distinctive mark and are called wove papers. Laid paper does show a pattern when held up to the light. It comes from the lines of wire that make up the mesh base of the mould.

## False deckles
As a deckle on all four sides of a sheet is a sign that it is handmade, many attempts are made to create false deckles. Mould-made papers have false deckles made on the machine: a wire across the web leaves a line of thinner paper fibres that is easily torn when the roll is being divided into sheets. Alternatively a water jet is used to cut the paper while it is still wet. You can make a false deckle by tearing a sheet against a straightedge or using a kitchen grater to roughen up a stack of sheets with guillotined edges. Japanese paper is difficult to tear because of the long fibres, so fold the sheet and moisten the fold – it will then tear neatly.

## Cast paper pulp
Many contemporary printmakers use paper pulp in unconventional ways. Pulp can be poured on to relief blocks, cut in lino or wood and allowed to form deeply embossed three-dimensional sheets. Any shape of sheet can be made by inventing special moulds. Dye can be added to the pulp and various coloured pulps poured on to a mould to make up a multi-coloured sheet. Pulp can be dribbled over a mould to form an open trellis-like pattern. Such cast paper can be an end in itself or it can be a base for the addition of printed work.

## PAPER TYPES AND SIZES

| Name | Size in mm | Size in inches | Furnish | Manufacture | Comments |
|---|---|---|---|---|---|
| ARCHES VELIN | many | many | 100% rag | France, mould-made | white and buff |
| ARCHES INGRES | 660 × 1020 | 26 × 40 | 75% rag | mould-made | white, cream, buff and black |
| ARCHES 88 | 560 × 760 available in rolls | 22 × 30 | 100% rag | mould-made | white |
| BASINGWERK PARCHMENT | 510 × 660 660 × 1020 | 20 × 26 26 × 40 | esparto and sulphite | Britain machine-made | smooth, used for wood engravings |
| BFK RIVES VELIN CUVÉE | many | many | 100% rag | France mould-made | white |
| BFK RIVES EXTRA RUGEUX | 560 × 790 | 22 × 31 | 75% rag | France mould-made | textured surface, white |
| CRISBROOK | 560 × 790 | 22 × 31 | 100% rag | Britain handmade | waterleaf, white |
| GOYU | 530 × 480 | 21 × 19 | mostly kozo with sulphite | Japan handmade | white |
| HERITAGE | many | many | sulphite also made with 100% rag | Britain machine-made | acid-free |
| HOSHO | 480 × 610 | 19 × 24 | part kozo | Japan handmade | waterleaf, white |
| INOMACHI NACRÉ | 560 × 760 | 22 × 30 | 100% kozo | Japan handmade | textured, pearlescent |
| KOCHI | 510 × 660 | 20 × 26 | part kozo | Japan handmade | waterleaf, natural colour |
| MULBERRY | 610 × 840 | 24 × 33 | kozo and sulphite | Japan handmade | thin, natural colour |
| OKAWARA | 915 × 1830 | 36 × 72 | kozo | Japan handmade | opaque, natural colour |
| SOMERSET | 560 × 760 | 22 × 30 | 100% rag | Britain mould-made | waterleaf, white and cream |
| SUZUKI | 915 × 1830 | 36 × 72 | kozo and sulphite | Japan handmade | textured surface white |
| T.H. SAUNDERS | many | many | 100% rag | Britain mould-made | white |
| TABLEAU | 510 × 760 rolls 1020 wide | 20 × 30 rolls 40 wide | hemp | USA machine-made | white, feels like oriental paper |
| TORINOKO | 530 × 790 | 21 × 31 | kozo and sulphite | Japan handmade | heavy, soft, absorbent |

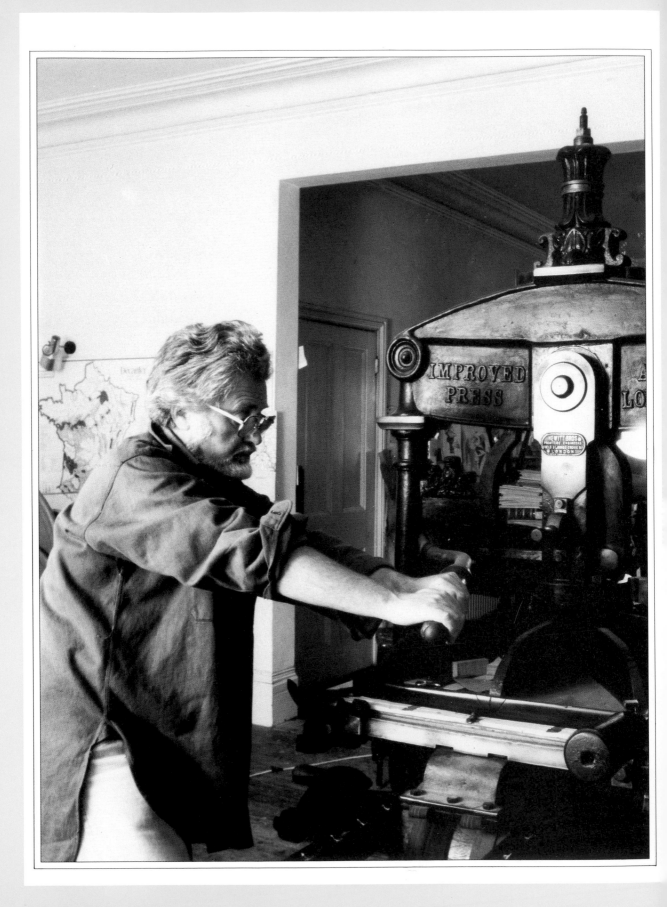

# Printing

*Printing is simply the transferring of ink from block to paper by means of pressure. Each impression follows a sequence: applying ink to the block, placing the paper in contact and applying pressure, taking off the printed sheet and putting it to dry. The sequence then begins all over again.*

*One of the joys of relief printing is that, unlike with intaglio and lithography, it is not essential to own or to have access to a printing press. Indeed many printmakers prefer the great flexibility, subtlety and individuality that non-mechanical methods offer.*

*Presses have their advantages simply because they can exert far greater pressure in a controlled way. Papers that are too hard to burnish because of their size content or surface treatment can still be used with a press. Two kinds of press are used by relief printmakers, based on the principles of the platen and the cylinder. Platen presses have a plate that is lowered on to the block resting on a similar plate called the press bed – thus pressure is exerted evenly all over. Cylinder presses have a revolving roller in place of the platen, and the bed with the block sitting on it is pushed under the cylinder, travelling from one side to the other – thus the pressure is exerted in a line across the block.*

*Presses range from the simple screw press to the beautifully decorated Columbian press, and take in converted mangles as well as modern hydraulic presses. They can print very small prints or extremely large ones. The old 19th-century cast-iron presses remain ideal for relief prints, though many modern presses made specifically for printmakers are excellent as well.*

*The actual process of printing, whatever the method used, is enormously rewarding. The coordination of all the previous work of preparing and cutting the blocks, the choice of paper and colour is realized at last. The moment of peeling off a print from the block after printing and seeing the result for the first time is nothing short of magic.*

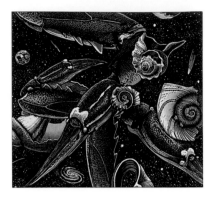

**A world apart**
**ARTIST Holly Berry**
**SIZE 36 × 33cm (14 × 13in)**

Linocut from a single block with hand colouring using watercolour paint. Hand colouring of prints was frowned upon but has recently been revived in the same way that monoprints and unique prints are now accepted as bona fide prints.

**The satin cushion**
**ARTIST Ivy Smith**
**SIZE 59 × 39.5cm (23 × 15½in)**

Colour linocut using several reduction blocks.

**Gum trees out back**
**ARTIST Edwina Ellis**
**SIZE 12.5 × 9.5cm (5 × 3¾in)**

Colour engraving done on three Delrin blocks. This tough, extruded homo-polymer is used as an alternative to end grain wood blocks. The three colours were printed in the order yellow, red and blue.

## By hand or in a press

Looking at prints may not always reveal the method of printing, but certain signs will give you some clues. If the print has large areas of flat colour evenly printed, it has almost certainly been printed in a press. If there is an overall mottled texture and the pattern of the paper fibres is obvious this indicates low pressure and probably the print has been burnished. If the ink is variable in strength where you would expect it to be even, this suggests burnishing and inconsistent hand pressure. If many colours are used in very tight registration it could be that a press would have been the easier method. A single-colour print without registration problems could be just as quickly printed by hand as in a press. A long edition makes it worth organizing the press and its pressure so that the result is always the same, but a unique or experimental print can benefit from the use of a wider number of effects during burnishing.

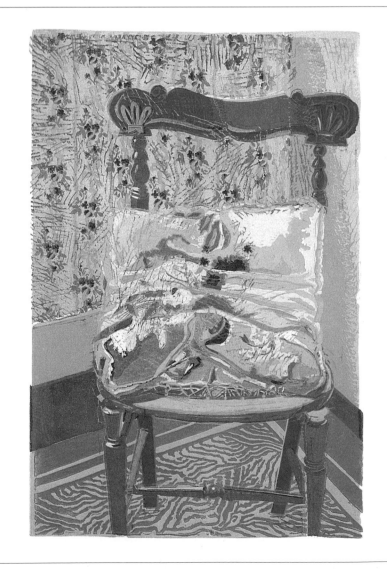

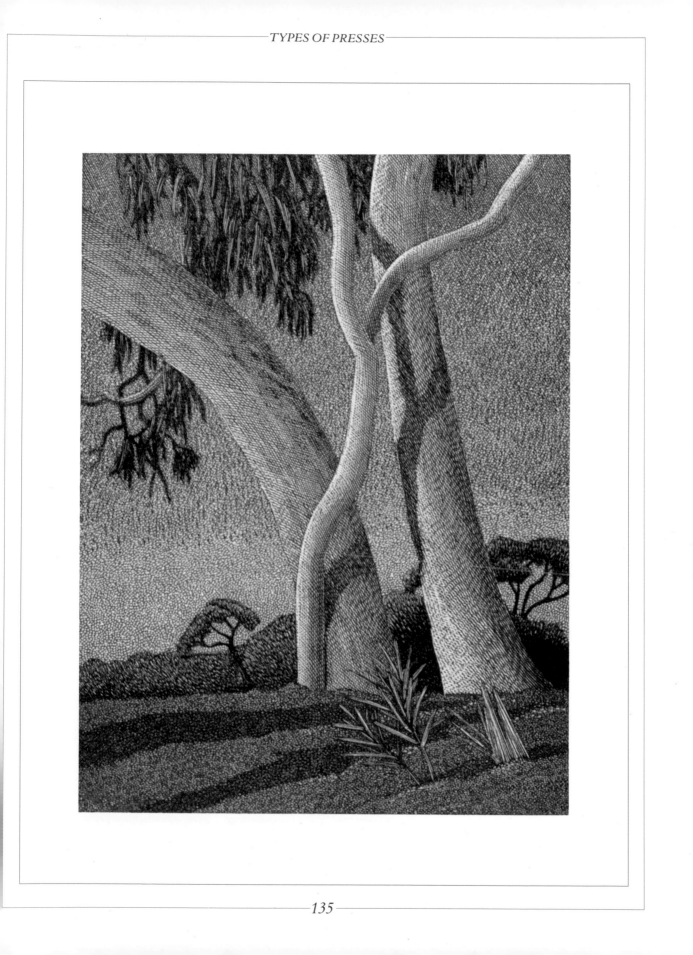

The Albion press

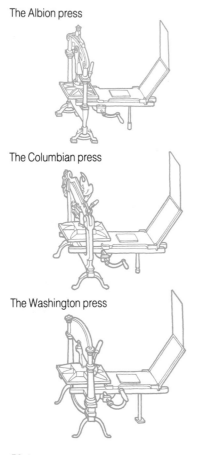

The Columbian press

The Washington press

### Platen presses
The three most common platen presses are shown above. The sequence in the printing cycle is shown in the three pictures below featuring the smallest size table-top Albion.

# PRINTING PRINCIPLES
## Platen presses

The best method of applying pressure in relief printing is undoubtedly by the vertical platen of a strong metal press. From the middle of the 15th century until the end of the 18th century presses were made of wood reinforced by pieces of metal. In 1800 Earl Stanhope invented and produced the first iron press, and in 1807 the Columbian press was invented in Philadelphia and brought to England in that same year. The Albion press was made in London from 1827, while the Washington press was developed in America. These presses were used by jobbing printers until recently and, sadly, many have been broken up for scrap metal. Occasionally one is discovered at a printer's sale, and those that have lasted are now treasured by printmakers.

The simplest platen press is the screw press, which is also called a bookbinder's press, a stand press or a nipping press. As the name suggests these presses were used to press books during binding. They are generally rather too small for printmakers. They are made of cast iron and so are very heavy, but wooden versions also exist. The sandwich of inked block and paper has to be slid between the upper platen and the base and the platen is screwed down. Ingenious printmakers have been known to make a pair of rails and a winding mechanism to shift the block in and out easily in imitation of the larger platen presses.

The Columbian, Albion and Washington presses, as well as variations such as the Atlas, share the same principle mechanism. The block and paper rest on the bed, which is rolled under the platen. A waist-high lever is pulled, which converts the horizontal pressure to the much higher vertical pressure, which lowers the platen on to the block. The action is reversed by pushing the lever back, unwinding the bed so that the print can be removed. In many ways the Albion is the superior design, since its piston-and-toggle action

## PRINTING ON A TABLE-TOP ALBION PRESS

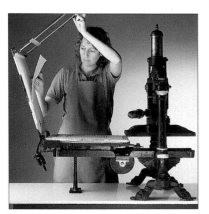
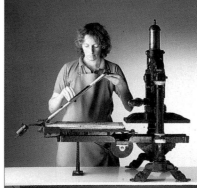
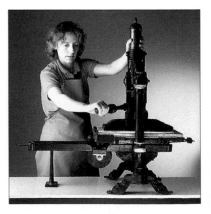

**1** The left hand raises the frisket while the other hand places the paper in the gauge pins on the tympan. The frisket is stretched with tape to keep the paper in position.

**2** The frisket and tympan are held together while they are lowered bringing the paper on to the block, which is placed on the bed of the press.

**3** The bed is rolled under the platen and the pressure handle is pulled towards the printer. This applies the pressure. The actions are reversed to release the paper.

joint gives the greatest conversion of energy, and it has four points of adjustment of pressure against the Columbian's one. The Columbian is, however, much the most beautiful and extraordinary. Its power is produced by a system of weights and counterweights decorated by snakes, dragons, foliage and rivets, and on top is an eagle that moves up and down.

## Cylinder or roller presses

The cylinder presses used by printmakers include letterpress proof presses (which were once used by jobbing printers to proof metal typesetting), intaglio and convertible presses and mangles.

Proof presses are now also obsolete in an industry that is dominated by offset lithography and photo-typesetting, but they were made in various sizes and can still be found. The block is placed on the press bed and a roller runs on a toothed track over the block. The action may be motorized or, in simpler models, a handle is used to revolve the cylinder along its track. In simpler models the ink has to be rolled on by hand, in others the inking is mechanized. In some the paper is placed on the inked block, in others the paper is laid at one end to be picked up by the cylinder and held on it as it travels over the block. These presses are finely engineered and the height of the block must be type high.

Intaglio presses are designed for printing metal plates at very high pressure – more than one would normally use in relief printing – but they are used by many printmakers. The block and paper are placed on the bed, which is moved under a revolving cylinder driven either by a hand-operated wheel or a motor. The action is reversed to bring the block back to the front again. This means pressure is applied twice, though some artists use single pressure only and take the block off the back before reversing the bed. The main problem is that relief blocks are often too thick and the press may not have sufficient adjustment to raise the cylinder. To overcome this difficulty a new sort of convertible cylinder press has been designed where the cylinder can be raised enough for most relief blocks or lowered for metal plates. Any block thicker than 3mm (⅛in) presents an obstacle to the roller, so a slender triangular strip of wood is needed to help the cylinder ride up over the block along its front and back edges.

The larger old-fashioned mangle that stands on its own feet can make a useful press. It must, however, have a means of adjusting the pressure – either a central screw acting on a leaf spring or two side screws. It is necessary to provide a bed, preferably with guide rails, and a tympan (see p.000). You will find some details about converting a mangle on p.155.

The basic principle of the cylinder press is seen in many office copying machines such as small offset litho and stencil copying machines. The older types with simpler mechanisms can be adapted by anyone with basic engineering skills. Another possibility is to cannibalize some of the parts. The cylinder and its supports can be used to build a relief press.

## CYLINDER PRESSES

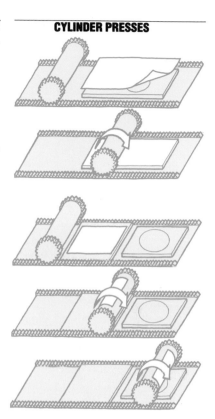

**Letterpress proof presses**
Above are shown the two basic types of letterpress proof presses. Top, the paper is placed by hand on the block and the pressure cylinder travels over. Below, on the more sophisticated press, the paper is picked up and wrapped round the travelling cylinder as it moves over the block.

## Packing

Whatever method of printing you adopt, some degree of packing will be needed. Packing consists of one or more sheets of paper or other material placed over the block and printing paper. Its main function is to protect the printing paper from the source of pressure, but it also serves to make up any finer differences in height between the platen or cylinder and slight irregularities on the block.

When burnishing, the printing paper would receive a great deal of rubbing if there was not a protective sheet placed over it. Fine papers are easily rubbed away, and even strong papers need a thin but tough sheet to protect them from the burnishing tool.

### STRETCHING THE TYMPAN WITH PAPER

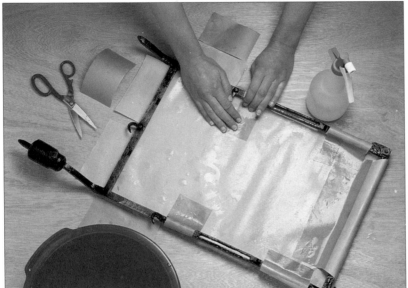

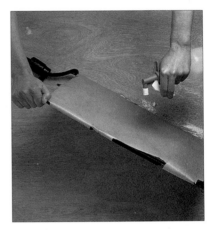

**2** Dampen the loosely stretched tympan. Spray all over evenly and leave to dry. The paper will contract and become drum tight. Repeat for the other half of the tympan frame.

**1** Cut strong brown paper to size and dampen it. Cut pieces of strong gummed strip (parcel tape) to attach the tympan paper to the metal frame by wrapping right round it.

### MAKING A PACKING PAD

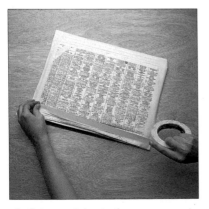

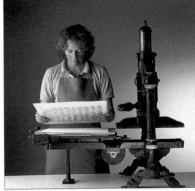

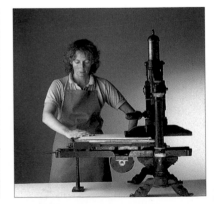

**1** Cut several sheets of newspaper and a slightly larger piece of card and tape together.

**2** Place the packing soft (newspaper) side down on the block. Note the tympan has been removed on this press.

**3** Without a tympan the bed with the block and packing must be guided carefully under the platen for printing.

Platen presses need a pad of several sheets of paper placed on top of the block and printing paper to protect the printing paper from the platen. The packing is also used to increase or decrease the pressure by adding or subtracting sheets from the packing. Some platen presses have a hinged flap made of a metal frame in two interlinking sections called a tympan. Each section is covered in stretched fabric or strong paper and the packing is placed between them. They lock together and form a consistent pad that is lowered on to the block and printing paper before the bed is rolled under the platen. The tympan was devised in an attempt to semi-mechanize packing.

You will decide while proofing what is the ideal pressure for each particular block and either fit the packing into the tympan or tape loose sheets together so they do not get lost. There may be, however, some small areas on a block that still print too light. There are two ways of adding small pieces of packing to correct these faults. Either take thin paper and tear it to the shape of the light area – do not cut it as it leaves a hard edge if the block is made of thin material. Or use more than one patch rather than a single layer. You can paste this "make-ready", as it is called, under the block or on to the packing.

Letterpress proof presses have thin packing attached to the cylinder, but make-ready goes under the block. With intaglio and convertible cylinder presses felt blankets are used instead of paper packing, but as they are soft you might need to put one sheet of stiff paper or card over the printing paper and under the felts. Make-ready must go under the block.

Converted mangles with a metal sheet tympan will need some packing between the tympan and the printing paper. Make-ready must go under the block.

The hardness or softness of packing can be varied to give different effects. Hard packing will give a very crisp impression whereas soft packing, which could include a sheet of felt or foam, will partially fill the cut lines in the block and give a slightly embossed effect.

### PACKING THE TYMPAN

This tympan has been covered in linen (book cloth), which lasts longer than paper. The packing of several sheets of newspaper is placed between the two sections of the tympan. The frames are then clipped together firmly.

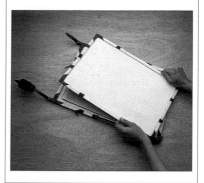

## TYPES OF PACKING AND MAKEREADY

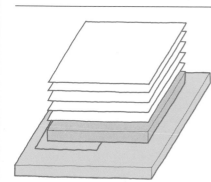

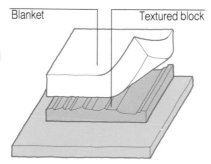

Blanket — Textured block

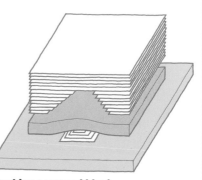

### Packing and makeready
Packing is made of several sheets of paper placed on top of the block to give even pressure. Makeready is made of several sheets of variable size placed under the block to correct small areas of unevenness.

### Soft packing
Felt blanket or foam sheet will give a very soft packing for use when the block is very fragile or when deep embossing is required. Several sheets of soft blotting paper provide a slightly more resilient packing.

### Packing a warped block
When a warped block must be printed in a press some remedial packing is essential to even out the pressure and prevent damage to the press. Cut the lower packing sheets to the profile of the block surface.

## PENCIL LINE REGISTRATION

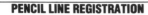

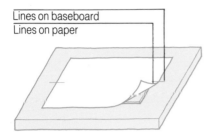

Lines on baseboard
Lines on paper

### Simple pencil lines
Two lines are marked on the baseboard on the two short sides. Matching pencil lines are marked on the back of the sheets of paper. The lines are matched.

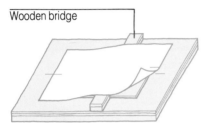

Wooden bridge

### Gladys McAvoy's method
To make aligning the pencil marks easier this artist uses a simple wooden bridge to support the paper while matching the lines; the bridge is then slid out.

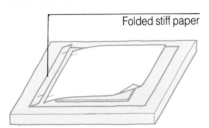

Folded stiff paper

### Walter Hoyle's method
A fold of stiff paper is taped to the left side of the bed. Two pencil lines are marked on it and matched with lines on the back of the paper.

# REGISTRATION

Every multi-coloured print necessitates a system of registering the blocks in the correct position so the colours fit together. If each colour block is an identical rectangular shape and size it is easier than using blocks of differing shapes. Very precise registration needs careful measurement of all the elements, but loose fitting areas of colour might well be registered by eye alone.

## Eye registration
Place the sheet of printing paper face up. Ink the block and turn it upside-down, holding it over the paper. Keep your eyes central by bending over it and sight the block position in relationship with the paper edges. Lower the block and flip the block and paper over to the usual position for printing. The tackiness of the ink should hold the paper in place. This method is widely used for single block prints but is also used for multi-block prints where the registration is not tight.

## Pencil line registration
This simple system is widely used and considered accurate by many professional printmakers. Mark a sheet of paper that will sit on the press bed or burnishing table with an outline of the printing paper and the position of the block within. Mark two pencil lines in the centre of the short sides from the paper edge out at right angles. Mark two pencil lines on the back of every sheet of printing paper to correspond. The paper is lowered and the lines matched by eye.

## Needle registration
Two needles can be used to aid simple eye registration though this method needs some dexterity and is more difficult with large sheets of paper. A needle is held between each thumb and forefinger and pierced through the back of the sheet of paper on opposite sides while the sheet is held with the other fingers. The needles are pierced through in diagonal corners or on opposite short sides. The sheet is lowered while engaging one needle in a prearranged hole in the block or in a piece of lino, wood or metal fixed in the margin area. The second hole is located with the other needle and the whole sheet lowered. Needle holes can be made in all the sheets in advance or needle points can be fixed upside-down in the holes of the first block

### REGISTERING DECKLE-EDGED PAPER
The feathery deckle on hand-made and mould-made paper prevents accurate butting-up to registration stops. The deckles can be trimmed right off on the lower long and one short (see right) or short strips can be trimmed just where the stops meet the paper, or the same places can be covered with masking tape.

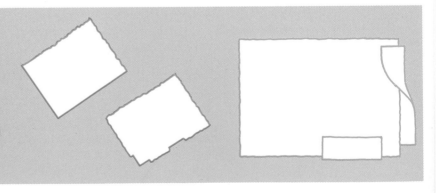

to pierce all the sheets at the first printing. Note that needle holes in a lino or soft wood block can easily become enlarged while printing.

## Cross and triangle registration

Cut a small cross in two opposite margins of the printing paper with a sharp knife. Then cut through from one end of the cross to the next cross end and take out the small triangle of paper; do the same to the opposite triangle. Mark two identical crosses on a sheet of paper that will rest on the press bed or burnishing table. The cut-out triangles should match up with the crosses and are registered by eye. This method is all right for proofing but ruins a final print, so it must be framed with a window mount to hide the crosses.

## Base sheet registration

In the most common system, suitable for rectangular or free form blocks, a sheet of paper or card is marked out with the position of the block and the paper. This sheet is taped to the press bed or to the burnishing table. The base sheet should be larger than the printing paper. You can glue two strips of card along the marked printing paper edges at right angles to make it easier to locate the paper in position. If your paper has deckle edges these will have to be trimmed square to fit or covered with masking tape temporarily. The position of the blocks is also marked on the sheet and similar card stops can be glued in place whether the blocks are identical rectangles or free-form shapes.

Some printmakers cut a base board from thicker board in which they cut out holes for each block. When the blocks are dropped into their respective holes they are held quite firm.

## Modified Kentō registration

The use of traditional Kentō, where the paper guide stops are carved as part of the woodblock, is described on pp.124–5. Western printmakers have developed the same idea to allow for much wider margins. Japanese prints did not need wide margins because they were mounted on to scrolls or into albums.

A base sheet is used to give more space round the image. Mark out the paper size on the base sheet and glue a short strip of card along one long edge and a short right angle into one corner. Remember that you always place a block centrally on a press bed, with its longest dimension parallel to the longest sides of the bed, and that it is easier to hold a sheet of paper by its short sides. It follows that the paper stops are on the bottom edge and in either the left- or right-hand bottom corner. If you are left-handed you might find it more natural to place the sheet into a right-bottom corner. The motion of handling the sheet on and off again after printing should be comfortable. Similar stops are glued on to guide the block if it is removed to the inking table between impressions. Other printmakers prefer to make the base sheet from something more substantial, such as blockboard, and to nail the block in position so it cannot move. Kentō is a good, basic system.

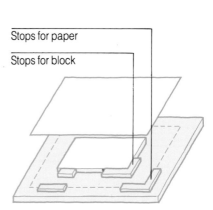

**Modified Kentō method**
Stops for the block and paper are glued to a base sheet or board. Stops can be made from strips of thick card, lino or wood but they should be the same thickness as the block material.

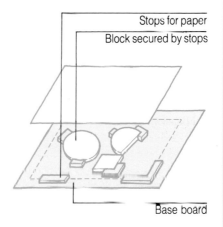

**Registering free form blocks**
Irregularly shaped blocks can also be given stops to ensure they are placed accurately each time on the base – if the fit is tight they can be dropped in from above.

## Misregistration

Most problems of misregistration will be discovered during proofing. The commonest fault is that the size of the blocks is slightly inaccurate from the beginning. If one of a series of rectangular blocks is fractionally out it will show up all too obviously when printed. If a free-form block is slightly too small a margin will appear round the colour, which is much worse than the block being slightly oversized. Another fault arises from inaccurate tracing, transferring or offsetting for each new block.

The other major fault that appears during proofing and, unfortunately, during editioning, is due to the fact that the block was not placed on the press bed or burnishing table accurately, or the paper was not fitted to the registration system well. Misregistering can also happen when you lose control of the paper just as it touches the inked block so that it smudges. The same thing can happen when lifting the sheet off after printing. Keep one hand to hold the paper down on the block so it does not shift, while gently raising the other side. Do not snatch the paper off but peel it slowly.

An easy way to find out what has gone wrong is to take a pull of each block on to sheets of acetate and mark the position of the registration system. When the pulls are dry lay one over the other and you should be able to see where the fault lies. It may mean trimming the edges of one rectangular block or re-cutting part of the design to fit. It may mean cutting out part of the block and fitting a new piece of lino or wood (see "Correcting Techniques", p.91). Occasionally there is no easy remedy but to throw out one block and cut it again. The fault may lie in the registration system. Are the guide lines on the base sheet accurate? If not, re-draw them. Are the Kentō stops correctly cut on the block? If not, cut the stops out more or insert slips of wood if they were over-cut in the first place. As modified Kentō stops are made from strips of card or similar material they are easy to renew. Other systems using needles, studs, punched holes, etc. should be checked for accuracy and reset. But do not forget to check the paper. Are the deckles trimmed correctly or covered with tape, concealing the fact that a corner is not a true right angle?

### PICASSO'S INTRODUCTION TO LINOCUTTING

When Picasso left Paris to live in the South of France he intended to continue to make lithographs long distance. The Parisian Atélier Mourlot sent prepared litho plates to Vallauris, where Picasso drew on them. He put them on a train to Paris and eventually proofs were sent back to him. He was never a patient man and frequently drew six plates in a day only to be frustrated by the long delay in seeing the results of what he had drawn. A solution to this impossible undertaking came from an unexpected source. The local bullring had been closed for many years and in 1952 when it was about to reopen a local printer called Arnerá asked Picasso to do a linocut for a poster. He often used lino to print short runs of posters.

He gave Picasso a proof the very next day. Picasso did several posters and in 1958 did his first linocut, in the form of a print rather than a poster. This is variously known in English as *Bust of a Woman, Portrait of a Girl* and *Seated Woman*: whichever the translation, the image is after Cranach; Picasso was once again indulging in re-working a well known work by another artist.

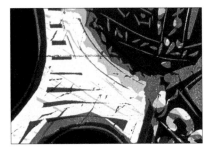

Picasso cut six separate blocks, one for each colour in the usual way. When they were printed on top of each other the registration was very unsatisfactory. Picasso found it difficult to cut blocks with the necessary accuracy and he nearly abandoned lino altogether. Arnerá introduced him to the reduction method, which he used as an economy measure in his print shop and, unexpectedly, Picasso found it a sympathetic way of working and, thereafter, he used no other. There is no doubt that the risky element of cutting away parts of the block before seeing the final result appealed to Picasso.

In 1959 he did seven prints of the bullring, then 24 prints of Bacchantes and women in various poses and then nine more bullfighting scenes – all in the same year. In 1962 he did more linocuts but came to a halt the next year. During this amazing period of creativity, 1952-63, starting when he was already 77 years old, he did 24 posters, and 107 linocuts.

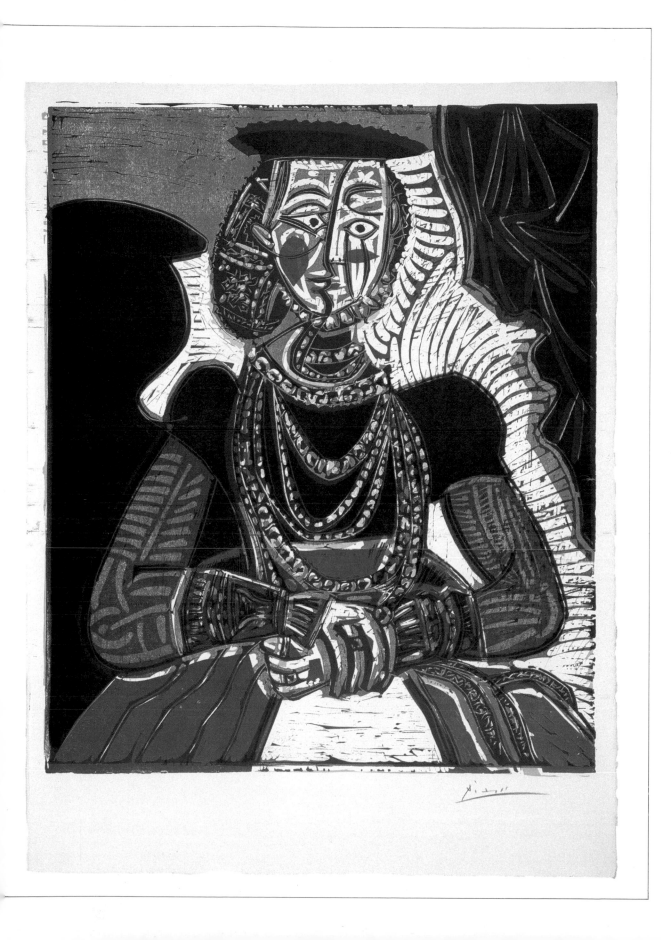

### Temporarily fixed studs and holes

Two studs punched out of metal or plastic are taped to the baseboard or press bed. Two tabs, each with a hole, are taped with masking tape on to the back of the paper. The holes locate and fit on to the studs.

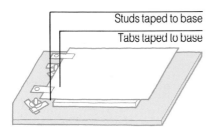

Studs taped to base
Tabs taped to base

## Fixed paper registration

Letterpress proof presses have a series of studs across one end of the press. Holes are punched along one short side of the printing paper which fit on to the studs. Each block is accurately fixed to the press bed by filling the surrounding space with blocks of wood and metal called "furniture". Thus the paper will always be in the same relationship to the block. The disadvantage is that the print will have a row of unsightly holes that will have to be trimmed away – allow for this when positioning the margins. A similar system on the same sort of presses has a long clamp instead of studs and holes.

Studs and clamps are integral to most letterpress proof presses, but equivalents can easily be constructed for use on the burnishing table, platen or cylinder presses. One method is to take a strip of strong card or thin wood, the same length as the short side of the printing paper, and to push drawing pins along its length. Push them right through, turn the strip over and tape it to the press bed or burnishing table. The paper is impaled on the points, always in the same place.

Another system involves two small tabs made out of thin plastic, each with a hole punched in the centre. These are fixed with masking tape to the back of the sheet on one short side, so they protrude just enough for the hole to locate the punchings taped to the press bed. When printing is completed the tabs are removed without damaging the paper. It follows that you need twice as many tabs as sheets of printing paper in your edition.

A slight modification involves a length of stiff paper, as long as the short side of the printing paper. Fold the strip in half lengthways and tape it to the left-hand side of the press bed or burnishing table. Mark two pencil lines on the top at right angles to the long edge about one-quarter and three-quarters of the way along. The printing paper is inserted into the registration fold and two pencil marks, previously put on the back of each sheet of printing paper, will line up.

## PAPER REGISTRATION METHODS

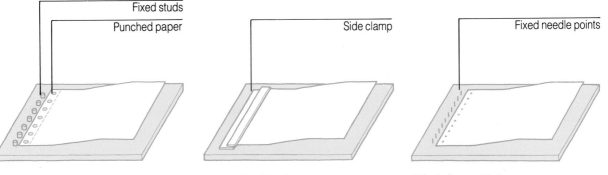

Fixed studs
Punched paper

Side clamp

Fixed needle points

### Fixed studs and holes

Letterpress proof presses often have integral stud registration. Holes to fit the studs must be punched in the paper.

### Automatic side clamps

Some proof presses have a fixed side clamp into which the short side of the paper is inserted. The clamp is then tightened.

### Fixed pins and holes

A row of needle points or upside-down drawing pins is fixed to the baseboard. The sheet of paper is impaled, making holes.

## Frisket registration

Albion, Columbian and Washington presses usually have a frisket attachment. This is a metal frame hinged on to the tympan, which holds the paper in the correct position. It must be used in conjunction with firmly fixed blocks, either sitting into a right angle guide taped to the bed, or using furniture in the same way as with the letterpress proof presses. Using a frisket is described in detail below.

### FRISKET REGISTRATION

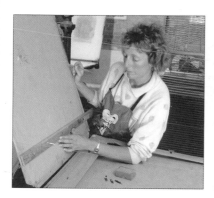

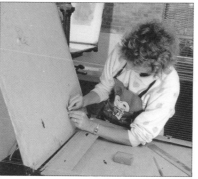

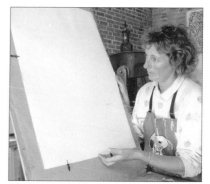

**1** Measure the tympan to determine the position of the paper and mark the position of the gauge pins to hold the paper.

**2** Insert two gauge pins at the bottom and one or more at the side depending on the size of the paper. Make sure the pins are firm.

**3** Place the paper into the gauge pins at the bottom and side. The tympan leans slightly backwards so the paper stays in place.

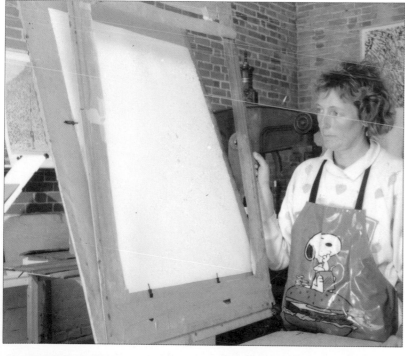

**4** The hinged frisket has a hole cut in the cover to allow the paper to make contact with the block on the bed but the edges of the frisket prevent the paper from falling out as it is lowered. This frisket is hinged at the bottom, others are hinged from the top.

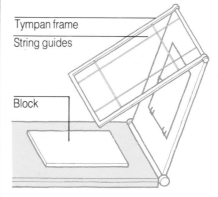

Tympan frame
String guides
Block

### String method of holding paper
The frisket need not be covered with paper with a hole cut out. You can stretch four pieces of string or flat tape across. The object is to hold the paper but give access to the area to be printed.

### Gauge pins
These small metal pins have two lower spikes that dig into the covering of the tympan and two upper spikes or fingers that hold the paper.

# PRINTING WITHOUT A PRESS

Pressure can be applied by burnishing with a hand–held object such as a wooden spoon, a Japanese baren, a smooth stone or any other object of suitable shape. Large prints can be very well printed by foot pressure, and ingenious printmakers have been known to use garden rollers, cars or even road rollers. Very delicate surfaces that would break in a press can still be printed by using a hand-held roller.

## Burnishing

Roll the block with ink and lay the printing paper on top. Place a sheet of smooth, hard paper such as glassine on top and rub all over with the burnishing tool in a circular motion. Do not forget the corners. A sprinkling of talcum powder will allow the burnisher to move easily. Use weights (old kitchen weights or even a brick) to keep the papers in place. You can check the progress from time to time, remembering that burnishing can be varied deliberately. By changing the pressure you can go from a very soft impression to a hard one within a small area. You can also add more ink to parts of the block as long as the paper is held firmly in place by weights while you peel it off the area to be re-inked.

Wooden spoons have long been the favourite Western burnisher and after they have been used for some time the wood becomes very smooth. Press on the bowl with one hand while you guide the

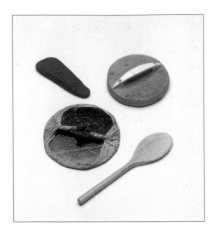

## Tools for burnishing

The humble wooden spoon from the kitchen makes an excellent burnishing tool especially once it has become smooth and polished with use. The baren is a purpose-made tool for burnishing that comes from Japan and is now used world-wide by printmakers. Many other objects can be used such as a well-worn flat stone or a smooth paper knife.

## BURNISHING METHODS OR TECHNIQUES

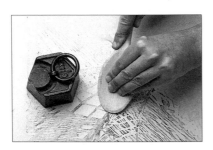

**1** Burnishing with a wooden spoon. Pressure is applied to the bowl of the spoon. You can see the image appearing through the back of this thin Japanese paper.

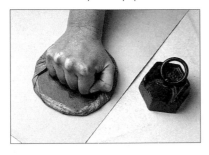

**2** Burnishing with a baren. All the weight of the body can be put on the baren while moving it in a circular motion. Do not forget to work the corners.

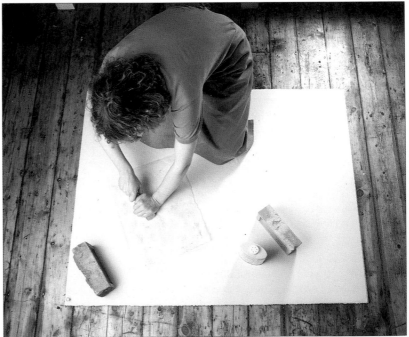

**3** Burnishing a large linocut. Katie Clemson is using an oriental food crusher to work over the print in a consistent way. A sheet of smooth paper is placed over the printing paper to protect it and to keep the back of the print clean as she moves over it. Bricks are used as weights and talcum powder is sprinkled as a lubrication.

direction with the other hand on the handle. The use of the baren is described on p.124. Printmakers often devise their own substitute or use a well-worn stone that fits the hand comfortably.

## Foot pressure

Make a pad of newspapers on the floor. Place the inked block and printing paper on the pad. Put another sheet of strong smooth paper on top, add a few more sheets of newspaper and start walking all over. Use weights if there is any chance of the printing paper moving. Bare feet are more sensitive, but flat rubber-soled shoes can be worn. Check progress as with hand burnishing and re-ink if necessary.

---

### USING FOOT PRESSURE

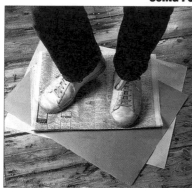

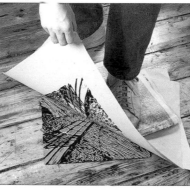

**1** Applying foot pressure. Use two or more sheets of protective paper and a pad of newspaper to prevent damage. Tread evenly.

**2** Check the print from time to time. Some areas may need more pressure or more inking. Use weights to keep the paper in position.

## Large rollers

Printing with a large heavy roller such as a garden roller needs a different technique. As the roller touches the block it tends to push it away rather than roll over it, so keep the block thickness to lino or plywood. It helps to place the block and paper sandwich between two much larger sheets of hardboard or similar board. Car wheels are narrow so the car must be driven backwards and forwards many times to cover the area to be printed – it is quite difficult to get even pressure, but perhaps your design calls for random pressure.

## Transfer printing

A delicate surface such as driftwood, expanded polystyrene, balsa wood or botanical specimens can be inked using a roller, dolly or brush in the usual way. Then take a clean, soft roller and take it over the block to pick up the ink. Immediately roll this transfer on to the printing paper. The roller must be of a large enough diameter to take the transfer in only one revolution: a 7.5cm (3in) long block needs at least a 7.5cm (3in) circumference roller, which should of course be as wide as the inked area. The roller must be cleaned between impressions. Very tight registration on to the paper is difficult.

### Using large rollers

Very large prints can be printed using a garden roller, a farm roller, a road roller or even a car. Use thin block material such as lino or plywood. Place the inked block and paper between two larger boards made of plywood, block- or chipboard to protect them. Place triangular fillets of wood in front and behind the sandwich to help the roller ride up over the top board and off again without pushing it away. The picture below shows Katie Clemson at the controls of a road roller while printing a very large print.

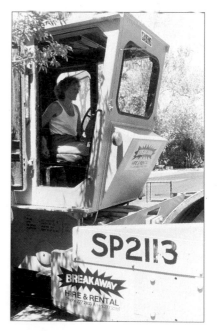

# PRESSES
## Screw and hydraulic presses

These presses work on the same principle, though the old-fashioned screw presses are small, and gigantic hydraulic presses are now being made specially for printmakers that generate up to 250 tons pressure per square inch (for comparison, a normal intaglio press generates 5 tons). In both cases the sandwich of block and printing paper is placed on the bed of the press and the platen is lowered. The large screw on top of the screw press is turned by hand until sufficient pressure is applied – count the number of turns to approximate the same pressure each time. The platen on a hydraulic press is lowered by the compression of oil in a cylinder linked to the platen. The mechanical advantage is such that a very high pressure can be generated and repeated accurately each time.

Cast iron screw presses are heavy but small enough to be moved by one person. Hydraulic presses are made in various sizes and are very heavy due to their robust construction. They should be moved, installed and serviced by a printer's engineer.

### USING A SCREW PRESS

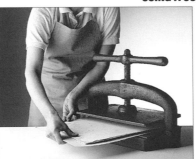 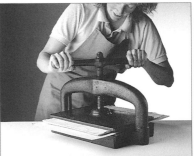

**1** Use a baseboard to support the block, paper and packing. Slide the sandwich under the centre of the screw press platen.

**2** Pressure is applied by turning the arms of the screw until they will turn no more. Reverse the screw and draw out the sandwich with care.

## Albion, Columbian and Washington presses

These presses share many features. The press bed is rolled out from beneath the platen so the block can be inked and the paper placed in position, after which it is returned under the platen. The platen is lowered and raised by operating a handle connected to the special toggle action joint that is their special feature.

The Columbian is the largest in size, though they are all heavy enough to need strong floors as they can weigh up to 2 tons. They should be moved and installed by a printer's engineer. They are made of cast iron, which will shatter if dropped or knocked badly. For this reason the bed should be rolled to and fro without force and the pressure lever should not be allowed to fall back out of the hand (children are usually too small to control this lever). There is little to go wrong with these presses beyond renewing the webbing that drives the bed or re-covering the tympan and keeping the rails greased.

---

**SIZES OF PLATEN PRESSES**
These are based on the maximum size of paper that can be printed:
Double crown: 88 x 57cm (34 × 22½ in)
Double demy: 91.5 × 58.4cm (38 × 23 in)
Double royal: 102 × 63cm (40 × 25 in)
These Albion, Columbian and Washington presses are no longer made but the table-top size Albion, which prints a maximum paper size 38 × 25.4cm (15 × 10 in) is now being made again as an accurate replica.

## THE ALBION PRESS

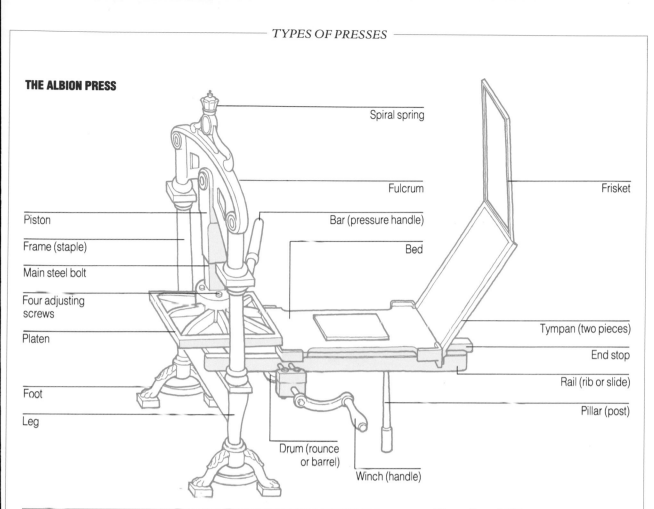

Spiral spring

Fulcrum

Piston

Bar (pressure handle)

Frame (staple)

Bed

Main steel bolt

Four adjusting
screws

Platen

Frisket

Tympan (two pieces)

End stop

Rail (rib or slide)

Pillar (post)

Foot

Leg

Drum (rounce
or barrel)

Winch (handle)

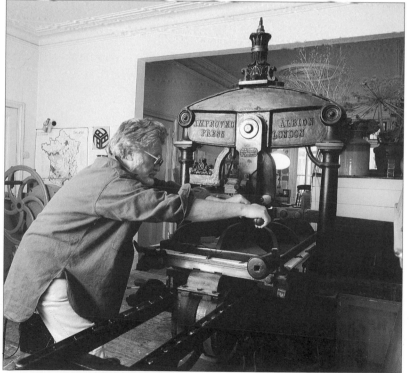

### The action of Albion press

The block is placed on the bed of the press in a central position. If the block has to be placed off-centre then equal height pieces of wood must be placed opposite to balance the pressure. Some printmakers fix the block to the bed by means of wooden furniture and quoins (wedges that expand and contract); the block is then inked in place. Alternatively the block is not fixed but removed for inking and replaced. The paper may be laid on the block using one of the many registration systems, or the paper is inserted into the gauge pins on the tympan, the frisket is lowered to secure the paper, and the tympan and frisket together are lowered on to the block. Correct packing is either inserted into the tympan or is laid by hand on the paper. The bed is then rolled under the platen and the bar or pressure lever is pulled towards the printer. The process is reversed and the print peeled off. The picture left shows James Burr mid-pull. Columbians and Washingtons have similiar actions.

## THE COLUMBIAN PRESS

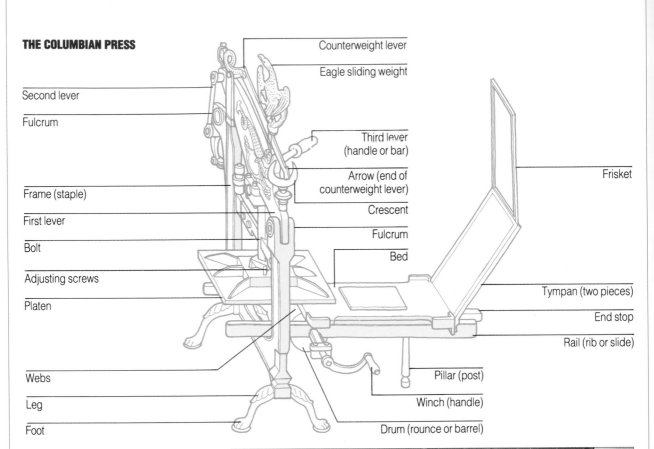

Counterweight lever

Eagle sliding weight

Second lever

Fulcrum

Third lever (handle or bar)

Arrow (end of counterweight lever)

Crescent

Frisket

Frame (staple)

First lever

Bolt

Fulcrum

Adjusting screws

Bed

Platen

Tympan (two pieces)

End stop

Rail (rib or slide)

Webs

Leg

Pillar (post)

Winch (handle)

Foot

Drum (rounce or barrel)

### The development of Columbian and Albion presses

George Clymer (1754-1834) of Philadelphia invented the first iron press in the New World in 1807. He called it the Columbian Press and charged 400 dollars for it. The press became an immediate success in America and it was soon imported into Britain where it superseded Earl Stanhope's Iron Press.

R. W. Cope started manufacturing the Columbian Press in England as it was very highly regarded for printing wood engravings. Soon after, Cope invented the Albion Press, which was lighter in weight and lighter to pull. It had more points of adjustment but still gave ample pressure. A bank of ten Albion presses was used to print *The Times* newspaper. The Albion was also used by William Morris in the 1890s to print his finest books. Columbian and Albion presses are treasured by printmakers today.

### Pulling a Columbian press

The Columbian needs rather more pulling than the Albion and if a really strong impression is needed the printer will have to brace him or herself, in order to utilize the full body weight when pulling the bar; see the picture right.

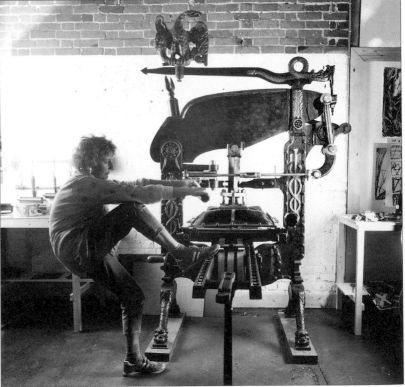

## CYLINDER PRESSES

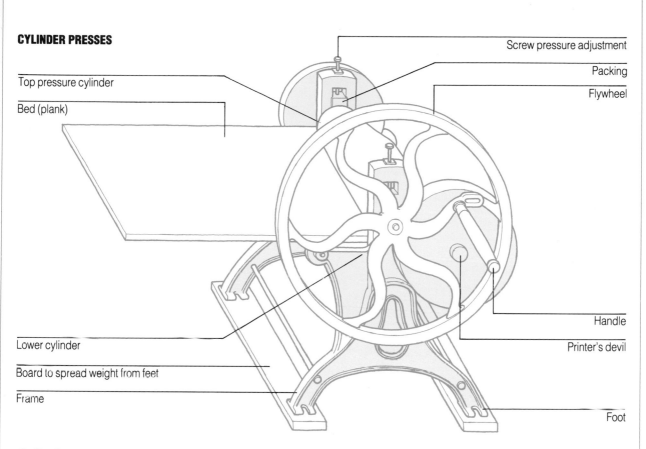

Top pressure cylinder

Bed (plank)

Screw pressure adjustment

Packing

Flywheel

Lower cylinder

Board to spread weight from feet

Frame

Handle

Printer's devil

Foot

## Cylinder presses

These presses are divided into those where one cylinder travels along a track rolling over the block and printing paper, and those where two rollers remain in a fixed position and the block and paper move between them.

Letterpress proof presses are single cylinder and generally not very large, though they vary from those designed to proof a galley (a tray holding metal type), which are either 30.5 × 20.5cm (12 × 8in) (quarto galley) or 61 × 18cm (24 × 7in) (slip galley), to large presses that were used to proof assemblages of many pages of type and illustrations together. There is little adjustment of height or pressure so the block should be type high and of an even material. The larger models are heavy and well engineered, so they should be moved and installed by printers' engineers, as should all large presses.

Intaglio, convertible intaglio/relief presses and converted mangles are all examples of double cylinder presses. Intaglio presses, also called copperplate or etching presses, are available in many sizes, from small table-top models to large floor-standing presses with rollers wide enough to print a sheet 183 × 91.5cm (72 × 36in) or even larger.

Intaglio presses with upper rollers that can be raised sufficiently to take lino or wood blocks can be used for both intaglio and relief printing. These presses are relatively modern and are usually equipped with micrometric vernier scales for accurate pressure

### Intaglio presses

Of all the cylinder presses, the printmaker is likely to have access to an intaglio press. Every teaching establishment where printmaking is taught will have an intaglio press. It may be an old-fashioned one or one made very recently from new materials that make it much lighter in weight, and it will probably be motorized, which means back sufferers can use it with ease.

### Using an intaglio press

The inked block is placed on the bed and the paper is placed on top. Two or three felt blankets are placed over the paper as packing. The bed is cranked between the upper and lower cylinders and then reversed to the starting position.

## Letterpress proof presses

These presses were designed to be used by commercial printers to proof type and metal blocks of a standard height and they do not have much adjustment. They vary from make to make but the basic principle is the same: the block is placed on the bed and fixed in position with furniture and quoins. It must be inked while in place. The paper is either placed on the block by hand or on some presses the paper is picked up mechanically and wrapped round the impression cylinder as it is cranked over the fixed bed and back again.

control. Very small presses of this type are not made and the average sized one prints paper 122 × 61cm (48 × 24in).

Mangles with rollers smaller than 46cm (18in) wide are not usually strongly made; the ideal kind worth converting into a printing press should have rollers 61cm (24in) wide. The frame should be undamaged and the screw adjustments intact. If the wooden rollers are slightly damaged or worn in the centre they should be skimmed on a woodworker's lathe down to the good wood. If the damage is greater more wood should be skimmed off and a heavy plastic or metal sleeve slid on. A bed must be made from composition board or ply to run between supporting rails, and you may like to add a brass sheet or plastic tympan. If this seems a great deal of work, remember that a converted mangle could cost you one-twentieth of the price of a new intaglio press.

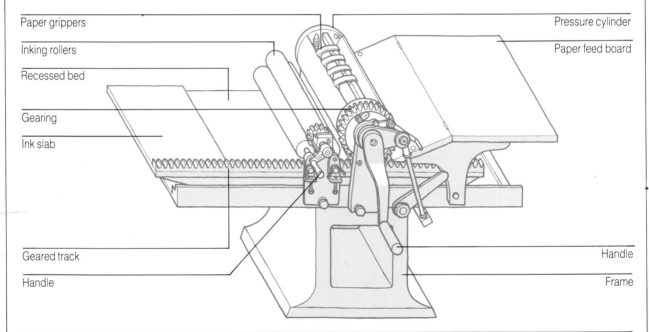

Paper grippers · Pressure cylinder
Inking rollers · Paper feed board
Recessed bed
Gearing
Ink slab
Geared track · Handle
Handle · Frame

## USING A PROOFING PRESS

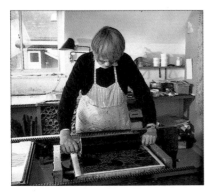

**1** The block is fixed in position on the bed of the press. Ink is rolled on the block by hand.

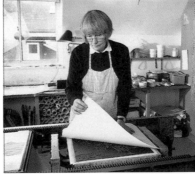

**2** The paper is placed on the inked block by hand or using a simple registration system.

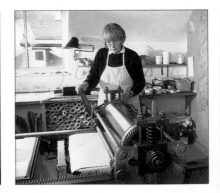

**3** The cylinder is cranked by a handle which rolls it over the block and paper to apply pressure.

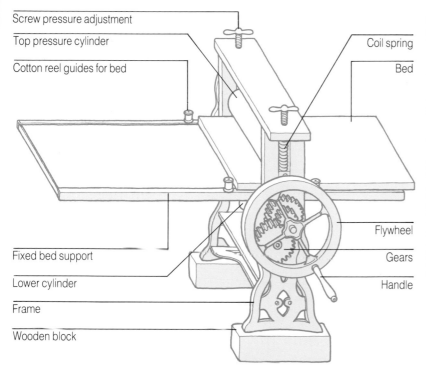

Screw pressure adjustment
Top pressure cylinder
Cotton reel guides for bed

Coil spring
Bed

Flywheel
Gears
Handle

Fixed bed support
Lower cylinder
Frame
Wooden block

## Gladys McAvoy's method of avoiding creep on a cylinder press
This artist uses lino mounted on hardboard. Her baseboard is made of chipboard with a border of hardboard and lino glued on top leaving a void the same size as the block in the centre. The block is then dropped into this hole and wedged firm. The surround and the block are of identical height so there is no creep.

## Converted mangles
The principle and method of the mangle press is the same as for an intaglio press. The cylinders are fixed to the press frame and the bed moves between the upper impression cylinder and the lower one. These converted presses can not exert as much pressure as a purpose-built intaglio press but are very acceptable as relief printing presses.

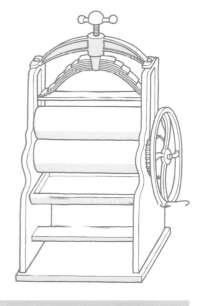

## TIPS ON CHOOSING A MANGLE
■ Make sure the frame is sound.
■ Make sure the springs are still flexible.
■ Avoid split rollers.
■ Avoid worn bearings.

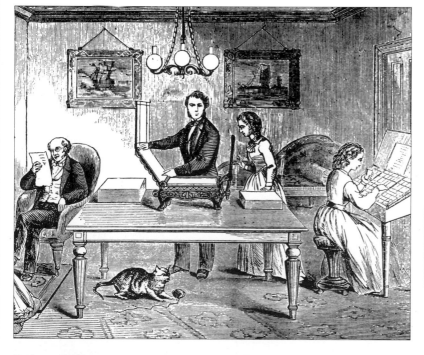

## Parlour printing
By the date of this illustration, 1870, printing as a hobby was fashionable and small table-top presses such as the one shown here were numerous. The girl on the right is seated at an elegantly styled case of type which she is setting in a 'stick'. The standing man is fitting a sheet of paper into the tympan with the frisket ready to be lowered over it. In this type of press the pressure lever on the right rocks over on to the back of the tympan. The two rectangular shapes are presumably piles of paper.

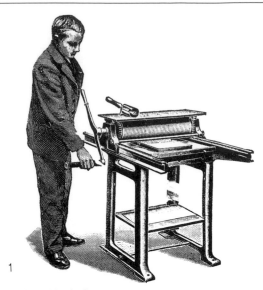

1

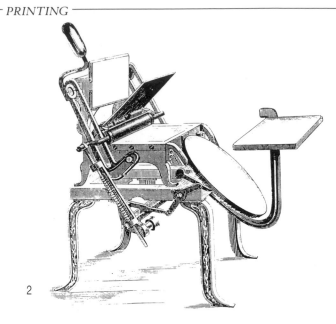

2

## Buying old printing presses

19th century presses of various kinds are still
occasionally seen at auctions and junk sales.
The examples shown here come from contemporary advertisements.

1 Letterpress proof press. Note the ink slab
and inking roller on top.

2 Jobbing platen press with automatic inking
suitable for printing wood engravings and
type.

3 Direct lithographic proof press or scraper
press, which can be used to print relief blocks
with some small adaptations.

4 The Stansbury Hand Press had a platen
area of 33 × 43cm (13 × 17in). Its acorn-
shaped frame is typical of early iron presses
designed in America.

The Washington Press shown right is an
early example of this very popular press and
this one is adorned with medallions of George
Washington and Benjamin Franklin.

3

4

## SIMPLE PROOF PRESS

This hand press was offered in 1882
specifically for the proofing of type set on
galleys (long narrow metal trays). The
basic principle is one that can be adapted
by printmakers today using scrap materials. High pressure is not possible since
the weight of the frame constitutes the
force but it should be sufficient for printing
lightweight papers. Some method of
fixing the block (in place of the galley) and
of fixing the distant end of the paper would
be an improvement.

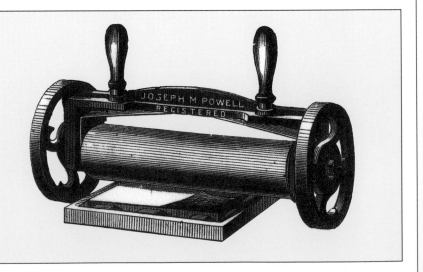

# Patent Washington Printing Press.

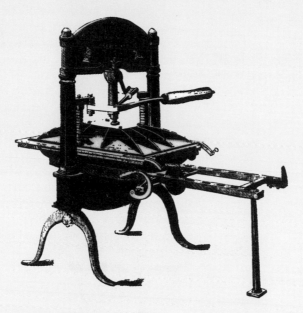

THE celebrity which our Patent Washington and Smith Hand-Presses have obtained during the last forty years, renders any remarks upon their superiority unnecessary. They are elegant in appearance, simple, quick, and powerful in operation, and combine every facility for the production of superior printing. Each press is tried at the manufactory, and warranted for one year.

## DIMENSIONS AND PRICES.

| | Bed. | | | | Matter. | | | | | | | |
|---|---|---|---|---|---|---|---|---|---|---|---|---|
| No. 1, | . . . | 17 × 21 inches, | . . . | . | 13 × 17 inches, | . . . . . | $ |
| No. 2, | . . . | 20 × 25 " | . . . | . | 15 × 20 " | . . . . |
| No. 3, | . . . | 24 × 29 " | . . . | . | 19 × 25 " | . . . . |
| No. 4, | . . . | 26 × 34 " | . . . | . | 21 × 29 " | . . . . |
| No. 5, | . . . | 29 × 42 " | . . . | . | 24 × 37 " | . . . . |
| No. 6, | . . . | 32 × 47 " | . . | . | 27 × 42 " | . . . . |
| No. 7, | . . . | 35 × 51 " | . . . | . | 30 × 46 " | . . . . |

Price includes two pairs of Points, one Screw Wrench and Brayer, one Slice, and one extra Frisket.

If the frame is made to be taken to pieces, $ extra.

*Grand, Broome, Sheriff, Columbia, and Gold Sts., New-York; and Dorset St., Salisbury Square, London, England.*

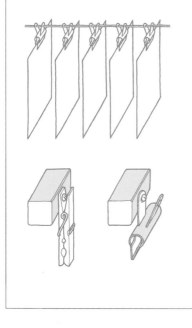

### Purpose-made drying racks
The diagram below shows the principle of the ball-and-socket hanging system. Balls may be made of glass, plastic or rubber and the framework may be metal or wood or a combination of both. Hang prints back-to-back to double the number. The picture, right, shows a wire drying rack in use. Each tray is hinged upwards to allow access to the one beneath.

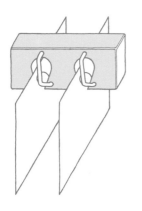

# DRYING TECHNIQUES
Oil-based inks are usually allowed to dry before the next colour is printed on top. If the underneath colour is still tacky it will tend to pull off under pressure. If, however, the ink film is very thin it is possible to print wet-on-wet. One way to get a thin ink film is to strip off excess ink by laying a sheet of tissue paper on the just-printed colour and rubbing gently all over. Peel off the tissue and the excess ink with it, and throw the tissue away. This stripping technique leaves an attractive matt, satiny surface, the very opposite of the squelchy oiliness associated with over-inked relief prints. Ink usually dries in 24 hours when the ink film is of a normal thickness, but this can vary with the absorbency of the paper, the number of colours underneath and the temperature of the drying area.

Small scale prints can be dried by interleaving them between the pages of a telephone book. Larger prints need to be hung up or laid on drying racks. The simplest hanging system involves two strings and ordinary spring pegs of the sort used to hang out the washing. If you drill the pegs and thread the strings through it holds the prints level, or the pegs can be screwed to a couple of wooden battens for greater stability. Purpose-made hanging systems have parallel sockets fitted with either a small ball or sometimes a cylindrical shape. The paper is slid into one side of the socket and is held there when the ball drops down by gravity. Wire racks are also specially made for drying prints, but they hold the print horizontally – one each per hinged tray. Wire racks are better for large prints as sheets can be damaged while hanging.

Water-based inks are usually printed on dampened paper and require different drying methods. If sheets are hung up or laid to dry

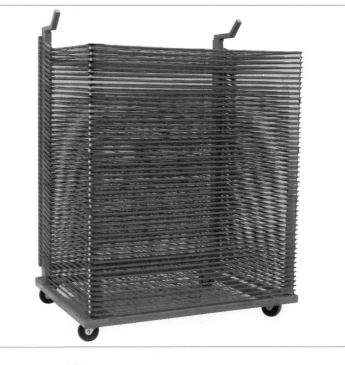

on racks they will cockle. The paper is kept damp throughout the printing session until all the colours are complete; if it does dry it will shrink and it will be impossible to register colours accurately. When the last colour is printed each sheet should be covered with a larger sheet of acid-free tissue. Up to five prints can be batched together with thick blotting boards between batches. The stack of drying prints is put under ply or similar board and under weights. The blotters must be changed for dry ones, four or five times, until the prints are quite dry and flat. Blotting paper or boards can be replaced with wood fibre insulation board.

Paper that has cockled can be flattened in the same way. First dampen between newspaper (see box on right) and allow the paper some hours to relax. When all signs of cockling have gone, dry as above. Slow drying over a number of days will give the best result.

Dampened paper can be dried quickly by sticking it on to a drawing board with gummed tape. The paper will dry flat but will have to be cut off the board. Either the deckle will be lost or the print will have an unsightly taped edge.

## EMBOSSING

Relief blocks are ideal for embossing with or without colour. Embossed prints have a special liveliness because the paper is actually formed into the cut marks as well as the surface being printed, so that the energy of the cutting is seen and emphasized.

Lino, wood and all kinds of boards, as well as built-up textures, can be embossed. The embossing can be "blind", that is uninked, so that it relies entirely on the play of light on the moulded paper. The surface of the block can be inked or the ink can be applied to the cut areas, or a combination of both, but in general the simplest methods are also the most effective.

The paper must be strong and heavy, otherwise it will not hold the embossing well and may crack. It should be sized to give it strength, and it must be dampened to allow the paper fibres to be moulded. Deep embossing can only be achieved using an intaglio or hydraulic press. Platen presses give shallower embossing. In all cases plenty of soft packing is essential to drive the paper into the deepest parts of the cuts. Some printmakers use a lamination of sheets to strengthen the embossing. The first, thinnish, sheet is left on the block and is given a thin coat of paste. Another sheet of paper is laid on top and the block is put through the press again. Each time the embossing is deepened. An alternative method is to paste a second sheet on the first at the edges only and to print only once. The sheets are left to dry on the block. Thin aluminium sheet, not dampened of course, takes embossing very well, and relief blocks can be used as formers for vacuum moulding. Other materials can be used to take casts from relief blocks. Plaster of paris and potter's clay are used to make three-dimensional tiles. Lightly oil or soap the block before casting to get a good release from the set plaster or clay.

A form of embossing using paper pulp instead of sheet paper is popular. It is an area for experimentation without any rules.

### DAMPENING PAPER
The easiest way to dampen paper evenly is to first take an old newspaper and spray each leaf with water. It should feel damp but not wet. Interleave each sheet of printing paper between the newspaper leaves, and then wrap the whole bundle in polythene sheeting. Place between two boards and weight. The time the paper takes to reach a state of even dampness depends on the weight of the paper and the ambient humidity. A light paper will be ready in half an hour. Many printmakers leave a heavyweight sheet a full week before printing. The dampened paper should be evenly damp, not spotty, and it should not glisten with surface water. Heavyweight sheets will take up a lot of water and the newspaper may have to be resprayed. Do not spray the printing paper directly.

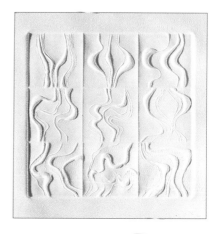

**Chimes**
**ARTIST Birgit Skiöld**
**SIZE 23 × 23cm (9 × 9in)**

One of seven blind embossed relief etchings that illustrate poems by Dante Gabriel Rossetti. This limited edition book won a major European prize for artists' handmade books.

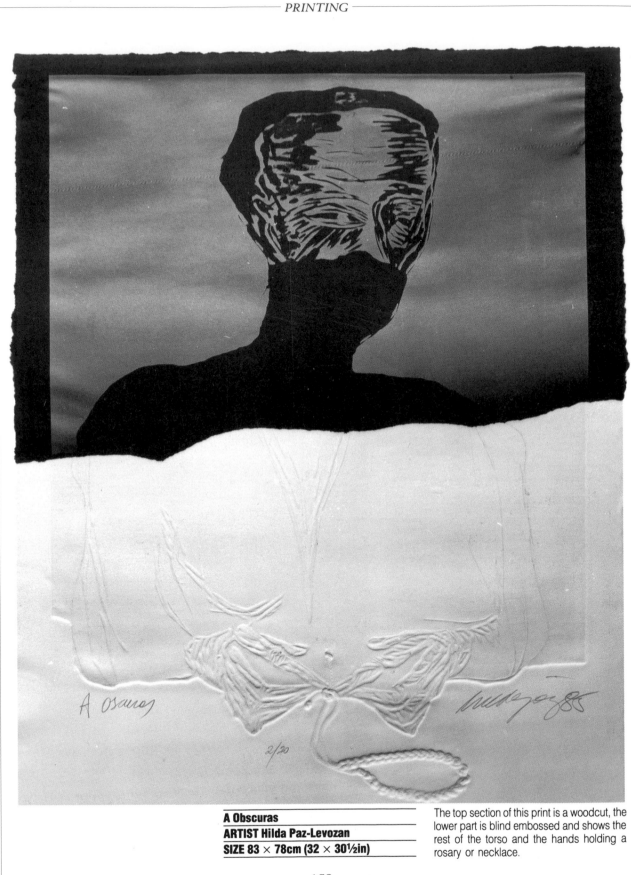

A osares                                                    [signature] 85

2/20

**A Obscuras**
**ARTIST Hilda Paz-Levozan**
**SIZE 83 × 78cm (32 × 30½in)**

The top section of this print is a woodcut, the lower part is blind embossed and shows the rest of the torso and the hands holding a rosary or necklace.

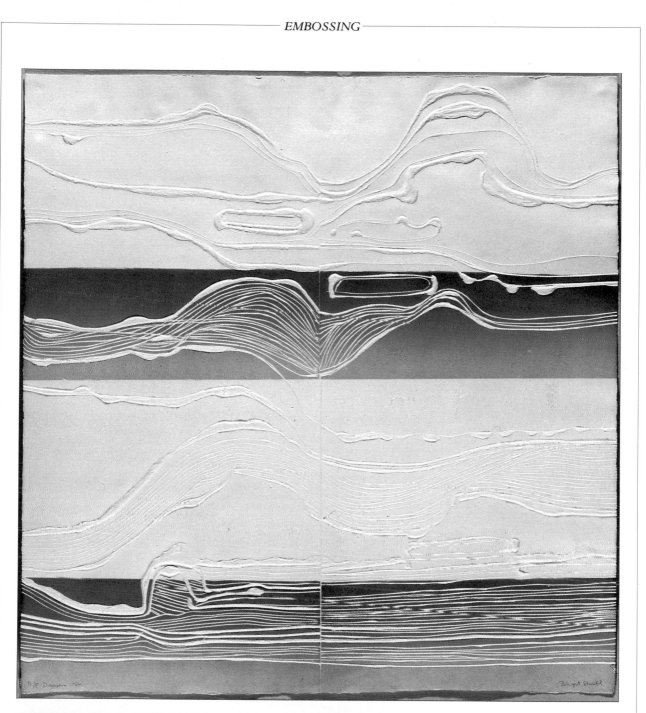

### Daisen-in I
### ARTIST Birgit Skiöld
### SIZE 58 × 59cm (10¾ × 11in)

Embossed linocut with surface-rolled bands of blended colour. It was printed on very heavy dampened paper in an intaglio press with soft felt blankets that press the paper right into the cut lines. Note this print is bled – no margins to cockle.

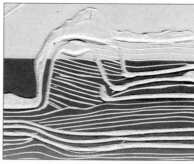

### Enlargement of detail

You can see that the inked area is not a separate block but the ink edge is straight – this suggests that the ink was rolled on to the block while the non-inked area was masked with strips of paper. The height of the embossing indicates that the lino is deeply cut in the areas that show white in this detail.

After experimenting with printing linocuts by driving a car backwards and forwards over a print and using a farm roller, Katie Clemson is seen below in Australia driving a road roller to print a very large print.

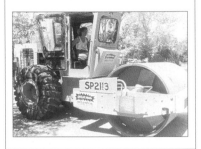

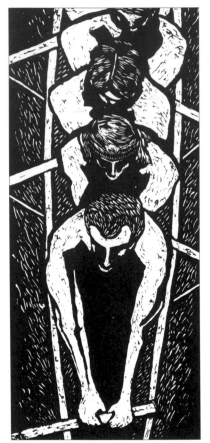

**Crew I**
**ARTIST Mary Pacios Humphrey**
**SIZE 198 × 89cm (78 × 35in)**

Large monochromatic linocut printed by burnishing on Tableau paper, which is made in rolls. Note how the partial clearance enlivens the white areas.

# PRINTING VERY LARGE PRINTS

The trend today is towards very large prints, which need unorthodox printing methods. Large sheets of paper are difficult to control single-handed, so you will need someone to help. Some excellent printmaking papers are available in rolls, which gives greater choice in size. Burnishing is the preferred printing method, but if you need greater pressure consider large rollers such as garden rollers, or farm or road rollers (see p. 146). Ingenious printmakers have also devised ways of printing rolls of paper in a platen or cylinder press. Relief blocks can be printed on canvas, which is then stretched and painted. Edward Bawden used lino blocks to stamp print designs directly on to his walls. He was able to print a border round the features of the room; round the fireplace, doors and windows, to make a unique and delightful decoration. Other Bawden designs have been printed on sheets of paper rather than the usual rolls.

**USING FOOT PRESSURE**

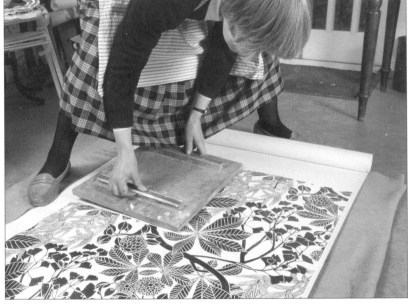

**Printing wallpaper by hand**
**1** The block is made of lino and is mounted on wood with two narrow wooden handles attached to the back. The block is inked, turned upside-down and its position sighted by eye. The paper is laid on a pad of felt blankets.

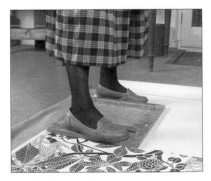

**2** Pressure is applied by standing on the block. The design is printed in repeats to cover the long length of paper.

## PRINTING FABRIC ON A CONVERTED PROOFING PRESS

Ian Gardiner prints long paper in a platen press – it can be no wider than the bed, see diagram below. The image is printed from several blocks, starting at one end. The printed area is covered with clean newsprint and rolled and held with paperclips.

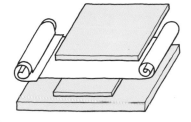

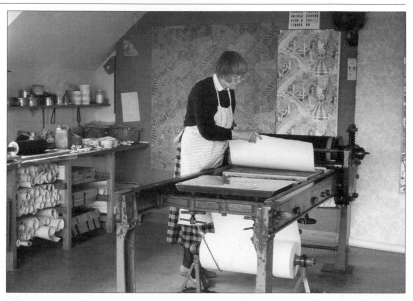

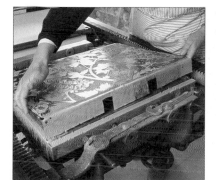

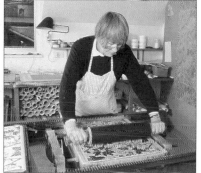

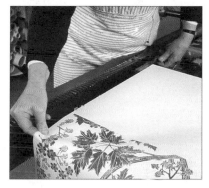

**1** The block is mounted on a metal plate and it slots firmly into place on the press bed.

**2** The block is rolled up with ink while it is fixed on the bed. The ink slab is on the work bench behind.

**3** The paper is held steady with the right hand while the left hand applies the gripper to hold the paper.

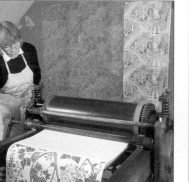

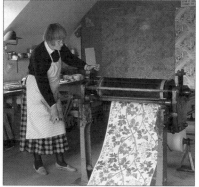

**4** The cylinder is wound over the block and paper by means of a handle. As it travels it applies pressure.

**5** The cylinder is wound back again to its original position ready for the next impression to be taken.

Marthe Armitage started printing her wallpapers by hand on short lengths of paper (see the pictures on the previous page). She acquired an offset lithographic proof press and found a supplier of better quality paper that came in large, heavy rolls. She had the press adapted to print a continuous pattern by attaching a paper gripping device. The reel of paper is supported on axle stands underneath the press (see top picture).

## California Pearl Gazes and Contemplates her Future
**ARTIST Elaine Kowalsky**
**SIZE 122 × 152.5cm (48 × 60in)**

Four-colour linocut on a large scale. It was burnished by hand on the artist's studio floor Though she has kept the registration of the colours loose it is nevertheless difficult to handle such large sheets of paper and maintain tight registration.

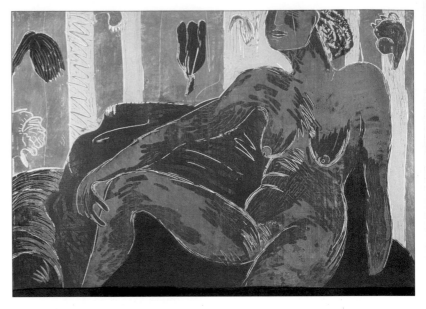

## PRINTING WALLPAPER BY HAND

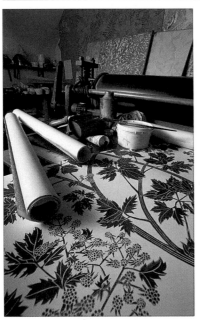

As the printing of wallpapers in the quantities required for a room is laborious, most handmade wallpapers are printed in one colour.

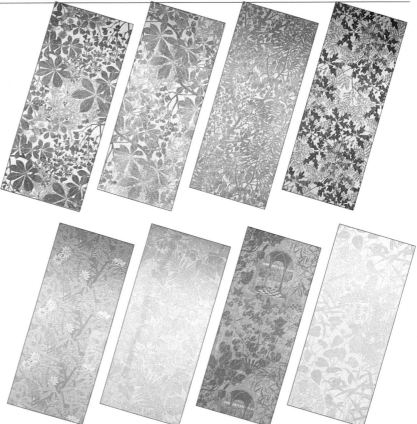

### Wallpaper designs
The first two examples of wallpapers by Marthe Armitage, shown above, are the same design but look very different. The other examples are all different and show the ingenuity with which she interweaves foliage to make wallpapers that look equally good in old and new buildings.

# RELIEF BLOCKS USED IN GRAPHIC DESIGN

Before the development of photography most magazines and books were illustrated with woodcuts and wood engravings. The earliest use of lino by artists was as a material for illustration. Although up to 15,000 impressions have been made from a lino block and 900,000 impressions from a woodblock, usually the blocks for runs over 1000 were electrotyped, that is a facsimile copy was made in metal, largely to preserve the original work.

Apart from printing directly from blocks or electrotypes, graphic designers have always used cut and engraved blocks for the specific quality of the cut or engraved line. Usually the resulting block pull was photographed and reproduced just like a drawing. An interesting transfer technique was popular between the wars in which a linocut was transferred on to a lithographic stone or plate. The block was rolled up in litho transfer ink and a pull taken on smooth paper. This was then laid on a prepared plate, run through a litho press and processed. Many large linocuts were transformed by this method into posters, lithographic prints and wallpaper.

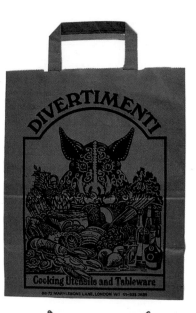

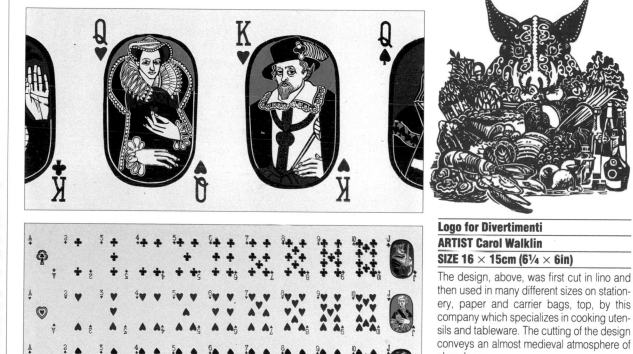

### Logo for Divertimenti
#### ARTIST Carol Walklin
#### SIZE 16 × 15cm (6¼ × 6in)

The design, above, was first cut in lino and then used in many different sizes on stationery, paper and carrier bags, top, by this company which specializes in cooking utensils and tableware. The cutting of the design conveys an almost medieval atmosphere of abundance.

### Scottish Historical Playing Cards
#### ARTIST Willie Rogers
#### SIZE 6 × 8.5cm (2¼ × 3¼in) each card

The designs for these playing cards were cut entirely in lino – every pip and symbol. Three colours are used: red, black and gold – the reverse side shows an abstract design in gold on red, also cut in lino. The effect is very sumptuous.

Eric Thake's witty monochromatic linocut was originally a print called *An Opera House in Every Home* until it was transformed into a poster, right, which commemorates the open-opening of Jorn Utzon's unmistakable building in Sydney.

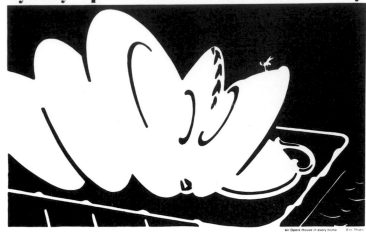

**Sydney Opera House Tenth Anniversary**

An Opera House in every home · Eric Thake

**Art Gallery of New South Wales**
**Exhibition 1st~31st January 1983**

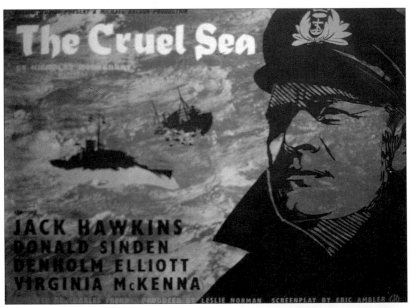

EALING STUDIOS PRESENT A MICHAEL BALCON PRODUCTION

**The Cruel Sea**

**JACK HAWKINS**
**DONALD SINDEN**
**DENHOLM ELLIOTT**
**VIRGINIA McKENNA**

DIRECTED BY CHARLES FREND · PRODUCED BY LESLIE NORMAN · SCREENPLAY BY ERIC AMBLER

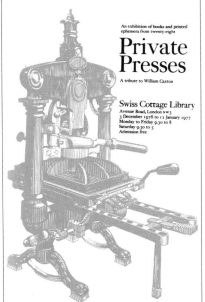

An exhibition of books and printed ephemera from twenty-eight

**Private Presses**

A tribute to William Caxton

**Swiss Cottage Library**
Avenue Road, London NW3
3 December 1976 to 12 January 1977
Monday to Friday 9.30 to 8
Saturday 9.30 to 5
Admission free

The Ealing Studio poster, above, was designed in 1953 by Colin Walklin. The background sea is photographic and the head and ships, overprinted in black, were cut from lino. The detail, right, shows the graphic interpretation of a cine still simplified to be understood as heroic and dramatic.

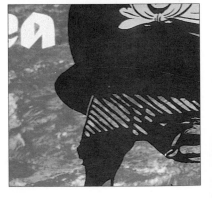

The poster, above, was designed and printed by Ian Mortimer for an exhibition in which his private press participated. He cut the picture of the Albion Press in lino, handset all the type matter and printed the poster on the very same press.

# PRINTING ON FABRIC

Woodblocks have been used to print on fabric from a very early date, and are still used for designer fabrics in the Western world and by most Third World countries. When lino became popular as an art medium during the '30s, it was also adopted by craftsmen to print lengths of fabric. Both wood and lino are still used today for fabric printing by craftsmen and amateurs who want to make something original, whether it is for furnishing or for clothing.

Artists' materials shops sell two kinds of colours for printing on fabric that are widely available. Oil-based fabric printing inks in tubes are very similar to those used for printing on paper. They are applied by roller to the block and require the same cleaning solvents. Fabric printing dyes, sold in jars or bottles, should be spread on a pad of felt or folded cloth – the block is pressed on to the dye pad to charge it with colour. The colours are fixed, so that the fabric can be washed, either by heat, usually by ironing, or sometimes by applying a special fixing agent supplied with the dye. Follow the manufacturer's instructions.

Professional fabric designers and printers use the more sophisticated dyes available commercially, which need more specialized equipment.

## Printing table

Blocks are placed on top of fabric instead of underneath as with paper, and pressure is applied by hand. A simple printing table on which the fabric can be fixed is easily made. Take a large piece of board, wider than the fabric, and cover it with several thicknesses of old blanket and finally a sheet of plastic. The fabric can be fixed to it with tape. A long length will have to be printed in sections. Professional fabric printers have very large sturdy tables covered in a smooth fabric to which the printing fabric is glued flat, but satisfactory experiments can be made with this simple padded board placed on top of your kitchen table.

## Blocks

Blocks should be mounted if they are thinner than 2.5cm (1in) to facilitate handling during inking, placing and printing. Pressure is usually applied by means of a mallet on the back of the block. The amount of colour picked up by the block can be increased by flocking the surface. Roll a thin coat of glue on to the block and dust it with flocking powder (usually powdered wool). When the glue is dry the excess flock can be blown away.

## Fabrics

Smooth, closely woven fabrics are the most satisfactory. Most craft printing inks and dyes are formulated for natural fabrics; synthetic fabrics need special dyes. Fabrics should be washed and ironed before printing as they usually contain some form of finish, which could prevent dye from taking evenly.

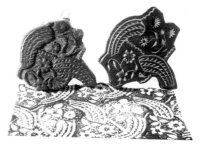

**Fabric and blocks**
The two blocks (above) were used to print the pattern "Peach" in black on honey coloured velvet. It was designed and printed by Barron and Larcher in the early 1920s and was made up into a wedding suit of jacket and skirt.

## Registration

Blocks are usually printed in a series of repeats to cover the entire area, but they can print just a border or perhaps a design around a garment neck. The fabric should be marked with chalk or another non–staining marker so the blocks can be placed by eye. Multi-coloured printing will need a system for each colour to register with the first printing as well as to keep the repeat position. The usual method is to embed two or more pins on the edge of the design in the same position on each block, so each time the pins are matched to similar marks from the first block.

### HAND-PRINTED FABRICS

**Barron and Larcher fabrics**
The lino block (below), mounted on wood, was used to discharge-print the pattern for "Bunch" (right) on silk velvet. It was designed and printed by the famous 1920s and '30s partnership.

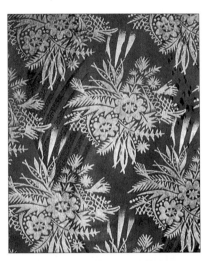

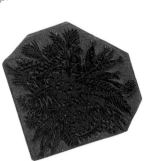

**Small repeated patterns**
The 19th-century carved wooden printing block, above, for the pattern "French Sprig" is 21 ×16cm (8¼ × 6¼in). The small pattern is carved many times on the block. Note the registration pins on the top and right-hand side. Larger patterns will occupy a whole block.

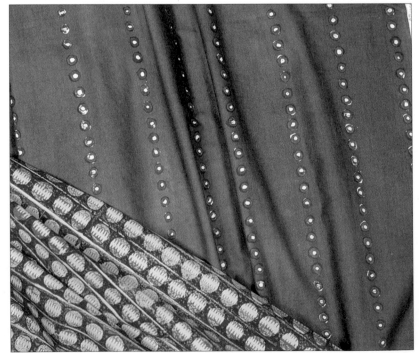

**Susan Bosence fabrics**
The dress length (right top) was printed with a line of circles in indigo Soledon dye, the centres waxed to resist over-dying with dark mossy green Caledon vat dye. The fabric (right below) is a two-colour print in tan and dark blue on a grey dyed poplin.

**Four scarves by Tsugumi Ota**
These scarves are hand-printed from lino blocks on to silk and fine wool. The coloured backgrounds (left) are shaded by the dye being sprayed on rather than the fabric being dipped in a vat of dye.

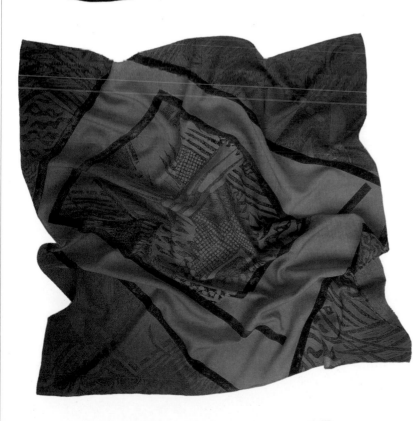

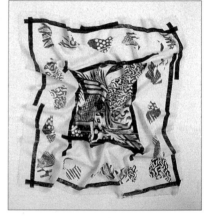

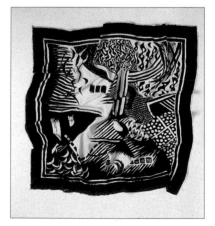

# PROOFING AND EDITIONING

The object of proofing is to iron out any problems before you start to print the edition. It is also the time for experimentation with different papers, the order of printing the colors, and the methods of inking and pressure for printing. Never underestimate the time allowed for proofing, for it will make editioning a pleasant and straightforward task. You will enjoy the variations and chance results that occur during proofing; you may not want to incorporate these discoveries at this point, but future possibilities will be enlarged. The experimental aspect of proofing has led to the acceptance of unique proofs (also called monotypes or monoprints) as bona fide exhibits at international print competitions.

## Block proofing

The first proofs taken from a block are to check the cutting and are usually taken in black, no matter what the final printing color, to show any mistakes and underclearing most accurately. A complex block will be proofed several times as work progresses. If you are unsure of what to cut next, stop and take a proof. Draw or paint on the proof, try out alternatives. It is better to spoil a proof rather than a block.

## Color proofing

Proofing in color is done to check the registration, the individual colors and the effect of overprinting. This is where you can have fun. Try, for example, to proof the last color, which is usually the darkest, in a light, opaque ink. Try reversing the order of printing. These unorthodox methods can reveal unexpected color combinations that may be more exciting than your original scheme. If you are not sure what the result will be, try proofing one color on a clear acetate sheet to lay over a proof. Acetate proofs are also useful for checking registration.

Keep a note of your color experiments by dabbing out small amounts of color and noting the proportions of reducing medium and color used. If you use the Pantone color matching system you need only note the color name. Wrap small amounts of ink in packages with greaseproof paper, foil or plastic – if well wrapped they will keep for some months without drying out.

## Progressives and Reduction block proofing

Color proofs that show all the colors as they build up are called progressive proofs; they are a guide to correct editioning. Proof one shows the first color: proof two shows the first and second color; proof three shows the first, second and third color, and so on.

You cannot proof a reduction block in advance, and if you want a record of each stage you will need quite a lot of extra paper. For a ten-color print you will need one sheet for each single color, plus nine more sheets for progressive overprinting.

A less extravagant method is to make roll-up color proofs as the

### TRIAL PROOFS

Proofs are variously called trial proofs, working proofs, stage proofs or stages, and, if the artist is important, they are of considerable interest to art historians and printmakers, as they show the development of a print.

When a satisfactory trial proof has been made it is marked p.p. (passed for press) or B.A.T. (*bon à tirer*). Any notes that will help printing are marked on this proof as it serves as the model for each print in the edition.

work progresses. Take a narrow roller and roll a band of the first color on a sheet of the printing paper. Before printing the second color roll it over the first roll-up proof to judge the effect of overprinting. Do this for each color before it is printed to check the effect obtained.

## The edition

The number of prints in an edition can vary from under ten to up to 500 or more. Most editions of relief prints are between 20 and 100. If the edition is commissioned, the publisher will usually determine the size. If the printmaker is working independently, the edition size may depend on the resources available and how successful the printmaker is at selling his or her prints. It is not unusual for a printmaker to print only part of the edition at first and the rest later. Printing a whole multicolored edition can take some time, and if you are preparing for an exhibition you will want many different images rather than a couple of complete editions. Keep a notebook with all the details of printing and how many prints have been completed.

Once the edition size has been decided it must be maintained. There has been a tendency for wood engravers in particular to do multiple editions. If a print proved popular they printed another edition, putting the Roman number II after the title or number. This practice is now frowned upon it as confuses the value of a print.

## Signing and numbering

Finished prints are signed by the artist in pencil to indicate that each one is approved. Pencil is used because it is difficult to erase or change without the paper fibers being disturbed. Prints are usually signed under the lower right corner of the image. If a print is to be titled that is usually centered.

All prints in an edition are given an individual number, which is usually written in pencil under the lower left corner of the image. Bleed prints are signed and numbered on the reverse of the paper. The number is usually expressed as, for example, 3/20, being the third print in an edition of 20. The number on a print does not necessarily indicate that it was printed before another because the order in which sheets are printed changes with each additional color. A low number is only important in some printmaking techniques such as drypoint (an intaglio method) where the plate can wear down quickly – most relief blocks are much more robust.

## Edition proofs

These are copies over and above the edition, but identical to it. There is a convention that the printmaker retains 10 per cent copies (five copies if the edition is 50), which can be kept as archive copies, given away or sold. They are marked artist's proof or A.P. Publishers, printers and editors all need archival copies. These prints should be annotated as printer's proof, etc.

### CANCELLING
Once the edition and its attendant proofs have been printed it is usual to cancel the blocks. This is done by cutting a prominent cross in the block. Metal plates are often drilled with a couple of holes. The method does not matter as long as the surface is clearly defaced. Take a few proofs as evidence of cancellation.

### Working from the original design

When the printmaker has a fully evolved design that is being used as a guide for the final print constant reference must be made to it during the proofing period. Colours will be selected and checked by comparing ink manufacturers' samples to the original design (see below). Specially mixed ink samples should be dabbed out and compared.

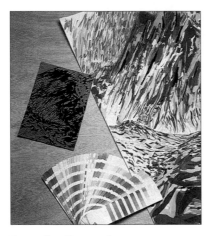

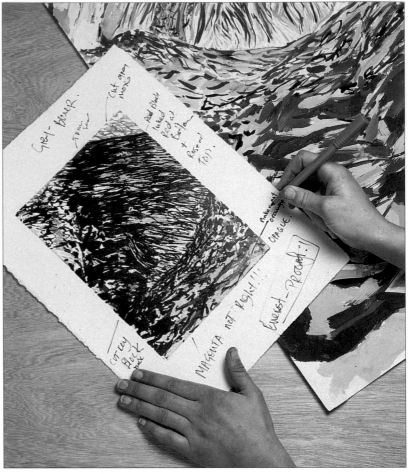

### Correcting the proof

The final correct working proof is annotated with every piece of useful information that will be needed to make sure the edition is printed correctly (see above right). This may mean that small modifications to the colours are still needed or minor adjustments to the pressure or registration.

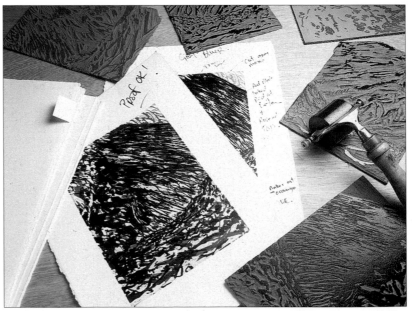

### Assembling the blocks and materials

Check the blocks (see right) for final work and make sure the non-printing areas are well cleared and will not pick up ink. Check the registration, all the tools and materials required for printing and drying and check and prepare the paper.

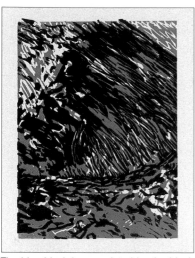

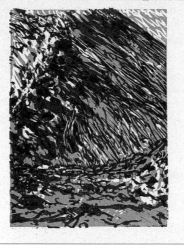

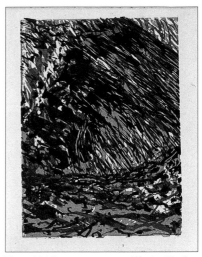

The blue block is overprinted by the black block.

Blue and black overprinted with the mauve block.

Blue, black, mauve overprinted with the orange block.

## The order of printing the blocks

An important aspect of proofing is to establish the order of printing the blocks. Though the blocks may have been cut in what seems a logical progression, that order may not be ideal and alternatives should be tried. The last colour to be printed, being on top, inevitably has a greater influence on the final image than a colour underneath. In addition the effects of warm advancing colours and cool retreating ones and the fact that some pigments are very dense make it all the more important to establish the order of printing the blocks at proofing stage.

Proofs of each of the blocks in their individual colours for Katie Clemson's linocut *Storm over Everest* can be seen on p.39. Here progressive proofs show the gradual effect of overprinting as the image is built up.

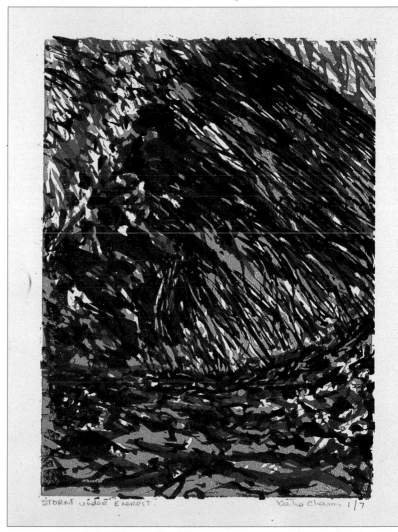

The final print: blue, black, mauve, orange overprinted with red.

The chart, below, lists the most common faults which are experienced no matter what method or materials you are using. Refer back to the detailed information on these pages: Preparing lino, p63, side-grain wood p64, end-grain wood p64, Repairing lino p93, wood p92, Choosing ink p110, mixing and additives p117, choosing paper p131, Applying inks p120, Registration p140, Printing p136, Finishing prints p176.

Faults which show up during proofing and editioning stem from poor craftsmanship at an earlier stage. The wrong choice of method, the ill considered selection of materials and slack discipline whilst printing are the culprits. The advantage of relief printmaking, however, is that most faults can be cured without too much difficulty and they should be found during the proofing stage. This can not be done with reduction blocks and every printmaker working in that method has, at some time in their career, been faced

## FAULT FINDING

### PAPER

| Fault | Reason | Correction |
|---|---|---|
| COCKLED | Paper is stored in a damp place or not allowed to acclimatize to studio, or paper is damp. | Store paper in even humidity. Bring into studio two days before printing. Flatten under weight. |
| CREASED | Sheet or just corner folded. | Reject sheet – use for proofing only. Can not eliminate crease. |
| WRINKLED AT EDGES OF BLOCK | Too much pressure is indenting the block and deforming the paper. Or paper is too hard (sized). | Reduce pressure, or dampen paper. |
| FOREIGN BODIES IN PAPER | Dust particles etc. within sheet. | Use needle to lift particle off surface. Reject sheet if particle is embedded; use for proofing. |
| MARGIN MARKS | Fingermarks in margins or ink picked up from press etc. | Handle sheet with paper 'fingers'. Clean press and surroundings. |
| SPECKLED INK | Paper too hard (sized) to absorb ink evenly. | Dampen paper. |
| SURFACE FIBRES PULLED OFF PAPER | Paper too soft (unsized) so loose fibres pulled off by ink. | Size paper. |

### INK

| Fault | Reason | Correction |
|---|---|---|
| PICKING (FRAGMENTS OF PAPER LIFT OFF) | Paper is dusty or the ink is too dry. | Wipe each sheet with a clean cloth to remove paper dust or thin ink very slightly. |
| SPECKLED INK | Insufficient ink applied or pressure too low. | Apply more ink to block or increase pressure with packing. |
| SQUASHED INK AT EDGES OF BLOCK | Too much ink or too much pressure. | Reduce ink applied or reduce pressure with packing. |
| SHINY INK | The ink is not absorbed by the paper because of underlying ink films or because the paper is too hard. | Strip off excess ink with tissue paper. |
| INK NOT DRYING | The ink will not dry because it is too oily, the paper is not absorbent or it is too cold. | Add driers to next batch of ink, use a softer paper, or warm the drying area. |

with a fault developing at a very late stage when most of the colours have been printed. If the last colour mis-registers and you can not find the fault within one or two impressions you can easily ruin the whole edition. It can be infuriating – but you learn to be extra careful next time. If you are a professional printmaker good planning always pays but if you are making experimental prints it is important to maintain flexibility and be open to insights and unusual effects which come about when a fault happens.

| Fault | Reason | Correction |
|---|---|---|
| UNEVEN IMPRESSION | The pressure is not even. | Check the press mechanism, check the packing. If the block is not centrally placed even out pressure with small blocks of the same height placed in unoccupied space on bed. |
| LINE ACROSS | A thicker line of ink appears across a printed area. | Check that a sheet of packing has not slipped or something got under the block. |
| BLOTCHY INK | Ink not mixed well enough with reducing medium or oil. Block surface poorly prepared. | Mix the ink and reducing medium or oil for longer. Fine sandpaper block surface. |
| LUMPS IN INK | Bits of dried ink making lumps. | Push ink through a mesh to remove lumps. |
| PICKING UP INK IN NON-PRINTING AREAS | The non-printing area has not cleared well enough or deep enough. | Clear any parts that still pick up ink. |

## REGISTRATION

| Fault | Reason | Correction |
|---|---|---|
| IMAGE RIGHT OFF POSITION | The paper was placed to block registration stops not paper stops or the sheet is placed top to bottom, in reverse. | Check the pile of paper waiting to be printed. Is it the bottom furthest away from you? It should be nearest. |
| IMAGE SLIGHTLY OFF POSITION | 1 Paper not placed snugly to registration marks or stops.<br>2 Paper not trimmed accurately or taped.<br>3 Block not accurately cut.<br>4 Block moved position on bed.<br>5 Registration marks, holes, studs etc. have become worn. | 1 Check placing of paper.<br>2 Check edges of paper where it meets the stops.<br>3 Re-cut blocks where required.<br>4 Check block position and fix it down if necessary.<br>5 Replace worn parts with new sections. |
| SHADOW IMAGE | 1 Paper smudged while putting down or lifting off.<br>2 Parts of press loose, particularly the frisket/tympan hinge.<br>3 If burnishing, the paper has moved while rubbing. | 1 Keep control of paper when putting down and lifting off.<br>2 Tighten up all loose parts of the press.<br>3 Put block on damp pad to prevent skidding and use heavy weights to keep paper in place. |

## COMMON FAULTS THAT CAN BE IDENTIFIED BY LOOKING AT A PROOF

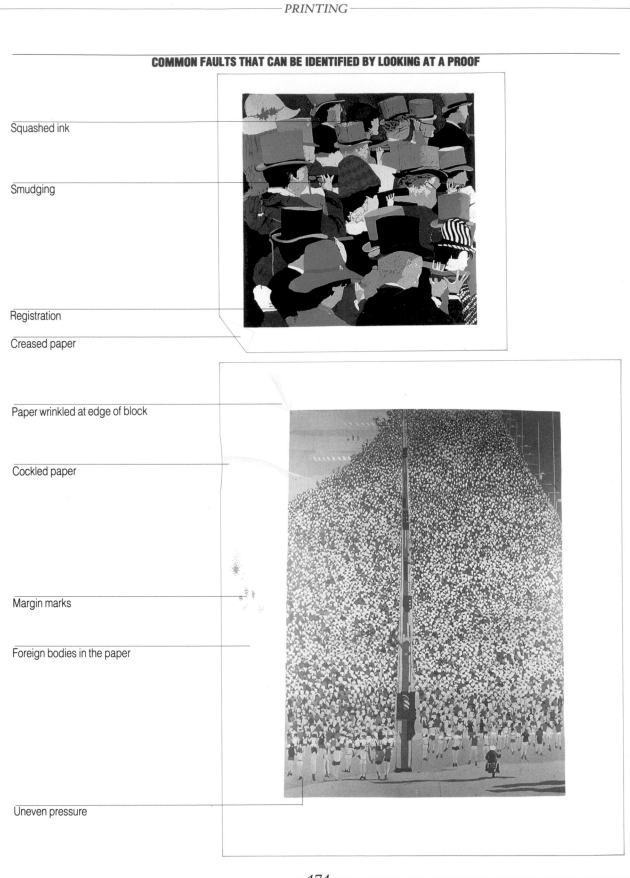

Squashed ink

Smudging

Registration

Creased paper

Paper wrinkled at edge of block

Cockled paper

Margin marks

Foreign bodies in the paper

Uneven pressure

## Planning the printing of the edition

Get everything ready before starting. Check paper, solvents, ink, blocks, presses, drying systems and every other piece of equipment or material that will be used. Not everybody has an ideal studio, so it may be necessary to rearrange work tables so that everything is to hand. You should aim for the minimum movement between elements to conserve energy. You should be able to ink the block, take up the printing paper and lay it on the block, apply pressure, remove the paper and put it to dry in one continuous and logical sequence.

## Calculating paper and ink quantities

In handprinting occasional mistakes will happen, so allow about ten per cent extra sheets of paper over the edition plus various edition proofs. The amount of ink to be used is more difficult to estimate because there are so many variables: the size of the block, the amount of cutting and the absorbency of both block and paper. One learns with experience, but in the meantime make sure you have a good supply of the basic colours and reducing medium or oil.

### ROLLING A TEST STRIP

The picture below shows the test strip for The Eight, a single block reduction linocut by Katie Clemson (see p.51). Each colour is rolled on the previous one, using a narrow roller, to make it easier to anticipate the effects of overprinting.

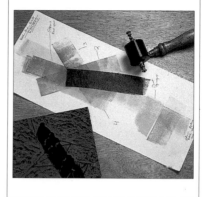

## USING ACETATE TO CHECK REGISTRATION

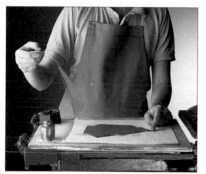

**1** Acetate is held by weights while a section of this free form print is positioned on the press bed.

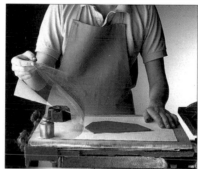

**2** A proof is taken on to the acetate. In this sequence it is used while the ink is wet; it can be used dry also.

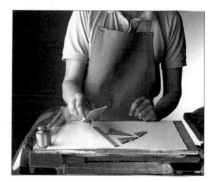

**3** Other free form blocks are positioned on the bed and printed on the paper beneath to provide a proof.

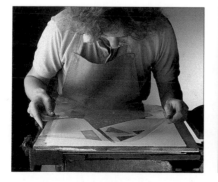

**4** The acetate with the ink still wet is lightly positioned on the proof just taken and adjusted by eye.

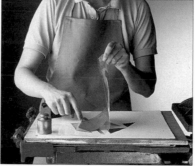

**5** The acetate is lightly pressed on to the proof so that it just marks the position of the blue block.

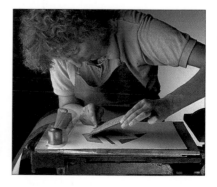

**6** The blue block is now registered to the faint marks made from the acetate. Variations are quickly made in this way.

### Records

Notes on materials and techniques are essential if the editioning is to be done in two or more parts, and such notes are also a valuable source of ideas for future work. Make notes about the idiosyncracies of your press – every one is subtly different and needs its own small adjustments. It is useful to be able to refer back to previous experience on, for example, how long a certain paper should be dampened before printing, or whether one colour, if mixed with a certain other colour, takes twice as long as normal to dry. Keep colour samples, mixing notes and records of pressure and packing.

Records of the edition are also essential if the printmaker is exhibiting and selling individual prints rather than complete editions. Use a large ruled ledger and give one line to each numbered print. Have columns in which you can note where a print is on show or on sale-or-return to a gallery, and finally when it is sold, to whom and for what price. Also note the basic information: date of publication, paper, size of paper, size of image, technique, number of colours, edition size and number of artist's and other proofs.

### Finishing prints

When the printing of all or part of the edition is complete and the prints are quite dry, each one should be inspected in detail. Look for any faults in printing and in the paper. Look for fingermarks in the margins. Minor smudges can be removed with the finest grade of sandpaper and then smoothed down with a flat burnisher. Trim off obtrusive registration marks or stud holes. Remove masking tape from deckles. Sign and number each print and add the title and date if required. Interleave each print with a sheet of acid-free tissue, and wrap a batch of prints in good quality paper to keep out the dust. Packages of prints should be stored on flat shelves in dry conditions. Large prints will need a sheet of stiff board at the base of the package to help handling. Remember that a fold or crack in a sheet of paper is very difficult to eliminate. Always hold a sheet in two hands at the short ends. Small prints can be stored in solander boxes, as they are in museums. Individual prints are usually stored flat in plan chests or they are framed for display.

### International print competitions

The easy transport of prints has made it possible to organize international contemporary print exhibitions when shipping a large number of paintings or pieces of sculpture would be hazardous and very expensive. Prints can be invited from individual artists without involving governments and arts council so a wider range of work is usually a feature of these exhibitions. They are held in many countries on a bi- or tri-ennial basis. They vary from miniature prints, nothing larger than 8cm (3in) allowed to those which specialize in a medium such as Xylon in Switzerland. It started for wood engraving alone but now encompasses all relief techniques. Your national printmakers society will have the details.

## Framing and display

The traditional way of framing a print is to cut a window mount in acid-free mounting board just large enough to reveal the image and the signature and number; the rest of the margin is covered by the mount. A sheet of glass is put in front, a backing sheet behind and the sandwich is held together with a wooden moulding. Traditionally thin wood was used for the backing, but this has been replaced with hardboard or ply, and metal extrusions are often used in place of wooden mouldings. Plastics are used as glass substitutes. Where the paper itself or its deckle edges are a feature of the print or the print is bled, a window mount destroys the effect. Such prints are often just hinged direct on to a backing or they are 'floated' so that they seem to be attached to the glass rather than the backing – this is done with pressure pads.

These effects can look dramatic but may be harmful to the print. Close contact with the glass can cause a reaction in the printing ink. Some cheap framing systems have clips to hold a glass-print-backing sandwich together but this should be considered only temporary as the dust will soon creep in. The value you place on a print will govern your choice of framing. Many prints are intended by the printmaker to be ephemeral and so can be displayed in less than conservationist conditions – important prints should be treated to museum standards for works on paper.

Since paper is vulnerable to excessive light, heat, humidity, insects and dust, it pays to follow a few rules. Hang a framed print out of direct sunlight and not too near spotlights or other light sources. Picture lights made to fit on the wall above a picture are not recommended. Do not hang a print over a radiator or fireplace. Most important of all, use conservation-grade acid-free materials in framing and do nothing that is irreversible.

Finally, you could revive an eighteenth-century idea and have a print-viewing party. Issue your guests with white cotton gloves and let them pick up unframed prints out of your plan chest and look at them close-to, as the printmaker sees them.

## Transport of prints

Prints are easily sent round the world, which is why ideas in printmaking travel from one country to another so quickly. A few heavily inked or embossed prints cannot be rolled and must be sent flat between the boards, but most prints can be sent safely in tubes by post or air freight. Choose a cardboard or plastic tube at least 10 cm (4 in) in diameter and 15 cm (6 in) longer than the print when rolled. Domestic plastic drainpipes make excellent tubes. Roll the print very slightly tighter than the interior of the tube and wrap it in tissue paper. Tape the tissue paper so the print does not unroll and make two pads of crumpled tissue paper to protect each end of the print and to stop it moving about inside. Tubes with specially made end caps are best, but otherwise cut circles of card and tape well in place. A rolled print will need several days to relax flat again so do not force it, but put it under a board with a light weight on top.

## THE WORKING ENVIRONMENT

While relief printmaking can be done on the kitchen table and prints can be stored under the bed, this arrangement soon becomes frustrating and a more permanent workspace becomes desirable.

If you print by burnishing, your minimum needs are a good, stout multipurpose table for preparation and cutting (later to be used for printing), a drying and flat-storage area for blocks, paper and finished prints and a storage cupboard for inks, solvents and rags. A simple paper rack can be made from sheets of chipboard with bricks to create open shelves.

If you have a press it is essential to have a good floor. The larger presses are very heavy, and even when taken to pieces for moving some of the cast-iron members are still large and you will need room to manoeuvre them during assembly.

Katie Clemson working out of doors in Australia. The sun warms lino until it is soft and very easy to cut. She has drawn directly on the surface with a felt-tipped pen, which acts as a guide for her vigorous cutting using a v-shaped gouge.

### THE OPEN WORKSHOP
Points to remember when organizing an open workshop:
■ Work out a method of charging print-makers or students. Should it be by the hour? By membership? Per finished prints? Does the charge include materials?
■ Devise a booking system.
■ Organize supplies of materials and stockkeeping.
■ Work out how much you will need to pay for light, heating and storage.
■ Estimate the cost of annual building maintenance.
■ Check your insurance for people, presses and buildings.

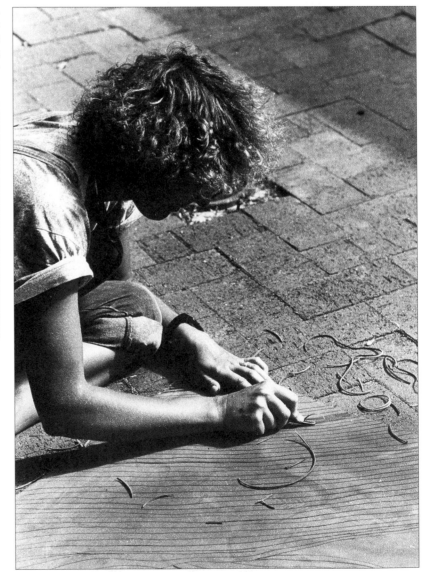

## Water, ventilation, light and heat

A good print workshop should have a water supply and sink for preparing blocks, etching lino, dampening paper and keeping the printmaker clean. Make sure the ventilation is good, especially if you are using oil–based inks; keep solvents safely and keep a dustbin for oil-soaked cleaning rags. Good, even light is essential for all stages of printmaking. An even temperature and humidity will keep paper from cockling and woodblocks from warping.

## Organizing the workspace

The preliminary drawing and the cutting of blocks should be done in a clean area away from the printing equipment. Paper and prints should also be stored in a clean area on flat, wide shelves or in a plan chest.

The printing area should be ergonomically organized so that the inking table is near to the press on one side and the fresh paper and drying system close on the other side. Inks, solvents and cleaning materials should be stored here away from the clean area.

## Teaching and editioning

If the print workshop is to be used for professional editioning or teaching it is essential to have plenty of space between fixtures to avoid congestion. Make sure the clean preparation area is well away from the printing area, and, in an editioning studio, have a separate, clean area for checking, signing, packing and storing finished prints. If you are holding classes, restrict the numbers according to the space and number of presses. Encourage good workshop practice of cleanliness, order and consideration of other workers in the studio.

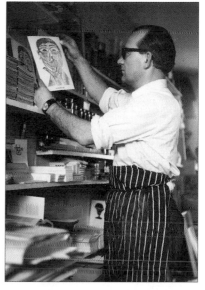

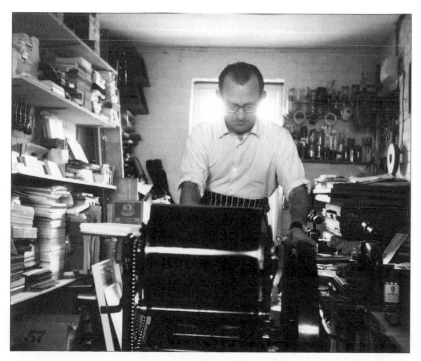

Paul Peter Piech working in his garage-studio. There is no room for a car anymore as every inch is occupied by blocks, inks and solvents, type, paper and his presses. It is all well organized but there is barely room for a second person in this studio. Under these cramped conditions he has produced a stream of poetry posters, books and other material in support of the Peace Movement. Everything is printed by him from lino and hand-set type.

## SETTING UP A WORKSPACE

Printmakers work in a variety of different places. Some use the kitchen table on which to cut blocks and print by burnishing – they put away their printmaking tools and bring out the culinary ones. Other printmakers integrate a beautiful antique press, such as an Albion, into their living area and make a feature of it.

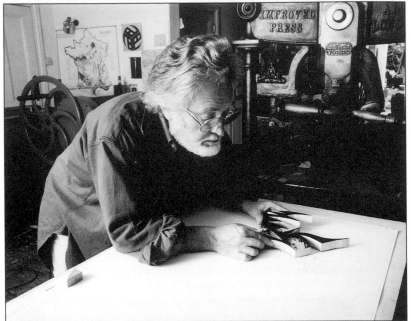

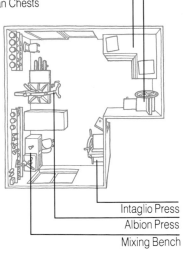

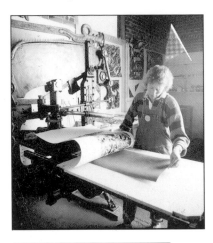

Intaglio Press

Plan Chests

Intaglio Press
Albion Press
Mixing Bench

James Burr has made his studio out of what was once his dining-room and sitting-room. There are windows at each end, three presses, an Albion and two intaglio presses as well as plan chests for storage and work benches. A very large slab of marble covers one end of a bench and is used for ink mixing and rolling up. He usually prints only ten prints in a session and leaves them to dry on top of the large surface formed by three plan chests, so he does not need a drying rack. Everything is within reach and there is plenty of space to move about.

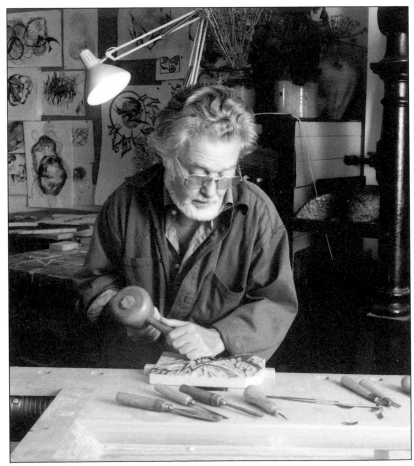

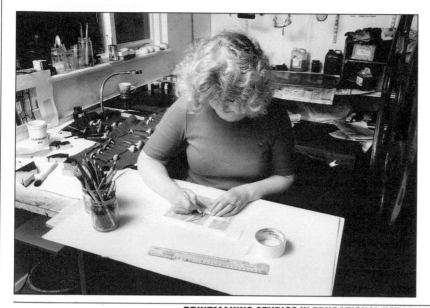

St Claire Allen works in a large purpose-built shed at the bottom of her garden. It has one long wall of windows in front of the workbench to utilize maximum natural light. Her intaglio press takes up a lot of space so she has to work in a disciplined way in what is quite a crowded space. In spite of this she undertakes editioning for other printmakers and also gives tuition in wood engraving and intaglio printmaking. Her other press, a letterpress proof press, sits in the living room of the house next to the piano.

## PRINTMAKING STUDIOS IN EDUCATIONAL ESTABLISHMENTS

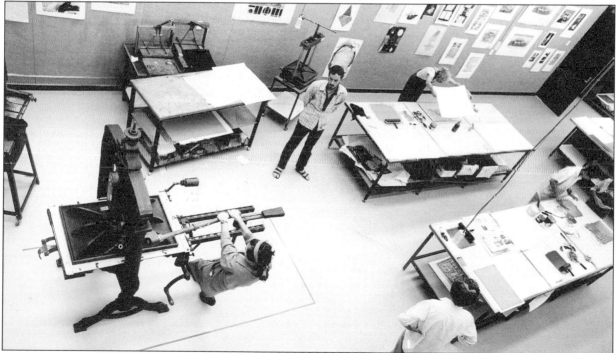

The department of printmaking in an art college or adult education centre is frequently shared between all the printmaking media. There may be an intaglio press side by side with a relief press, though this is far from ideal as printers have different requirements by way of inking slabs, hot plates, dry or dampened paper and drying methods.

It is usual to set aside one area that can be kept free of printing ink and solvents for all preliminary clean work such as designing and cutting blocks. Paper and proofs can also be kept in the clean area. Plenty of space around each fixture is essential when several students are working together. Storage cupboards with locks on doors are needed in place of open shelves for all inks, solvents and tools.

The picture, above, shows the new relief printing section on Mt. Lawley campus at the Western Australian College of Education.

Note the bench on wheels behind the Albion press. The two large benches are glass-topped and are used for mixing, rolling out ink and rolling up blocks and printing by burnishing. In the background is a screw press and a pair of small, simple proof presses. Preparatory work is done in a separate clean area adjacent to paper and print storage and a teaching area.

# Glossary

**Acetate film or sheet:** Used to set up accurate positioning for visual registration of printing blocks.

**Acid:** Corrosive liquid used to etch various materials. Those used to etch linoleum are alkalis, i.e. caustic soda solution or proprietary paint strippers.

**Acid-free:** Neutral pH state expressed on a scale 0-14, from alkalinity to acidity. pH7.0 is neutral. Used with particular reference to paper. Acid-free paper and boards are recommended for fine printmaking and framing.

**Acrylic modelling paste:** Used to build up a texture on the block surface.

**Anti-drying agents:** Additives to the ink that retard drying. Glycerine is added to water-based inks and either Vaseline, poppy oil or turpentine substitute is added to oil-based colour. Minute quantities are used. Aerosol sprays are made for the printing industry that retard formation of a dry film on ink in a tin or on the ink slab.

**Antiquarian:** Paper size used by print-makers – 79 × 135cm (31 × 53in).

**Artist's proof or AP:** Copies of a print over and above the edition (by general agreement this is not more than 10 per cent extra). These are intended for the artist's archives. They are identical to the edition copies.

**Baren:** Japanese burnishing pad made from a spiral of twisted string or wire placed between two circles of varnished cloth covered with a piece of bamboo sheath, the ends of which are knotted to form a handle. Measures 13-18cm (5-7in).

**BAT/bon à tirer:** French for 'good to print', marked on the correct working proof or trial proof which will serve as the guide for the edition.

**Bite:** The action of acid on metal or alkali on lino.

**Blanket:** Felt placed between the paper and roller in an intaglio press which is forced into the depths of the printing plate. Also a roller, covered in rubber or similar, on a letterpress proof press.

**Bled image:** The sheet of paper has no margins and the image extends to the edge.

**Bleeding colour:** When pigment spreads beyond the printed area causing a halo effect.

**Blended colour:** When two or more colours are blended by means of a roller or brush. Usually the colour is blended on the ink slab first but it can be blended on the block.

**Block:** Piece of linoleum, wood, slate, card etc. from which a print is taken.

**Bokashi:** Japanese method of blending colours in woodblock prints.

**Boxwood:** Hardwood made into cross-grain/end-grain blocks for wood engraving.

**Brayer:** Roller made of gelatine, rubber or plastic (American term).

**Brush inking:** Ink applied to the block by brush (often several colours). Emphasizes brush textures but each print will not be identical.

**Burin:** Engraving tool used on end-grain wood and metal. Also a term used to describe the characteristic line of engraving.

**Burnishing:** Applying pressure by rubbing with a piece of bone, a baren, wooden spoon, smooth stone etc. on the back of paper laid on an inked block.

**Cancellation:** Defacement of the printing block so no more copies can be printed.

**Chiaroscuro woodcut:** Early form of colour printing in Europe from several woodcuts and using a series of browns or greys.

**China paper:** Fine strong paper suitable for relief prints. Originally made in China from mulberry bark.

**Chop mark:** Blind embossed stamp in the corner of a print that denotes artist, printer or publisher, or a phrase such as 'printed by the artist' (American term).

**Collage block:** Printing surface created by modelling paste or glueing materials on a backing board. Can be printed relief or intaglio.

**Collagraph:** A print taken from a collaged block or plate. In USA both collagraph and collograph are used. Comes from the French *coller* to stick.

**Colour print:** A print using several colours.

**Colour separation:** A separate drawing made of each colour in a print.

**Coloured print:** A print with colour, usually water-colour, added by hand after printing.

**Commission:** A contract between artist and publisher; also a proportion of a sale taken by a print seller.

**Copyright:** The copyright of a print belongs to the publisher (who may also be the artist) unless otherwise agreed.

**Cushion:** A leather bag or pillow filled with sand placed under an end-grain block so it can be turned easily.

**Dabber:** Inking pad made of soft leather. Used to ink the block before the invention of rollers and still used occasionally today.

**Date:** Date of publication of a print, sometimes written on the print.

**Deckle:** The irregular edge of a handmade sheet of paper on all four sides. Mould-made paper has two deckle edges and two torn edges. False deckles are made by tearing, grating with a rasp or an irregular cutting blade.

**Dolly:** Poupée or tampon, a twist of cloth round a pad or a roll of felt used to put colour by hand in specific parts of a block in multi-coloured inking.

**Double elephant:** Paper size used by print-makers – 102 × 69cm (40 × 27in).

**Driers:** Additives to ink that speed drying. Water-based inks rarely need such additives as they usually dry too fast anyway; oil-based inks may need extra driers, though ready-mixed inks have some already incorporated. Driers come in paste form and consist of rosin plus some metal in the form of cobalt, lead or magnesium. Minute quantities are used and added only to the ink being immediately used.

**Edition:** The total number of prints published not including artist's proofs or other extra proofs.

**Editioning:** The printing of the edition once the definitive image is settled by proofing. In reduction prints proofing and editioning are combined.

**Editor's proof:** A proof reserved for the editor who has organized the publication of a print, or more often a portfolio of prints.

**Electrotype:** Metal duplicate printing plate made from the original linoleum or wood engraving where there is a long printing run; usually for book illustrations. Now almost obsolete as commercial letterpress printing declines.

**Embossing:** A raised design created when damp paper is moulded by pressure. Engraved blocks of lino, wood or metal are used, with or without ink, usually in a copperplate press, which gives greater pressure than relief presses. Japanese artists use the smooth end of a brush handle to push the damp paper into the engraved block.

**End-grain:** A block of hardwood cut through the trunk at right angles, showing the growth rings.

**Engraving:** A general term for an incised mark, an incised block, or a print taken from an incised block.

**Etching linoleum:** Caustic soda (sodium hydroxide) solution is usually used, though proprietary brands of paint stripper are also suitable. The process is unreliable, dangerous to the skin and breaks down the lino surface into an aquatint-like texture.

**Extenders (reducing and tinting mediums):** Transparent additives to inks that dilute the pigment colour but maintain the correct viscosity for rolling. Available for both water-based and oil-based inks.

**Film:** Transparent plastic sheet used as a support for photographic emulsion, or used to draw or paint upon as an aid to registration of colours or to make a photographic positive.

**"Fingers":** Strips of paper 2.5 × 13cm (1 × 5in) folded and used to hold a sheet of paper while printing and when fingers are inky.

**Flocking:** Wool or other fibres glued to a fabric printing block to increase the amount of ink it will take up during printing.

**Formed paper print:** Paper pulp manipulated to form a sheet, often irregular in shape and incorporating dyes, other paper and vegetable matter. Can be printed after the sheet is dry.

**Fourdrinier paper machine:** All machine-made papers are made in a continuous web on this machine, which was invented in 1798.

**Gesso:** A mixture of plaster of paris and glue used to create shallow texture on a linoleum block surface. Will last for a modest sized edition without crumbling.

**Glue:** Woodworking glue used to stick shallow objects on to a collage block, or to replace a section of linoleum block where cutting was incorrect. In diluted form PVA can be used as a sealant to prevent penetration of oil-based inks in very absorbent linoleum or collaged materials.

**Gouge:** V- or U-shaped tool to engrave lino, wood and plastics.

**Grain:** Pattern of fibres in wood.

**Graver:** See burin.

**Group print:** Invented by Michael Rothenstein for co-operative mural-scale projects.

**Gum arabic:** Principal element in water-based inks.

**Handmade paper:** Paper made by hand in single sheets, having a deckle on all four sides. Should be used unsized or only very lightly sized for relief printmaking.

**Hand-colouring:** Colour added to the print by hand after editioning.

**Hardboard cut:** An engraving in hardboard (Masonite in USA).

**Hardener:** A liquid used to seal and harden very soft and absorbent materials, usually water-soluble plastics; boiled linseed oil used to harden open-textured wood.

**Hors commerce or HC proof:** Prints outside the edition offered for sale. Usually those kept by the publisher or collaborators for reference only.

**Imperial:** Paper size used by printmakers – 56 × 76cm (22 × 30in).

**Impression:** Any printed copy; the indentation left in paper when high pressure has been used in relief or intaglio printing.

**Industrial resins:** Used to build up textures on printing blocks.

**Ink:** Pigment suspended in a semi-liquid medium, which may be gum arabic (water-based), oil, varnish or a complex mixture of chemicals (oil-based). Can be mixed by the artist using powder pigments, artists' oil paint or water-colour and gouache paint or bought ready mixed.

**Ink slab:** Sheet of white marble, plate glass or smooth white plastic on which ink is spread, mixed and rolled.

**Intaglio:** A large category of techniques used in printmaking: hard and soft ground etching, aquatint and lift ground aquatint (all produced by etching in acid); engraving, drypoint and mezzotint (all produced by direct working on the plate with tools). The ink is held in the incised portion of a block. Generally used on metal blocks but can also be used on linoleum blocks. Requires strong pressure from a copperplate press to effect transfer of ink to paper.

**Japanese paper:** Handmade paper using long fibres from mulberry bark and other plants indigenous to Japan. Sold unsized. Much favoured by all printmakers and particularly good for burnished prints, being very strong.

**Jigsaw blocks:** Printing blocks cut up into pieces, each section being inked in a different colour and the whole block reassembled to be printed together.

**Kentō:** Registration marks used in traditional Japanese woodblock printing and now widely used by relief printmakers. Consists of an L-shaped strip and long strip of wood or linoleum on the lower right corner and on one long side, into which the paper is slipped ensuring registration between the different blocks. A modified system employs strips of card glued on to a sheet of paper laid on the bed of the press with the position of the block(s) marked.

**Key block:** Where one colour carries the essential part of the design and is printed first so that subsequent colours are "keyed" to it. Occasionally the key design is not printed at all but is used as a guide only for the varied colours or it may be printed last in the actual editioning process.

**Laid paper:** The impression of the mould wires in handmade paper appears as light lines, also imitated in machine-made papers.

**Leather strop:** The undressed side of a piece of leather used for the final smoothing in sharpening tools.

**Letterpress:** Relief printing from type and blocks, usually commercial, now rapidly disappearing and being replaced by offset lithography and photocopying.

**Light-sensitive coating:** A coating on paper, film, metal plate or boxwood which reacts to light by hardening in exposed areas. Also acts as an acid resist in etching photo-relief blocks.

**Limited edition:** A printing of a declared number of prints supported by the numbering of each print as part of the total.

**Line-block, cut, engraving, plate:** Commercial printing term for a photo-etched relief block in letterpress printing where only line and solid areas are used – no tonal areas.

**Linocut, linoleum engraving:** A print taken from linoleum.

**Lithography:** A planographic technique used in printmaking based on the antipathy of grease and water. Originally the design was drawn on stone but today zinc or aluminium sheet are often substituted.

**Makeready:** Layers of thin paper pasted under a block or to a tympan to even out irregular pressure points.

**Margin:** Border of unprinted paper around an image.

**Master printer:** The head printer or owner of a studio specializing in editioning artists' prints.

**Matt:** Dull finish of printing ink when dry on paper.

**Medium:** In printmaking the main methods: i.e. relief, intaglio, lithography and screen-printing. Also: a substance that binds pigment.

**Metal cut:** Early engraved metal plate relief- or surface-printed.

**Mixed media:** Artists' prints that combine more than one basic method: linocutting and intaglio, embossing and lithography etc.

**Monochrome:** A single coloured print, sometimes but not always black.

**Monotype/monoprint:** A painting on a smooth surface that is transferred to a sheet of paper by burnishing or printing in a press. Further impressions can be taken but they get progressively weaker. Also: any unique print.

**Mould-made paper:** A machine-made paper from the same high quality pulp as handmade paper, but less expensive. Has two deckles. Ideal for relief printmaking.

**Mount:** Rigid paper board used to protect prints (called mat in USA). Ideally made of acid-free board and can be for background only or used in conjunction with a window mount.

**Mounted block:** Where linoleum or other material is glued on to a wood, paper or composition board for strength, ease of handling or to bring it up to type-height.

**Multi-block printing:** Where separate blocks are used for each colour. They may all be of the same dimensions or may have free-form shapes.

**Multi-coloured inking:** Where several colours are applied to one block. The areas of colour are usually separated from each colour. Ink is applied with a small roller, brush or poupée. Stencils can also be used to locate areas to be coloured.

**Multiple editions:** More than one edition of the same image, now frowned upon as not making it clear to the public the real size of the edition. Sometimes printed on a different paper from the first edition. Print number should indicate the facts.

**Multiple tool:** A tool for wood engraving that makes several parallel cuts.

**Number:** The number of the individual print from the total edition. Usually expressed as a fraction such as 2/75, 48/50, the edition size being the second number, written in pencil.

**Number of colours:** Number of separate colours used; does not necessarily coincide with the number of printings, see multi-coloured inking.

**Number of blocks:** Number of separate printing surfaces or matrices, which may not coincide with the number of colours, see above.

**Objet trouvé:** Any found object that can be inked and printed.

**Offset:** Short for offset lithography or commercial lithography. Also: to offset a proof on to a new block. Also: offset printing from fragile materials.

**Original print:** A print designed and printed by the artist or under the artist's supervision, signed, numbered and in a limited edition. Not a reproduction.

**Packing:** Several sheets of paper placed on top of the printing paper and block in a press to soften and distribute the pressure applied. Also used to describe the similar pad of paper placed beneath the block/printing paper sandwich when burnishing or using foot pressure. Soft packing of sheets of felt or foam is used to pack very delicate blocks where a degree of embossing is required.

**Paper:** A sheet made from matted vegetable fibres most commonly used as a support for printed images.

**Passed for press:** See BAT.

**Photo-mechanical:** A broad term for any reproductive process that uses photography to create a printing matrix.

**Plate:** Sheet of metal or plastic that is engraved, etched or collaged so that a print can be taken from it; thinner than a block.

**Plank:** Cut of wood parallel to the grain, used for woodcuts.

**Plaster print:** A print taken from an engraved plaster block; must be burnished.

**Plate mark:** The shape of a plate embossed in the paper, usually seen in intaglio but also seen in high pressure relief printing.

**Printed by the artist/by hand:** Sometimes written on the print or embossed by means of a stamp.

**Printing order:** The order of printing colours must take into account the effect of one over another, e.g. light over dark, transparent over opaque.

**Printer's proof:** When a professional printer is used one copy is usually made for his archives.

**Progressives:** A series of proofs that show each individual colour as well as the first and second colours, the first, second and third and so on.

**Proofing:** The taking of the trial impression prior to editioning, also called trial or working proof. May involve colour variations.

**Publisher:** The person who issues and sells prints, may be the artist arranging his own distribution.

**Publisher's proof:** A copy of the editioned image for the publisher's records.

**Punches:** Shaped metal tools that are hammered into the block making repeated marks often in the form of dots, stars, lines, circles etc.

**Pulp:** Paper pulp, which will be formed into sheets, webs or formed irregular shapes.

**Rainbow colours:** See blended colours.

**Reduction blocks:** Only one block of linoleum or wood is used to create a multi-coloured image. Parts of the block are cut away, a colour printed, then further areas cut away and another colour printed. Usually light colours are printed first ending with the darkest. No preliminary proofing of the complete image is possible. Also known as suicide prints as no second thoughts are possible.

**Registration systems:** The correct positioning of different colours in relationship to each other by various systems, which may be mechanical on automatic or semi-automatic presses, or by means of pins, strips of board or marks on a sheet or purely by eye.

**Relief:** Also known as surface printing – where all non-printing surfaces are cut away and ink is applied to the remaining surfaces.

**Relief etching:** Any intaglio plate surface-printed.

**Reproduction:** A printed copy of a drawing or painting usually made by technicians using photo-mechanical methods.

**Resist:** A substance applied to the surface of the block to protect it from corrosive attack. Can be wax, varnish or adhesive plastic sheet.

**Reverse:** When a preliminary design has to be reversed as a block cutting guide so that when printed the image will be the right way round.

**Riffler:** A small filing or scraping tool used by woodcarvers and wood engravers.

**Roller:** Used to spread ink in an even film on the inking slab and thence to the block surface; made in various lengths and diametres of gelatine, rubber or plastic (polyurethane).

**Royal:** Paper size used by printmakers, 31 × 67.5cm (20 × 25in).

**Rubbing:** A sheet of paper placed over a textured surface and rubbed with a wax crayon or block, which registers the raised surface beneath. Also burnishing.

**Scorper:** Type of engraving tool used for wood engraving.

**Screenprinting:** Also called silkscreen. A planographic method of printing in which ink is pushed through a mesh or screen, some parts of which are sealed, on to paper placed beneath.

**Sealant:** Varnish or diluted PVA used to seal the surface of a linoleum or wood block to improve the acceptance of ink and reduce the quantity of ink used.

**Separations:** Where each colour is drawn on a separate sheet as a guide to block cutting.

**Signature:** Each print in an edition is signed by the artist to denote approval of the print. Usually in pencil as it is difficult to change or remove without disturbing the paper fibres.

**Size:** The dimensions of paper or image. Also: gelatine or glue used to coat paper and other materials to seal and strengthen them.

**Spitsticker:** An elliptical tool used in wood engraving.

**Solvent:** One substance used to dissolve another. Basic solvents in printmaking are water for water-based inks, paraffin (kerosene), turpentine substitute or white spirit (mineral spirit), or petrol (gasolene) for oil-based inks. Gelatine rollers should be cleaned with paraffin only.

**Squash factor:** Halo of thicker ink around edge of printed shapes indicates the ink is too thin or the pressure too high.

**States:** Working proofs taken in sequence and used by the artist to judge progress in the work.

**Stencil:** Ink applied through a stencil on to the block surface (partial inking) or on to the print. Stencils are also used to mask part of the inked block or part of the print. Stencils are cut from stiff paper or stencil paper or are identical to the screens used in screenprinting. Ink is applied through the stencil by roller, brush or poupeé.

**Stones:** For sharpening tools. First use artificial stones (Axolite, carborundum or India) and finish with the finer natural stones (Arkansas or Washita). Use oil as a lubricant unless working with water-based inks, in which case keep separate stones and use water as the lubricant.

**Stripping:** Excess ink can be stripped from all or part of the inked block prior to printing or from the print by laying a piece of tissue paper on the area to be reduced and peeling off. Also used to keep a matt surface on the ink when dry.

**Strong copperplate oil:** Used as the ink medium in Blair Hughes-Stanton's method. Powder pigment, artists' oil paint or ready mixed printers' ink supply the pigment. Also sold as thick copperplate oil. Usually used by intaglio printers.

**Sulphite:** Paper merchants' term for wood pulp used in making some papers.

**Thinners:** Water-based inks are thinned with water; oil-based inks with linseed oil, copperplate oil, poppy oil, Vaseline or turpentine substitute.

**Tint tool:** A tool used for wood engraving that makes fine, even width lines.

**Trial proof:** A working proof used to try out different colours or orders of printing colours. Not part of the edition.

**Type high:** In letterpress printing the height of metal type is usually 2.33cm (0.918in). The measurement varies slightly in Europe and elsewhere.

**Unique impression:** One print which is not repeated in that form.

**Unlimited or unrestricted edition:** An edition that is not limited or numbered though there may be a stated total printed.

**Veiner:** A v-shaped cutting tool used in woodcutting.

**Viscosity:** The relative fluidity of a printing ink.

**Washing-up:** The cleaning of ink slabs, rollers, mixing knives and any other tools as well as the printing block(s); see solvent.

**Waste sheets:** Extra sheets of paper used during proofing or editioning which are used to set up the machine or test registration. Not part of the edition.

**Watermark:** Design in paper seen when the sheet is held against the light. Usually the manufacturer's mark but artists' devices or signatures are also incorporated.

**White line engraving:** A characteristic of wood engraving where the design appears as white lines on a dark background.

**Woodblock print:** The Western term for a traditional Japanese woodcut.

**Woodcut:** A print taken from a side-grain or plank woodblock or any manufactured board such as plywood.

**Wood engraving:** A print taken from end- or cross-grain woodblocks. Occasionally used for woodcuts that are very finely worked with engraving tools, particularly early woodcuts.

**Wove paper:** Paper without laid lines, i.e. most papers.

**Xylography -er:** Woodcutting -er, wood engraving -er, from the Greek *xylos*, wood.

## LOOKING AT RELIEF PRINTS

National collections of prints are often kept in art galleries or museums of art within a Department of Prints and Drawings. Sometimes it is called the Print Room. Some Print Rooms have an open policy and you can go without an appointment and ask to see specific prints in their catalogue. Other museums require an application in writing with details of your particular interests. They are usually very helpful to anyone with a serious enquiry.

Many of the major collections have both permanent and changing exhibitions. There are also a number of international and national print competitions in various countries: watch the art magazines for announcements. Art colleges with print departments are also worth contacting. Ask them when they have their graduation or diploma shows. Not only will you be in touch with the latest trends, but you can also buy prints by future major talents.

Most countries have organizations run by artists that put on exhibitions of members' work and act as the source for information on practical aspects of printmaking. They often hold slide libraries or plan-chest collections of members' work that may be consulted. Commercial galleries do not specialize in relief prints, but watch the listings for exhibitions.

### MAJOR COLLECTIONS
#### Great Britain
■ The Victoria and Albert Museum, South Kensington, London SW7 (the Print Room; the Library for books on prints and the Henry Cole Wing, where there is an excellent permanent display on the techniques of printmaking).
■ The Science Museum, South Kensington, London SW7 (permanent display on the history of printing).
■ The Tate Gallery, Millbank, London SW1.
■ St Bride Printing Library, Bride Lane, London EC4.
■ The British Museum, Great Russell Street, London WC1.
■ Holburne of Menstrie Museum, Great Pulteney Street, Bath (block-printed textiles).

#### United States of America
■ Museum of Modern Art, 11 West 53rd Street, New York, New York.
■ Brooklyn Museum, Eastern Parkway, New York.
■ Metropolitan Museum, Fifth Avenue at 82nd Street, New York, New York.
■ Library of Congress, 110 Second Street, Washington, D.C.
■ Los Angeles County Museum of Art, 5905 Wilshire Boulevard, Los Angeles.
■ University of California at Los Angeles, Grunwald Center for the Graphic Arts, 2122 Dickson Art Center, 405 Hilgard, Los Angeles.
■ California Palace of the Legion of Honour, Achenbach Foundation for Graphic Arts, Lincoln Park, San Francisco.

#### Canada
■ National Gallery of Ottawa, Lorne Building, Elgin and Slater Streets, Ottawa.
■ Art Gallery of Ontario, 317 Dundas Street West, Toronto, Ontario.
■ Glenbow Museum, 130 9th Avenue SE, Calgary, Alberta.
■ Burnaby Art Gallery, 6344 Gilpin Street, Burnaby, British Columbia.

### Australia
■ Australia National Gallery, Canberra, Australian Capital Territory.
■ Art Gallery of New South Wales, Art Gallery Road, The Domain, Sydney, New South Wales.
■ National Gallery of Victoria, 180 St Kilda Road, Melbourne.
■ Art Gallery of South Australia, North Terrace, Adelaide.

### Associations of printmakers

### Great Britain
■ Printmakers Council of Great Britain, 31 Clerkenwell Close, London EC1.
■ Royal Society of Painter-Etchers and Engravers, Bankside Gallery, London SE1.
■ The Society of Wood Engravers, c/o Hilary Paynter, Hon. Sec., 10 Riverdale Road, East Twickenham, Middlesex.

### USA
■ World Print Council, 1700 17th Street, San Francisco.
■ California Society of Printmakers, P.O. Box 3296, Berkeley, California.

### Australia
■ Print Council of Australia, 105 Collins Street, Melbourne, Victoria.

### Print workshops offering relief facilities
### Great Britain
■ Bristol Printmaking Workshop, MacArthur Building, Gas Ferry Road, Bristol BS1.
■ Bracken Press, 2 Roscoe Street, Scarborough, N. Yorks.
■ Dundee Printmakers Workshop, 38-40 Seagate, Dundee.
■ Glasgow Print Studio, in process of moving as we go to press.
■ Holland Park Studio, 50 Queensdale Road, London W11.
■ I.M. Imprimit, 219A Victoria Park Road, London E9 (contract printing only).
■ Inverness Printmakers Workshop, 20 Bank Street, Inverness.
■ Lowick House Print Workshop, Lowick, Near Ulverston, Cumbria.
■ Moorland House Workshop, Burrowbridge, Near Bridgewater, Somerset.
■ Oxford Printmakers Co-op, Christadelphian Hall, Tyndale Road, Oxford.
■ Peacock Printmakers, 21 Castle Street, Aberdeen.
■ Pigeonsford Printmaking Workshop, Pigeonsford Mansion, Llangranog, Llandysul, Dyffed.
■ The Printing Studio, 121 Honor Oak Road, London SE23.
■ White Gum Press, Fleetwater Farm, Newtown Minstead, near Lyndhurst, Hampshire.

### USA
■ Black Stone Press, 865 Florida Street, San Francisco, California.

■ Chicago Center for the Print, 1505-1513 W Fullerton Avenue, Chicago, Illinois.
■ Chip Elwell, 355 W 35th Street, New York.
■ Erie Lackawanna Editions, 404 3rd Street, Hoboken, New Jersey.
■ Experimental Workshop, P.O. Box 77504, San Francisco, California.
■ Flatstone Studio, 210 W Comanche Avenue, Tampa, Florida.
■ Impressions Workshop, 27 Stanhope Street, Boston, Mass.
■ Michael Berdan, Woodblock printing and cutting, 11 Shady Hill Square, Cambridge, Massachusetts (Japanese method).
■ The Printmaking Workshop, 114 W 17th Street, New York.
■ Rancho Linda Vista, Box E, Oragle, Arizona.
■ X Press, 116 W 29th Street, New York.

### Australia
■ The Newcastle Printmakers Workshop, Newcastle Community Arts and Adult Education Centre, Corner Union Street and Parkway Avenue, Newcastle, New South Wales.
■ Ritchies Mill Arts Centre, Gorge Street, Launceston, Tasmania.
■ Victoria Print Workshop, Corner Courtney and Blackwood Streets, North Melbourne, Victoria.
■ Workshop Arts Centre, 33 Laurel Street, Willoughby, New South Wales.
■ Zero Print Workshop, 68 Oxford Street, Darlinghurst, New South Wales.

### Suppliers of relief printmaking equipment and materials
### Great Britain
■ Atlantis Paper Co., Gullivers Wharf, 105 Wapping Lane, London E1 (paper, presses, general supplies).
■ Ault and Wiborg Ltd, 71 Standen Road, London SW18 (inks and rollers).
■ R.K. Burt & Co., 57 Union Street, London SE1 (paper).
■ Coates Brothers Inks Ltd, Grape Street, Leeds, W. Yorks. (letterpress inks).
■ L. Cornellissen & Son Ltd, 105 Great Russell Street, London WC1 (dry pigments, tools, general supplies).
■ Croda Ink Ltd, 170 Glasgow Road, Edinburgh (inks).
■ Dryads, Northgates, Leicester (school-grade tools and inks).
■ Falkiner Fine Papers, 76 Southampton Row, London WC1 (paper, books on printmaking and paper).
■ Daler-Rowney Ltd, Southern Industrial Area, P.O. Box 10, Bracknell, Berks and 12 Percy Street, London W1 (school-grade tools and general supplies).
■ Hunter-Penrose Ltd, Spa Road, London SE16 (presses, inks, rollers, chemicals).
■ Intaglio Printmaker, 323 Goswell Road, London EC1 (all printmaking supplies).
■ T.N. Lawrence & Son Ltd, 2-4 Bleeding Heart Yard, Greville Street, London EC1 (wood engraving blocks, tools, tool sharpening service, paper and inks).
■ T.J. Morgan (Barry) Ltd, Ty-Verlon Industrial Estate, Cardiff, Barry, Cardiff (Delrin engraving material).
■ Modbury Engineering, 311 Frederick Terrace, London E8 (presses and removal and maintenance).
■ Paintworks Ltd, 93 Kingsland Road, London E2 (paper, general and some printmakers supplies).

■ John Purcell Papers, 219 Eversleigh Road, London SW11 (paper).
■ Michael Putman, 151 Lavender Hill, London SW11 (tools, paper, inks and other printmakers' supplies).
■ Reeves Arts Materials, P.O. Box 91, Whitefriars Avenue, Wealdstone, Harrow, Middlesex and 178 Kensington High Street, London W8 (school-grade tools and general supplies).
■ Harry Rochat, Cotswold Lodge, Staplyton Road, Barnet, Herts (presses).
■ Alec Tiranti Ltd, 70 High Street, Theale, Bucks (woodcutting tools).
■ Winsor and Newton, 51 Rathbone Place, London W1 (school-grade tools and general supplies).
■ Yorkshire Printmakers and Distributors Ltd, 1 Windmill Lane, Emley Moor, Near Huddersfield, W. Yorks (printmakers' supplies).
■ Frederick Ullmer Ltd, City Gate Unit, Eleys Estate, Angel Road, London N18 (printers' engineers).

### USA
■ Andrews Nelson Whitehead, 31-10 48th Avenue, Long Island City, New York (paper).
■ American Printing Equipment & Supply Co., 42-25 9th Street, Long Island City, New York (presses and printmakers' supplies).
■ Apex Printers Rollers Co., 1541 North 16th Street, St Louis, Massachusetts (rollers).
■ Graphic Chemical and Ink Co., P.O. Box 27, 728 North Yale Avenue, Villa Park, Illinois (inks).
■ Fine Art Materials, 539 La Guardia Place, New York (wood engravers' supplies).
■ J.Johnson & Co., 33 Matinecock Avenue, Port Washington, New York (wood engraving blocks, tools, inks and general supplies).
■ Light Impressions Corp., P.O. Box 3012, Rochester, New York (mail order printmakers' and general supplies).
■ Edward C. Lyons, 3646 White Plains Road, Bronx, New York (wood engraving tools).
■ New York Central Supply, Dept. P.N., 62 3rd Avenue, New York (paper and general printmaking supplies).
■ The Paper Source Inc. 1212 Washington Avenue, Wilmette, Illinois (paper).
■ Printmakers Machine Co., 724 North Yale Avenue, Villa Park, Illinois (presses).
■ Rembrandt Graphic Arts, The Cane Farm, Rosemont, New Jersey (printmakers' general supplies).
■ The Sander Wood Engraving Co. Inc., 212 Lincoln Street, Porter, Indiana (wood engraving supplies).
■ Sculpture Associates Ltd, 114 East 25th Street, New York (wood engravers' supplies).
■ Daniel Smith Inc. 4130 1st Street South, Seattle, Washington (mail order paper, presses, inks and general supplies).
■ Zellerbach Paper Co., 245 South Spruce Avenue, South San Francisco (paper).

### Australia
■ Art Papers and Supplies, 243 Stirling Highway, Nedlands, Western Australia (paper and general supplies).
■ Melbourne Etching Supplies, 227 Brunswick Street, Fitzroy, Victoria (paper, presses and general supplies).
■ Tamarisque, 27 Albion Street, Surrey Hills, New South Wales (paper).

# Bibliography

The books listed here cover individual artists and groups as well as techniques used in relief printmaking and some basic books on other printmaking methods.

Ainslie, Patricia. *Images of the Land, Canadian Block Prints 1919-1945* Calgary 1985.

Bliss, D.P. *Edward Bawden*. Godalming 1981.

Bosence, Susan. *Hand Block Printing and Resist Dyeing*. London 1985.

Butler, Roger. *Melbourne Woodcuts and Linocuts of the 1920s and 1930s* (catalogue). Melbourne 1981.
*Australian Prints in the Australian National Gallery*. Canberra 1985.

Castleman, Riva. *Prints of the Twentieth Century, a History*. London 1976.
*Prints from Blocks*. New York 1983.

Chamberlain, Walter. *The Thames and Hudson Manual of Etching and Engraving*. London 1972.
*The Thames and Hudson Manual of Wood Engraving*. London 1978.
*The Thames and Hudson Manual of Woodcut Printmaking and Related Techniques*. London 1978.

Chibbett, David. *The History of Japanese Printing and Book Illustration*. Tokyo 1977.

Dawson, John, Ed. *The Complete Guide to Prints and Printmaking*. New York 1981.

D'Oonoh, Ellen G. and Joan Feinberg. *Jim Dine Prints 1977-1985*. New York 1986.

Deutcher, Chris and Roger Butler. *A Survey of Australian Relief Prints 1900-1950* (catalogue). Melbourne 1978.

Draffin, Nicholas. *Australian Woodcuts and Linocuts of the 1920s and 1930s*. Melbourne 1976.

Eichenberg, Fritz. *The Art of the Print*. London 1976.

Fine, Ruth. *Gemini G.E.L. Art and Collaboration*. New York 1984.

Fisher, Jean. *Frank Stella, Works and New Graphics* (catalogue). London 1985.

Gascoigne, Bamber. *How to Identify Prints*. London 1986.

Garrett, Albert. *A History of Wood Engraving*. London 1978.
*British Wood Engraving of the 20th Century: A Personal View*. London 1980.

Gilmour, Pat. *Modern Prints*. London 1970. *The Mechanised Image: An Historical Perspective on Twentieth Century Prints*. London 1978.
*Artists at Curwen*. London 1977.
*Artists in Print*. London 1981.

Gross, Anthony. *Etching, Engraving and Intaglio Printing*. London 1973.

Hacking, Nicholas and Frank Tinsley, Silvie Turner, Bernard Fitzsimmonds. *Practical Printmaking*. Newton Abbot 1983.

Hayter, Stanley William. *About Prints*. London 1962.
*New Ways of Gravure* (revised edition). New York 1981.

Heller, Jules. *Printmaking Today*.
New York 1972. *Papermaking*. New York 1978.

Jones, Stanley. *Lithography for Artists*. London 1967.

Lambert, Susan. *Printmaking*. London 1983.

Leaf, Ruth. *Etching and Engraving*. New York 1976.

Mackley, George. *Wood Engraving*. Old Woking 1981 (reprint).

Mara, Tim. *The Thames and Hudson Manual of Screen Printing*. London 1979.

McLean, Ruari. *Edward Bawden, a Book of Cuts*. London 1979.

Michener, J.A. *The Modern Japanese Print*. Rutland 1968.

Moran, James. *Printing Presses*. London 1973.

Moses, Cherie and James Purdham, Dwight Bowhay, Roland Hosein. *Health and Safety in Printmaking – a Manual for Printmakers*. Edmonton 1978.

North, Ian. *The Art of Dorrit Black*. Melbourne 1979.
*The Art of Margaret Preston*. S. Australia 1980.

O'Connor, John. *The Technique of Wood Engraving*. London 1971.

Anon. *Paper Art and Technology* (catalogue). San Francisco 1978.

Peterdi, Gabor. *Printmaking*. London 1959.

Petit, Gaston and Amadio Arboleda.
*Evolving Techniques in Japanese Woodblock Prints*. Tokyo 1977.

Proud, Nora. *Textile Printing and Dyeing*. London 1965.

Robertson, Bruce and David Gormley. *Learn to Print Step-by-Step*. London 1987.

Ross, John and Clare Romano. *The Complete Printmaker*. New York 1972.

Rothenstein, Michael. *Linocuts and Woodcuts*. London 1962.
*Frontiers of Printmaking: New Aspects of Relief Prints*. New York 1966.
*Relief Printmaking*. London 1970.

Rumpek, Heinrich. *Wood Engraving*. Geneva 1972.

Saff, Donald and Deli Sacilotto. *Printmaking*.
New York 1978.

Salter, Rebecca. *Japanese Woodblock Printing*.
London 1987.

Simmons, Rosemary. *Collecting Original Prints*. London 1980.

Smith, Lawrence. *The Japanese Print Since 1900*.
London 1983.
*Contemporary Japanese Prints*. London 1985.

Smith, Robert. *Noel Counihan 1931-81*. Sydney 1981.

Toale, Bernard. *The Art of Papermaking*. Worcester 1983.

Turner, Silvie Ed. *Printmakers Council Handbook of Printmaking Supplies*. London 1977.

Turner, Silvie and Birgit Skiold. *Handmade Paper Today*. London 1983.

Van Bodegraven, Kayes. *Handmade Paper-making for Beginners*. Melbourne 1976.

Vicary, Richard. *The Thames and Hudson Manual of Lithography*. London 1976.

Warner, Glen. *Building a Print Collection*. Toronto 1981.

Watrous, James. *A Century of American Printmaking, 1880-1980*. Madison 1984.

Wenniger, Mary Ann. *Collagraph Printmaking*. New York 1975.

# Index

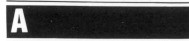
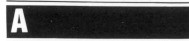
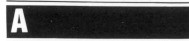
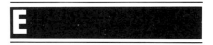
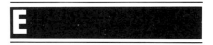

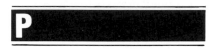

# Acknowledgements

*The authors would like to thank the following artists for permission to reproduce their work:*
Sarah van Niekirk (p.12), Roy Willingham (p.12), Michael Rothenstein (pp.18, 27, 46, 97), Edward Bawden (p.19), Monica Poole (p.26), Judith Ingram (p.27), Lynne Moore (pp.30, 123), Roy Lefroy (p.31), Tsugumi Ota (pp.33, 167), Gladys McAvoy (p.35), Simon King (pp.36, 55), Peter Daglish (p.37), Marthe Armitage (pp.38, 162), Carol Walklin (pp.39, 49, 163), Paul Peter Piech (pp.40, 69), Ann Conner (p.41), Peter Ford (p.41), James Burr (p.44), Ann-Marie Le Quesne (p.45), Paul Huxley (pp.47, 58), Bob Rain (p.60), Rosalind Cuthbert (p.61), John Muafangejo (p.69), Trevor Allen (p.72, 122), John Jackson (p.72), St Claire Allen (p.85), Fiona Hamley (pp.99, 123), Betty Bates (p.102), Yolanda Christian (p.104), Heinke Jenkins (p.105), Anne Jope (p.107), Holly Berry (p.134), Ivy Smith (p.134), Edwina Ellis (p.135), Mary Pacios Humphrey (p.160), Willie Rogers (p.163), Ian Mortimer (p.164), Colin Walklin (p.164), Susan Bosence (p.166).

*We would like to thank the following museums and galleries for permission to reproduce works in their possession:*
**Male Bather**, Edvard Munch (p.6), Oslo Kommunes Kunstsamlinger, Munch Museet; **Bogenshütze**, Wassily Kandinsky (p.7), Victoria and Albert Museum; **Painting in a Gold Frame**, Roy Lichtenstein (p.10), Tate Gallery; **Les Bandereilles**, Pablo Picasso (p.11), Galerie Louise Leiris, Paris, © ADAGP, Paris and DACS 1988; **Puddle**, Maurits Cornelis Escher (p.11), © M.C. Escher, c/o Cordon Art BV, Holland; **Mahana Atua**, Paul Gauguin (p.13), Victoria and Albert Museum; **Between Moments**, Akira Kurasaki (p.14), British Museum © Akira Kurasaki; **Charing Cross Mural**, David Gentleman (p.15), London Regional Transport Board; **Cubist Figure**, Josef Čapek (p.15), Museum of Modern Art, New York, gift of John Torson; **Untitled**, John Walker (p.17), Tate Gallery; **The Model in Thea's Chair**, Amy Kingston (p.18), collection: City of Ballarat Fine Art Gallery; **The Gust of Wind**, Ethel Spowers (p.18), reproduced by permission of the Australian National Gallery, Canberra; **Speed**, Claude Flight (p.19), Victoria and Albert Museum; **Portrait of Frau H.M.**, Max Beckmann (p.20), © DACS 1988; **Camouflaged Ship in Dry Dock, Liverpool 1918,**, Edward Wadsworth (p.20), Victoria and Albert Museum; **Christ on the Throne being Mocked**, Albrecht Dürer (p.21), Victoria and Albert Museum; **The Serpent**, Raoul Dufy (p.21), ADAGP, Paris and DACS, London; **'84 Katsura (XII)**, Seiko Kawachi (p.22), British Museum © Seiko Kawachi; **Bathrobe**, Jim Dine (p.22), Waddington Graphics; **Tobias and the Angel**, Leonard Baskin (p.23), Victoria and Albert Museum; **Sydney Heads**, Margaret Preston (p.23), reproduced by permission of the Australian National Gallery, Canberra; **Federal Sharpshooter**, Winslow Homer (p.24), Western Americana; **N for Epiphany**, Eric Gill (p.25), Victoria and Albert Museum; an illustration from **The Hansom Cab and the Pigeons**, Eric Ravilious (p.25), © Ravilious 1988, all rights reserved DACS; **A Page from Jerusalem**, William Blake (p.26), Victoria and Albert Museum; **Green Mud Wall**, Hodaka Yoshida (p.31), British Museum/Hodaka Yoshida; **Still Life**, Ben Nicholson (p.32), Victoria and Albert Museum; **The Wrestlers**, Henri Gaudier-Brezeska (p.33), Victoria and Albert Museum; **Pryde-Pierrot**, Eduardo Paolozzi (p.34), Victoria and Albert Museum; **Kopf im Doppelclicht**, Emil Nolde (p.37), Victoria and Albert Museum; **Improvisation, Lubrication, Humorous and Fanciful**, Josef Gielniak (p.38), The Museum of Modern Art, New York, John S. Newberry Fund; **Full Moon**, Richard Bosman (p.58), Experimental Workshop; **Then Came Death and Took the Butcher**, Frank Stella (p.59), graphics from **Had Gadya** by El Lissitzky, Waddington Gallery; **Swan Engraving Square II**, Frank Stella (p.98), printed and published by Tyler Graphics Ltd, © Frank Stella/Tyler Graphics Ltd 1982, photography by Steven Sloman; **Collection 85-10**, Haku Maki (p.106), British Museum/Haku Maki; **Paradise – Landscape with a House**, Hodaka Yoshida (p.106), British Museum/Hodaka Yoshida; **Bust of a Woman**, Pablo Picasso (p.143), Galerie Louise Leiris, Paris, © ADAGP, Paris and DACS 1988; **A Obscuras**, Hilda Paz-Levozan (p.158), British International Print Biennale, Bradford; **California Pearl Gazes and Contemplates her Future**, Elaine Kowalsky (p.162), © DACS 1988; **An Opera House in Every Home**, Eric Thake (p.164), reproduced by permission of the Australian National Gallery, Canberra.

*Special thanks also go to the following people who lent prints or generously gave advice and help:*

Jane Porritt and John Purcell, John Purcell Papers, London; David Muncey, Forbo Nairn, Kirkcaldy, Scotland; Michael Parkin, Parkin Gallery, London; Bernard Steinfield, Fieldbourne Gallery, London; Mary Leask, West Dean; Peter Bird, London; the Rev. John Wheeler, London; John Brodsky, London; Martin Lawrence, T.N. Lawrence and Son, London; Gordon Samuel, Redfern Gallery, London; Joseph Lebrovic, J. Lebrovic Gallery, Sydney; Chip Elwell, New York; Barley Roscoe, Holburne of Menstrie Museum, Bath; Judith Russell, Bristol; Penny Hughes-Stanton, London; Tim Mara, Chelsea College of Art, London; Ian Mortimer, I.M. Imprimit, London; The Experimental Workshop, San Francisco; Jane Hyden and Roger Butler, Australian National Gallery, Canberra; Phillip Jago, National Gallery of Victoria, Melbourne; Barbara Haddy, West Australian College of Advanced Education, Perth; St Bride Printing Library, London; James Burr; St Claire Allen; Marthe Armitage; Rebecca Salter; and Mary Pacios Humphrey, for Americanizing the text.